Lost at Guad

Lost at Guadalcanal

The Final Battles of the Astoria *and* Chicago *as Described by Survivors and in Official Reports*

JOHN J. DOMAGALSKI

McFarland & Company, Inc., Publishers
Jefferson, North Carolina, and London

LIBRARY OF CONGRESS CATALOGUING-IN-PUBLICATION DATA

Domagalski, John J., 1969–
Lost at Guadalcanal : the final battles of the *Astoria* and *Chicago* as described by survivors and in official reports / John J Domagalski.
p. cm.
Includes bibliographical references and index.

ISBN 978-0-7864-5897-4
softcover : 50# alkaline paper ∞

1. Astoria (Cruiser : CA-34) 2. Chicago (Cruiser : CA-29)
3. Guadalcanal, Battle of, Solomon Islands, 1942–1943.
4. Wold War, 1939–1945 — Personal narratives, American.
I. Title.
D774.A88D66 2010 940.54'265933 — dc22 2010024451

British Library cataloguing data are available

©2010 John J. Domagalski. All rights reserved

No part of this book may be reproduced or transmitted in any form or by any means, electronic or mechanical, including photocopying or recording, or by any information storage and retrieval system, without permission in writing from the publisher.

Front cover: *top* In what may be the last photo of the *Astoria*, the cruiser is seen during the voyage to the Guadalcanal area (U.S. Navy/ National Archives); *bottom* One of the last known pictures of the *Chicago* shows the damaged cruiser riding low in the water on January 30, 1943 (U.S. Navy/Naval Historical Center)

Manufactured in the United States of America

McFarland & Company, Inc., Publishers
Box 611, Jefferson, North Carolina 28640
www.mcfarlandpub.com

To
Sandy

Acknowledgments

Words cannot adequately express the appreciation that I have for the many individuals who helped make this book possible. Trying to recreate a story that is almost seventy years old is a truly daunting task. For basic research assistance, I thank the staffs at the National Archives in College Park, Maryland, and the Naval Historical Center in Washington, DC. Without these dedicated people, writing about American naval history would be a very difficult undertaking.

The project simply could not have been possible without the veterans who freely gave of their time to tell me about their World War II experiences. In some cases family members took the place of veterans by providing me with narratives that their fathers had written prior to passing away. The documents tell the vivid story of a war that they fought many years ago. There are two veterans who stand out from the rest: Don Yeamans and Art King.

It was during an evening telephone conversation that Don Yeamans first told me about his great ship, the *Astoria*. He mentioned that the ship was forgotten in history, sunk in a terrible naval battle that many would like to forget. Hopefully my project is able to change that notion.

Art King spent untold hours talking with me about his time aboard the *Chicago*. He explained in great detail the inner workings of the ship and the many people aboard. He was truly a memorable part of the project.

It seemed that each veteran I contacted wanted to make sure that I found someone else from their ship that also had a memory to share. With their memories fading and numbers dwindling, the project serves as a way to keep their stories alive. In many respects, the book is really their story. I just wrote it.

Finally there is my family, who provided me with much support and encouragement. I also cannot forget the important contribution of one special person. I would like to thank my wife, Sandy. Without her constant help, patience and encouragement this book would not have been written.

Contents

Acknowledgments	vi
Preface	1

PART ONE: ON THE ROAD TO WAR

1. Treaty Cruisers	5
2. Early Days	10
3. New Hands	22
4. Early Operations	27

PART TWO: GOING TO GUADALCANAL

5. Gathering Forces	33
6. Veterans	38
7. Rendezvous at Koro	43
8. The Voyage	46
9. Approach and Landing	51
10. Air Attacks	59
11. August Eighth	64

PART THREE: A NIGHT OFF SAVO ISLAND

12. Unheeded Warnings	75
13. Night Dispositions	79
14. The Enemy Arrives	84
15. A Torpedo Finds the *Chicago*	89
16. The Battle Moves North	95
17. Captain Greenman at the Helm	103
18. Below Deck	106
19. The Battle Continues	110
20. Escape	117
21. Help at Last	127

22. Commander Shoup at the Stern	135
23. The Fight to Save the *Astoria*	144
24. Abandon Ship!	152
25. Survivors	158

PART FOUR: THE FINAL VOYAGE OF THE CHICAGO

26. Stateside	169
27. Return to Guadalcanal	174
28. The Last Battle of the *Chicago*	178
29. Rescue	189
Epilogue: The Voyage Continued	199
Chapter Notes	207
Bibliography	217
Index	221

Preface

More than a generation ago a group of American and Australian warships gathered near tiny Koro Island deep in the South Pacific. On the afternoon of July 31, 1942, the ships weighed anchor and began a voyage into history. Seven days later the small armada arrived unannounced off the coast of the Japanese-held island of Guadalcanal. Representing the first American offensive operation in Pacific War, the invasion was a bold and daring move to gain a tiny foothold on the edge of the expansive Japanese Empire. For the next six months forces of the United States and Japan struggled for control of the small island in a battle that was fought on land, at sea, in the air, under the sea and in supply chain operations. The naval aspect of the campaign centered around six large battles and numerous smaller ones. The fighting at sea was fierce and the casualties were heavy on both sides.

Lost at Guadalcanal is the story of two of the ships that headed out to sea on that July afternoon. Both the *Astoria* and *Chicago* were American heavy cruisers designed and built almost a decade before the start of World War II by a navy that believed the next war would still be fought by battleships. Each ship played an important role in the Guadalcanal operation, but neither survived the campaign. The *Astoria* was destined to meet a fiery end in the opening days of the fighting, one of four allied heavy cruisers sunk in the disastrous Battle of Savo Island. Damaged in the same battle, the *Chicago* survived to fight another day. She eventually succumbed to an air attack in the final stage of the Guadalcanal fight, never seeing the victory that was only days away.

Lost at Guadalcanal combines two stories. First, the operations of the two ships during the Guadalcanal campaign are reconstructed using a wide variety of materials, including official U.S. Navy documents. The second is the individual stories of the men who manned these fighting vessels. Oral histories, interviews and previously unpublished firsthand accounts are used to give a human face to the ships. The text seamlessly weaves the stories together to provide a realistic account of men and ships in battle. The courage and fortitude displayed by the sailors aboard these two warships, often in the face of great danger, stands as a monument to the World War II generation of American sailors. The book that follows is their story.

PART ONE

On the Road to War

"We didn't know anything more than the suppositions that we made all along that pretty soon we would have a war with Japan and that it would take us about three weeks to whip 'em. That was the general attitude."[1]

Art King
Electrician's Mate First Class
U.S.S. *Chicago*

Chapter 1

Treaty Cruisers

Memorial Continental Hall was filled to capacity on the morning of February 6, 1922. The distinctive and elegant building with a palm decorated interior was located only blocks from the White House in downtown Washington, D.C. It had served as the setting for talks between the worlds's leading powers on the issue of limiting naval armaments. For almost three months delegates sat at tables arranged in a horseshoe fashion discussing a variety of pressing issues. On this day a single green table located inside the horseshoe held the fruits of the conference, a series of treaties, the capstone of which was an agreement to limit naval armaments.

The audience in the galleries applauded as delegates entered the chamber. Promptly at 10:10 A.M. United States secretary of state Charles Evans Hughes called the session to order. After formally adopting the previous session's meeting minutes, he directed the delegations, in alphabetical order by nation, to sign the treaties laid out on the green table. He himself began the procession by leading the American delegation. As his colleagues stood by, and the audience once again roared with applause, Hughes sat down and signed the various documents. Thus came into being the Treaty for the Limitation of Armament of 1922, also known as the Washington Naval Treaty.

Ratified by the United States Senate almost two months later, the Washington Naval Treaty was lauded as a monument to peace. Little did any of the delegates know that the treaty provisions would have far reaching implications for the world's navies, many of which would be embroiled in a world war less than two decades later.

A key goal of the treaty was to end the expensive arms race in capital ships, the big-gunned battleships and battlecruisers that were showcased in World War I. A ratio system for total capital ship weight, measured in tons, was established for the three largest naval powers: Great Britain, the United States, and Japan. The treaty also mandated a ten year period during which no new capital ships could be constructed. Afterward, each new replacement ship was to be limited to 35,000 total tons. As a result of the various treaty provisions, a large number of battleships and battle cruisers already in service would be sent to the scrap yard and others planned or under construction would be cancelled altogether.

The agreement would also have far reaching implications for a second type of ship known as a cruiser. The idea of an intermediate sized warship was not new. It had been around since the days of sail. As shipbuilding technology progressed from wood to steel and from sail to boiler, so evolved the cruiser. With the development of modern battleships, the need existed for a smaller and faster warship to serve a variety of roles within the fleet.

With the restrictions imposed on capital ships, treaty negotiators had feared that unless limited, the size and armament of cruisers could be gradually increased. If this were to happen, the naval arms race might well continue with larger and more powerful cruisers being built to fall just short of capital ship specifications. As a result, a section of the treaty was developed to set limitations on cruisers. Specifically, no such warship could be constructed that exceeded 10,000 tons or have a gun armament larger than an eight-inch diameter.[1] The cast had now been set for a new generation of warships, officially to be known as heavy cruisers because their displacement and guns would be larger than their predecessors. However, the new type of ship was quickly dubbed treaty cruisers.

Like other treaty signatories, the United States wasted no time in starting to develop heavy cruisers that met the maximum guidelines. The limitations meant that hard decisions had to be made about balancing armament, protection (armor), and speed.[2] American naval planners wanted the new ships to be as close as possible to the 10,000 ton weight limitation.

A mini naval arms race, unforeseen and unintended by the treaty negotiators, was soon underway. In late 1924 Congress authorized eight new heavy cruisers, providing funding for the first two. The resulting two ship *Pensacola* class represented the first U.S. Navy heavy cruisers to be built under the treaty guidelines.

Authorization bills in 1926 and 1927 funded the remaining six ships, which were soon designated as the *Northampton* class. With funding approved in March 1927, the fourth ship of the class was laid down at the Mare Island Navy Yard near San Francisco on September 10, 1928. Designated as heavy cruiser number twenty-nine, or CA-29, the ship was named the *Chicago*. She would be the second ship in history to bear the name. Starting with the keel, shipyard workers slowly built and assembled the ship. The *Chicago* would be the first American warship that was welded. The process helped to eliminate excess weight, a critical issue given the treaty weight limitation.[3] Like two of her sister ships, the *Chicago* was built as a flagship with extra space needed to accommodate an admiral and his staff. The cruiser was ready to be launched on April 10, 1930, exactly twenty months since the start of construction.

From the earliest days of shipbuilding, the launch of a new ship has been surrounded by ceremony. The launch of the *Chicago* was to be no exception with a crowd of almost 20,000 people gathered for the event. Tradition dictates that a ship must have a sponsor. In the case of the *Chicago*, it was Miss Elizabeth Britten, the sister of a Chicago congressman. The new ship was christened with the traditional breaking of a bottle of champagne against the hull by her sponsor. Amid wild cheering from the crowd, the cruiser slowly slid down the ways for a near perfect launch. It was then off to a nearby dock to be fitted out. As yard workers installed equipment and completed the interior compartments of the ship, the beginnings of her crew began to arrive.

Almost one year later on March 9, 1931, the *Chicago* was commissioned as a fighting vessel of the United States Navy. The ship's sponsor was once again on hand for the ceremonies. As the ship's four scout seaplanes circled overhead, Miss Britten unveiled a tablet bearing two seals: one of the navy and the other of the City of Chicago. With an overall length of 600 feet and a width (beam) of sixty-six feet, the *Chicago* was a sleek and modern warship. The ship was designed to attain a speed of just over thirty-two knots.[4] Under the command of Captain M. H. Simmons, the new cruiser headed out to sea for a short trial run. A longer cruise soon followed to Hawaii, Tahiti, and American Samoa.

After the reduction of the third class of treaty cruisers to just two ships, the final cruisers were ready to be built. Designated the *New Orleans* class, these ships embodied improvements designed to correct the deficiencies of the three previous classes. With prior ships

The *Astoria* test fires her eight-inch guns off Hawaii on July 8, 1942. The ship was soon en route to the South Pacific for the Guadalcanal operation (U.S. Navy / Naval Historical Center).

coming in well under 10,000 tons, it was decided to use the extra available weight for better protection. The result was a slightly shorter cruiser with somewhat of a low profile. Heavier armor lined the hull beltline to protect critical internal machinery. Protection was also bolstered around the magazine, bulkheads and turrets.

The first ship of the new class to actually be started was the *Astoria*. The vessel honored the Oregon city that was situated near the mouth of the great Columbia River. Designated hull number thirty-four, she was laid down on September 1, 1930, at the Puget Sound Naval Yard near Bremerton, Washington. For almost three years the yard workers toiled in constructing the ship, delayed at one point as certain design features were modified.

The launch ceremony took place on the afternoon of December 16, 1933. The *Astoria* was sponsored by Miss Leila McKay, the great-granddaughter of John Jacob Astor. It was Astor's fur company that established the trading post which later became the city of Astoria. After almost ten minutes of opening music provided by the Navy Yard Band, the base commandant introduced the mayor of Astoria, J.C. Ten Brook. On behalf of the Astoria area school children, he presented the ship with a memorial plaque of the city. Next was a speech by the former governor of Oregon and a prayer. After christening by her sponsor, the *Astoria* slowly slid out of Dry Dock Number Three. The new cruiser was about 85 percent complete.[5] As the band played the *Star-Spangled Banner*, the *Astoria* slowly moved across the yard. She was 588 feet in length with a beam of slightly less than sixty-two feet.[6]

The *Astoria* was commissioned on April 28, 1934. Under the command of Captain Edmund S. Root, the new warship ventured out to sea. During the summer of 1934 the *Astoria* conducted a lengthy shakedown cruise across the South Pacific. She arrived back in San Francisco on September 25, 1934.

* * *

Although of different designs, both the *Astoria* and *Chicago* shared a basic configuration that was typical of all American treaty cruisers. Each ship mounted nine eight-inch main battery guns divided among three turrets. A secondary armament of eight single five-inch guns was mounted four to a side in the middle section of each ship. Considered dual purpose, these guns could fire at either surface targets or aircraft. The armament was rounded out by a small number of light machine guns.

Located directly behind the two forward turrets, the superstructure was a series of raised decks that contained the bridge, main radio room, chart house, and various lookout points. The top of the area housed an assortment of fire control equipment used to direct the fire of the various armaments. The superstructure of the *Chicago* was dominated by a large tripod mast with a lookout point perched high on top. The *Astoria* had a somewhat lower superstructure with a single pole foremast.

Directly behind the superstructure were two smokestacks and an aviation area. Known as the well deck, the aviation area contained a hangar and two catapults. Both cruisers normally carried a compliment of four seaplanes.

Below the main deck was a complex network of rooms and compartments interconnected by narrow passageways and ladders. Frame walls, known as bulkheads, supported the hull and divided up the interior of the ship into various compartments.[7] The entrance to each compartment was either a door or hatch. Once closed tightly, or dogged down, these provided a waterproof barrier that sealed and separated areas of the ship.

The area below deck contained a wide variety of compartments ranging from crew quarters to engineering spaces. The forward area located under the superstructure was the living quarters for the ship's officers. Known as officer's country, the area was commonly off limits for the enlisted men. The wardroom was the officer's club, used as a place to eat and meet. In many ways the officers lived a separate existence from the enlisted men.[8] The living quarters for the enlisted men were located in the back half of the ship behind and below the boat deck and aviation area.

Under each of the main battery turrets was an ammunition storage area. Individual shells and bags of gunpowder were sent up to the turrets by way of a mechanical hoist. For the smaller guns a limited amount of ready-to-use ammunition was stored in ready boxes that were located near each gun mount.

Deep below the waterline in the middle part of the ships were a cluster of three important rooms. Central station, the main battery plotting room, and the interior communications room were all adjacent to each other. Central station was where the damage control officer was positioned during battle conditions. He would be in telephone contact with each of the various repair parties that were stationed at different parts of the ship. The main battery plotting room served as the fire control center for the eight-inch guns. It was the destination for information from lookouts and fire control equipment on a potential target. Information, such as speed and range, were fed into a rudimentary computer that calculated the estimated future position of the target.[9] The result was a firing solution that would be sent back to the turrets and used to aim the guns. The interior communications room contained the main switchboard for the various communication circuits that tied the functional areas of the ship together.

Taking up a large amount of space below decks were the engineering spaces that provided the power to run the ships. Firerooms contained boilers that burned fuel oil to generate steam that was piped to the adjacent engine rooms. Each of the four engine rooms contained a turbine that used steam to turn one of the propeller-ended screws. The rooms also contained generators that produced electricity for use throughout the whole ship. The vessels had a forced draft ventilation system that used fans to blow outside air into the various compartments below deck.

Hundreds of sailors were required to man these fighting vessels. Each cruiser carried a crew that consisted of a small group of officers, large number of enlisted men, and a small marine detachment. The normal peacetime compliment of the *Astoria* consisted of 868 men. The *Chicago* carried 617 sailors, plus additional flag staff if an admiral was aboard.[10] Many more sailors were needed to operate the ships under wartime conditions. In less than a decade, the crews of both the *Chicago* and *Astoria* would be tested in grueling naval combat in the South Pacific.

Chapter 2

Early Days

As the *Chicago* and *Astoria* began their time at sea, the Great Depression ravaged the economy at home. Factories idled and unemployment soared. The navy also endured some tough times with temporary pay and benefit cuts for enlisted men resulting from fiscal constraints. The construction of new ships gradually brought about the need for more manpower. With few employment and educational opportunities available, many young men decided to join the navy.[1] The circumstances gave the service an influx of capable young men, many of whom would be veteran sailors by the time the next world war began. Some of these sailors were assigned to the *Chicago* and *Astoria*.

* * *

The new *Chicago* pulled out of Mare Island on July 27, 1931, bound for the East Coast and service as the flagship of the Scouting Force. Later years in the decade saw the *Chicago* spending most of her time on the West Coast with her home port at San Pedro, California. Her voyages took her to various parts of the Pacific and occasionally to the Caribbean and Atlantic.[2]

In August 1940 the cruiser was one of the first ships to be fitted with a radar set.[3] The CXAM long wave search set was mounted high atop the main mast and resembled a bed spring. Basic and crude compared to models that came out later in the war, it could be used to provide the range and bearing of surface ships and aircraft.[4]

Born while World War I was still raging, Art King grew up in a poor neighborhood in Louisville, Kentucky. He spent a typical childhood spinning tops, shooting marbles, and playing ball. Upon graduating from high school, he did not see much opportunity in his hometown. "That was during the Depression and there was no possibility for work," recalled King.[5] Always having a thirst for travel, he decided to join the navy. He enlisted on May 11, 1936, and shipped out to Norfolk, Virginia, for thirteen weeks of boot camp.

After completing training King was able to take a short leave to go home. Prior to departing he took an exam to see if he qualified to attend one of the navy specialty schools, called service schools. He passed the test and after returning from leave went directly to the school. It was a sixteen week program that focused on five different subject areas. Students had to decide on one subject after the first eight weeks. Prior to starting the class King had a temporary job assisting the officer in charge of the electrical school. During this time he was able to look over a number of different electrical books and began to get interested in the subject. So when the time came to pick a specialty, he decided on electrical school.

Upon graduation, King was made seaman second class with a monthly pay of thirty-six dollars. Before long, King was one of almost 2,200 men who boarded the transport *Chaumont* for the long voyage to California. On route the ship made a stop at Guantanamo

Bay, Cuba. "That was used as sort of a disciplinary barracks at the time," King remembered. "So we had a couple of people to drop off there and we picked up a couple of graduates." The *Chaumont* continued through the Panama Canal and eventually made it to Mare Island.

Arriving at the navy shipyard, the passengers of the transport were divided up for duty assignments. King was one of eight men who were assigned to the *Chicago*. At the time, the cruiser was in the yard for a regularly scheduled overhaul. The transport had docked at one end of the navy yard while the *Chicago* was at the opposite end. With sea bag and hammock in hand, King and the seven other sailors walked the length of the island to their new boat. The *Chicago* was now out of the drydock and tied up to a pier. He boarded the cruiser during high tide, meaning the gangway was at a steep angle. "We had to struggle up that thing," he recalled, "with our bag and hammock on our shoulder and still be able to salute the colors while we went aboard." It was the spring of 1937 and Art King had boarded the ship that would be his home for almost six years.

Art King had obtained the rank of chief electrician's mate just prior to the sinking of the *Chicago*. He narrowly made it off the cruiser as she went down near Rennell Island (courtesy Art King).

In boarding the cruiser King felt like he had entered a new world. The language and terminology on the ship seemed very different from his days back at Norfolk. It was difficult to understand what some of the sailors were saying. "You just hope that you get by long enough until you learn something and you don't seem so foolish," King recalled of the time.

Like most new arrivals in the pre-war days, King's first duty was a three month assignment in the mess hall. The three large rooms, located just below the main deck and after the second stack, served as the eating place for the hundreds of enlisted men aboard the *Chicago*. There was no cooking involved in his duty, just setting up and cleaning. All of the meals were served family style on large tables that were stored overhead when not in use. Before each meal King was responsible for setting up two large tables and four benches, enough to serve twenty hungry sailors. King continues with the story: "Then you just stood by and waited until they blew the mess hall on the bugle. And then you would dash up to the galley and try to be one of the first in line ... the goal was to be one of the early ones to go through there and get the food." After the meal, King took the dirty dishes back to the scullery for cleaning by dishwashing machines. The routine was followed three times a day, every day.

In addition to the duties during meal time, each mess attendant had to help load food supplies aboard the ship during port calls. The sometimes strenuous work involved hauling crates of fresh fruits and vegetables from the main deck down to the refrigeration spaces. King remembered that occasionally some of the supplies never made it to their intended destination. "You got a friend that would be stationed in the cleaning gear locker and as you come by there with a case of apples or oranges he would step out and grab them."

After three long months in the mess hall, King was given his first real assignment: duty in the fire room. As part of his new assignment, his rating was changed to fireman third class. An officer told him just to do what he had to do to get by so that he could serve his time and move on to the electrical division.

Each fire room aboard the *Chicago* contained two large boilers and fifteen burners. At first King did nothing more than menial jobs, such as making the coffee. However, he soon learned the basics of boiler operations. The ship operated only the number of burners for the basic power needed at that particular time. King learned the procedures of the area that often centered on opening and closing certain valves to provide more or less fuel oil or air pressure. A chief petty officer would always be on hand to give direction based on orders received from the bridge. After almost two years in the navy, Art King made fireman second class. He would soon make it to where he really wanted to be, the electrical division.

Don Wallace decided at a young age that he wanted to join the navy. He was all of seven years old when several navy ships paid a visit to Santa Cruz, California, in 1928. Visiting from the nearby town of Soquel, he was greatly impressed with the clean appearance of the warships and how neat the sailors looked. He soon made up his mind that the navy was somehow going to be in his future.

Years later as he attended high school, his thoughts once again turned to the navy. Although he was getting good grades, he did not think that his family would have the money to send him to college. His father had steady work doing odd jobs for local farmers who paid him mostly in food. Although Don and his brother brought money into the household by working two paper routes and setting pins at a local bowling alley, the money for college just was not there.

One day after his seventeenth birthday, Wallace went to a recruiting station in San Francisco and joined the navy. Being under the age of eighteen, both of his parents had to give their written consent. They both did, believing that it was just a dream and that their son would never go through with it. On September 6, 1938, he passed the required preliminary exams and went home to wait for the call to active duty.[6]

Almost seven months later a call came to report for a physical. After passing the rigorous daylong exam, Wallace was sworn into active duty. He and other recruits were taken by bus to a YMCA building in San Francisco. Each recruit was given a meal ticket, assigned a room, and instructed to stay in for the night. Instead of following orders Wallace and another enlistee ducked out to see a Sherlock Holmes movie. The next morning began early as the recruits boarded a train for San Diego and boot camp.

During the next three months the recruits were kept busy learning all about the navy. They learned how to march, swim, tie knots, and stuff all of their belongings into a seabag. They learned how to sleep in a hammock and then tie it around their seabag. Each recruit was required to spend two weeks working in the mess hall and standing guard duty. It was during mess hall duty that Wallace learned an important lesson about the navy. During an early morning breakfast preparation he found himself cracking eggs into a large mixing bowl. Part way through the process of cracking hundreds of eggs, he noticed the pungent smell of a rotten egg. He had already dropped it into the mixing bowl. He immediately called over the cook, told him what had happened and suggested that the whole bowl be dumped. The cook looked at the new recruit and said, "Son, you might as well learn right now that there is no such thing as a rotten egg in the navy."[7] Wallace continued his work, but would always remain suspicious of scrambled eggs in the future.

After graduating from boot camp as an apprentice seaman, Wallace awaited transfer to sea duty. Each recruit was given the opportunity to fill out a request card. "I requested a heavy cruiser for the simple reason that I heard that battleships were sticklers for spit and polish and that destroyers were rough riding things," he would later write. "So I figured that a cruiser being in between might be the best choice." On July 29, 1939, Don Wallace received orders to report to the heavy cruiser *Chicago*.

Hopping on the tanker *Neosho*, Wallace and sixteen other boot camp graduates went on an overnight trip to the cruiser's home port of San Pedro. It was clear and sunny when the old tanker moored just inside the breakwater. The *Chicago* was just a short boat ride away. "A beautiful heavy cruiser, gleaming and sparkling in the sun," he recalled. "It was like a bit of heaven to me."

Boarding the ship, he was assigned to the fourth division. It was a deck division, responsible for maintaining a portion of the main deck. The result was a lot of hard work. Among the regular duties was cleaning the deck. The process started with a holystone, which was a type of porous brick. It had a hole drilled through the middle to fit a mop handle. The instrument was moved back and forth over a mixture of lime and sand to brightly polish the teakwood deck. Scrubbing the deck was hard labor for a man of any age. For all of his hard work, Don Wallace was paid seventeen dollars per month. Before long he had comfortably settled into navy life.

After talking his parents into giving their permission, Howard Fortney went down to the Clarksburg, West Virginia, recruiting office and joined the navy on March 1, 1938. Growing up on a farm outside of town, he had just graduated high school and did not want to go to college. "I just wanted to go out and see the world," he later recalled of his decision.[8] Fortney was soon on his way to Norfolk for basic training. He scored high enough on his entrance exam to gain admission to electrical school. After graduation in early December he was made fireman third class and went home for a short leave.

Fortney soon boarded a train bound for the West Coast and his first assignment. "We went by Pullman car, first class," he recalled of the trip. The riders traveled over the holidays and were served a special Christmas dinner. After pulling into San Diego after the long journey, a few men were assigned to the destroyers that were in port at the time. Fortney, along with most of the

Howard Fortney is seen aboard the *Chicago* in 1939. The young sailor was on his way down a ladder when the cruiser shuddered from a torpedo hit off Guadalcanal. He knew that he had to go to his battle station deep below the waterline and so pressed on (courtesy Howard Fortney).

others, went by bus up to San Pedro. The men were soon divided up for assignment among the various battleships, aircraft carriers, and cruisers that were in port. Two sailors were assigned to each battleship and aircraft carrier, while only one man went to each cruiser. By the luck of the draw, Fortney was assigned to the *Chicago*.

On December 28, 1938, Howard Fortney boarded the ship that would be his home for the next four years. Although rated as a fireman third class, he aspired to become an electrician's mate. After only three short weeks, he was able to get out of the normal mess hall and engine room duty given to new assignees. Having learned to type in high school, he was given a job as a log room messenger. His journey to become an electrician's mate had now begun.

Charles Germann knew that there was not much to do in his hometown of Exline, Iowa. Even as he worked in a local grocery store he was also aware of the gathering war clouds in the world. One day while talking about the troubled times in Europe, a co-worker gave him some advice. "I think that these young guys around here should go into the service now so that they'll have a rating before the war starts," the friend told him.[9] Listening intently Germann made a decision that would change his life. In June 1940 he joined the navy.

Germann took no special courses while attending basic training at Great Lakes Naval Base near Chicago. After completing boot camp he went directly to his assignment aboard the *Chicago*. He boarded the cruiser in September 1940 at San Diego. Almost immediately, the ship set sail for Hawaii. He boarded the ship with two others, but there were no available bunks. "They put us up by a gun mount," he recalled, "somewhere in a ... like a sail locker or something. That was the first night that we were there."

Assigned to the third division, Germann was soon put to work scrubbing the deck. After a few days he moved on to painting, at one point working high up on the main mast. He was eventually assigned to work in the powder handling room directly below turret three. It did not seem to bother him that he was below deck and could not see what was going on above. However, he did not like the smell of the ether and sought duty in another division.

In his early days aboard the *Chicago*, Germann took notice of the seaplanes taking off, landing in the ocean, and then being pulled back aboard the ship. He knew next to nothing about the aviation area. After three or four months in the powder handling room, he noticed an ad in the ship's newspaper for a yeoman in the V division, the aviation area. The yeoman position was an administrative office job that involved writing letters, preparing reports, and keeping personnel records.[10] Although pretty good at typing, he was not sure if that was the kind of job he wanted. He decided to drop by the aviation office to investigate further and was immediately accepted for the position. Germann soon began work in the aviation area, the field in which he would remain for the rest of his navy years.

Ken Maysenhalder always wanted to see the world. Growing up in California he loved to watch the navy ships that always seemed to be sailing in and out of San Francisco Bay. He would go down to the Embarcadero every Fourth of July to tour the ships that were open to the public. The San Francisco resident was working at Shelly's Restaurant for fifteen cents an hour when he started to seriously think about joining the navy. The soda fountain's owner, Mr. Shelly, tried to dissuade him, "Six years is a long time if you change your mind," he told the young man. "I will raise your pay to twenty cents an hour if you will stay."[11] Maysenhalder declined the offer and joined the navy on September 6, 1940. He enlisted for six years.

With almost fifty other enlistees, Maysenhalder boarded a train bound for boot camp in San Diego. He recalled the trip taking several days. "It took us several days due to being sidetracked for more important trains to pass us. We had a lot of fun on the train, and all the meals were free. I was now being taken care of by the U.S. Government." At the end of basic training he wanted to go aboard a submarine, thinking that subs had the best food and duties. Instead, he was assigned to the *Chicago*, which at the time was in Pearl Harbor. He boarded the old light cruiser *Milwaukee* for the trip to Hawaii. It was his first time at sea, and he soon became violently seasick. He was not alone: most of the new recruits were also sick and many looked green.

Maysenhalder boarded the *Chicago* in Pearl Harbor in early 1941. He fondly remembers seeing his new ship for the first time. "Being a flagship and seeing this large ship and knowing it was going to be our home ... I was really enjoying the whole thing." Like most of the other new sailors, he spent plenty of time cleaning and working in the mess hall. He remembered the first below decks inspection, a routine that normally took place on Fridays. "I witnessed the officer going down with a flashlight and looking under a generator, and with a white glove passing his gloved hand over an upper door ledge. I made sure these areas were extra clean."

Maysenhalder aspired to become a storekeeper. The position involved keeping track of supplies and maintaining records. In the meantime, he fell into learning the routine of the ship.

George Pursley grew up a Midwesterner in Cayuga, Indiana. He joined the navy on June 4, 1940, just two weeks after graduating from high school.[12] Other than working in a coal mine or local canning factory, there was not much to do in Cayuga. Joining the navy seemed like a good idea at the time. He enlisted for six years.

While attending boot came at Great Lakes, Pursley often did extra work. "I volunteered for everything so I could get my choice for ships," he later recalled. His extra activities included extended mess hall duty, running on the track team,

Ken Maysenhalder manned one of the *Chicago*'s five-inch guns during the air attacks off Guadalcanal. "It was spellbinding to look up and see these big planes," he later wrote (courtesy Ken Maysenhalder).

After completing basic training in 1940, George Pursley requested assignment to the *Chicago* based on the ship's good reputation. His request was granted. In the year before the war he learned how to operate fire control equipment (courtesy George Pursley).

singing in the choir, and playing on the company's baseball team. When it came time for ship assignments he requested the *Chicago*. He did so because the cruiser had a good reputation. She was known to have a great swing band, good food, boxing matches, a baseball team, and other shipboard activities. Pursley would later write of his request. "The reason for choosing this ship was it had a reputation of being alive ... there was something for everybody."

His request was granted and Pursley boarded the *Chicago* in late 1940 as an apprentice seaman. He was initially assigned to the fourth division. In the year before the war started he worked his way up to seaman first class. He was striking to become a fire controlman, a position responsible for operating and maintaining the optical equipment used to track targets and aim guns. It would not be long before he achieved his rating and was called to use his skills in combat.

Enlisting in the navy in May 1940, Fred Tuccitto soon was on his way from Omaha, Nebraska, to Great Lakes for boot camp. After graduation he was part of a group of almost thirty men assigned to the *Chicago*. At the time, the cruiser was undergoing an overhaul at Mare Island. The new recruits boarded a train for the West Coast. One man came down with meningitis and the whole group ended up quarantined. While staying at Mare Island Naval Hospital, he met another new recruit named George Pursley. When the quarantine was lifted, they boarded the *Chicago* together.

Fred Tuccitto scored high marks in gunnery practice as a pointer on one of the *Chicago*'s five-inch guns. His skills were put to good use when the ship battled Japanese planes in the Coral Sea and off Guadalcanal (courtesy Fred Tuccitto).

Like Pursley, Fred Tuccitto became part of the fourth division. However, he eventually ended up as part of a five-inch gun crew. He spent the last year of peace learning the fundamentals of operating the gun mount. Tuccitto became a pointer, a crewman who moved the gun vertically. He remembers well how he was chosen for the job. "When we were in Hawaii they sent us over to the marine base and they put us on a firing range with a forty-five caliber pistol," he later recalled. "And I was the only one that got five bulls-eyes. I was pretty good at it because I grew up on a farm with guns. From there I was put on to a pointer. I had a pretty good eye for aiming the gun."[13] Unbeknownst to the young sailor at the time, his aiming skills would be a great asset off the shores of a far away island deep in the South Pacific.

* * *

After completing her shakedown cruise, the *Astoria* was assigned to Cruiser Division Seven and was based in San Pedro. In early 1939, as the cruiser was participating in the annual fleet exercises in the West Indies, she was ordered to proceed immediately to the East Coast. The *Astoria* was assigned to travel to Japan with the remains of the late Japanese ambassador to the United States, Hirosi Saito. Under the command of Captain Richmond K. Turner, the *Astoria* departed Annapolis, Maryland, on March 18. With Saito's ashes aboard she began the long journey to Japan via the Panama Canal and Hawaii. Accompanied by three Japanese destroyers, the *Astoria* slowly entered Yokohama harbor on April 17. After firing a twenty-one gun salute, the ambassador's remains were transferred ashore.[14]

The cruiser spent the next month visiting various ports in China and the Philippines. In May she participated in the search for adventurer Richard Halliburton, who was missing after departing San Francisco on a voyage to Hong Kong in a small Chinese junk. Unable to find any trace of Halliburton, the cruiser returned to her home port. Like the *Chicago*, the *Astoria* benefited from the influx of navy enlistees during the Depression.

When Don Yeamans enlisted in the navy on December 10, 1940, he was acting on a decision that he had made almost three years earlier.[15] After his family moved to Portland, Oregon, from Salt Lake City, he developed an interest in ships. He soon made a decision about his future.

Navy ships were scheduled to visit the city during the 1937 Portland Rose Festival, an annual civic event. Living about five miles from the harbor, Yeamans rode his bike to take a look. One ship in for the festival happened to be named for the nearby city of Astoria. Taking a tour of the new cruiser had a great impact on him. He snuck away from the main tour and decided to go on his own. Going down a roped off passageway he went through the crews quarters, carefully looking at the rows of bunks. While passing through the galley, a sailor noticed him and asked if he wanted a hot dog. He had just cooked up the dogs and wanted to know if they were any good. Yeamans though the dogs were exceptionally good and ate more than one. While touring the *Astoria*, Yeamans made up his mind: he would join the navy when he was old enough.

With the completion of basic training in San Diego, Yeamans was offered the opportunity to attend a specialty school. Asked to list three choices he put down, in order of preference: machinist mate school, aviation machinist mate school, and sea duty. He did not get any of his choices, but instead was assigned to bugler's school. He soon remembered that he put down on his enlistment application that he had played the bugle in high school. After completing the school, he was again asked for three choices, this time for a ship assignment. Yeamans put down the *Astoria* for all three and boarded the ship in June 1941.

Given that each cruiser carried only two buglers, Yeamans did not like the advancement

Don Yeamans decided to join the navy after touring the *Astoria* while the ship was visiting Portland, Oregon, in 1937. Almost five years later he jumped off the vessel as she was sinking off Guadalcanal (courtesy Don Yeamans).

opportunities in that field. His assigned bunk was with the quartermaster group. Quartermasters worked in the bridge area and were responsible for maintaining the ship's log book and assisting the navigators. After hearing about their duties, he approached the executive officer about making a change. A move to the quartermaster group was approved, but only if he could find and train a suitable replacement. Yeamans soon found a candidate who in casual conversation expressed interest in learning to play the bugle. After spending a great deal of time training his replacement, the change was made official. Yeamans was now part of the quartermaster gang.

It was a Sunday visit to family friends in Citronelle, Alabama, that started to get Richard Tunnell thinking about joining the navy. He was about sixteen years old. "It was just a Sunday afternoon, you know, get in the car and go driving and go visit. That's what you did in those days," he would later say.[16] The friends had a son who was attending the Naval Academy in Annapolis, Maryland, so there was no shortage of monthly academy magazines for him to flip through as the grownups conversed.

As he read the materials, Tunnell started to think about his future. His parents did not have the money to send him to college. The Naval Academy seemed like a good opportunity, but one that would require a congressional appointment. His father wrote their local congressman only to find out his annual quota of appointments had already been filled.

A year out of high school, Tunnell was notified that he had been selected as a first alternate. He would take the entrance exam. If he passed he would be allowed one of the available appointments only if one of the principal candidates had failed. He hit the books with the help of tutors. "My high school grades and record were good enough so that I only had to take what was called a substantiating exam, which was mathematics and English," he later said. "I didn't have to take the physics and the chemistry and all that stuff. So, my mother hired two of my high school teachers to coach me in the evening and I had about ten hours coaching, at night, over a period of about a month."[17] After some hard studying, he took the exam and passed it, but just barely. At the same time a principal candidate failed to make the grade and Tunnell received the appointment. "I was delighted that I did. It was a whole series of unplanned events that turned out in my favor." He officially entered the Naval Academy on June 17, 1935.[18]

While at the academy, Tunnell participated in tennis, track, and swimming. The annual *Lucky Bag* yearbook described him as being "sorta quiet, shy, and good natured." However, it continued, the Gulf Coaster was "officer material through and through, with a deep-rooted love for the service."[19] After graduating with the class of 1939, he was commissioned an ensign in June of the same year. For his first assignments he spent time aboard the heavy cruiser *Salt Lake City* and the destroyer *Mugford*. Tunnell eventually decided to pursue a career in the growing field of naval aviation. In August 1941 he traveled to the Pensacola Naval Air Station to attend flight school. Upon graduation in February 1942 he earned his wings and became a lieutenant (jg). His next assignment would be to the *Astoria*.

John Powell joined the navy in August 1937. He would later say that he enlisted "so I could eat three meals a day."[20] He was from Coos Bay, Oregon, a small coastal city just over 200 miles from Portland. It was during the Depression, and the prospects for getting steady work anywhere in the state did not look good. He went south for basic training. "It was boot camp in San Diego for three months," he recalled.

Powell really wanted to get into the aviation area. At the end of basic training he took the test for the aviation machinist mate's school but did not make the cut. He ended up being assigned to the *Astoria*. Like Don Yeamans, he had been aboard the *Astoria* during the Portland Rose Festival in the summer of 1937. "They brought a whole bunch of cruisers in there," he remembered. "I just went aboard the *Astoria* because it was named for a city in Oregon. That was the only ship that I visited in Portland. I walked around the main deck a little bit and walked off. That was it. I was surprised when I got orders to the *Astoria*. I didn't put two and two together until I got aboard ship." It was his first ship, and he would remain on her until the day she went down.

Catching the old transport *Chaumont* for the ride up to Long Beach, Powell didn't make it to the cruiser until 3:30 A.M. He and a small group of other apprentice seaman were directed to string up their hammocks in the mess hall and get some sleep. He gladly obliged until being suddenly awakened at 5:00 A.M. It was time to get ready for breakfast.

After his first meal aboard ship, the chief master-at-arms told the new group to report to the ship's office for division assignments. In turning in his papers to the yeoman, Powell requested assignment to the F division, mistakenly believing it to be the aviation area. The yeoman was startled, apparently not used to new people making requests for assignments. Sometime later the executive officer showed up and began to call out assignments. Powell's name was called for the F division. The apprentice seaman thought to himself, *Oh boy. I'm going to the flying division!* It did not take long before Powell learned that the F division was not the aviation area, but rather the firecontrol division. The group was responsible for operating and maintaining the various pieces of equipment used to track targets and fire the guns. In time he would be striking for a fire controlman rating. "It was a good rate to have," he recalled, "because there was not much competition."

Bob Schiller was twenty-four years old when he entered the navy. A native of Shoshone, Idaho, he had spent a number of years working at the Sun Valley ski resort. "I had been working for quite awhile," he recalled. "It was brand new then. I lived close by there and I went to work up there." He spent time doing a variety of jobs ranging from construction work to a hotel bellhop. "That's the way it was in those days. That was in the middle thirties. There weren't too many jobs floating around."[21]

One day Schiller noticed an ad in the paper. "They were looking for people to learn how to fly, to become aviators. You just had to sign up to learn how to fly." He decided to join up. "I wasn't doing anything else very important, and it seemed like a good idea." Schiller was activated from the U.S. Naval Reserve and went to flight school in Pensacola. "By that time things were looking a little grim," he said. It seemed pretty clear to him that the United States and Japan were headed towards a war.

Earning his wings, Schiller was commissioned an ensign. He had hoped to be assigned to an aircraft carrier.[22] However, he departed for Pearl Harbor in late October 1941 for assignment aboard the *Astoria*. At the time the cruiser was in

Astoria aviator Bob Schiller flew a morning mission over Guadalcanal on the day of the invasion. Two days later he survived the sinking of the warship (courtesy Kathy Judkins).

the Philippines. In the interim he spent time aboard the cruisers *Minneapolis* and *San Francisco*. He boarded the *Astoria* in November upon her return to Pearl Harbor. "Just before the war started," he remembered.

Twenty-year-old Beverly Hills resident Gene Alair joined the United States Naval Reserve in June 1940.[23] At the time he was a student in the reserve officer training program at the University of California, Los Angeles. He was not sure what started his interest in the navy. "My parents had lived in Seattle for a while, and I was attracted to fleet week," he said. "I wasn't doing well in school, and I just didn't have the interest required to maintain the grade point level. I was probably border-line at that time. It was an opportunity to capitalize on what I had invested in the naval reserve program."[24]

Alair was selected for the relatively new V-7 program. It was designed to train young men for duty as line officers in the naval reserve.[25] It was open for any college junior or senior. Candidates were required to complete a one month preliminary course. Those who continued attended a three month Midshipman's School. The course provided instruction on key naval areas, including navigation, seamanship, and gunnery.[26] Completion led to active duty with the rank of ensign. "They had three locations they could send you to, and I was sent to Northwestern University in Chicago," he said.

Alair was commissioned as an ensign in March 1941. Having done a cruise aboard the battleship *New York*, he requested to be assigned to a destroyer. "I didn't enjoy my time on the *New York*. It was just too big. I wanted a smaller ship." He was assigned to the *Astoria*. It was not a destroyer, but at least it was smaller than a battleship.

The cruiser happened to be in California at the time. However, the young ensign did not travel to the ship by conventional means. "A classmate of mine named Woodside and I drove a car at the request of a dealer. We drove that car out there, he disconnected the speedometer, and we drove it all the way to Los Angles. We were alternating hot seats." It was a pretty good deal because the navy paid time and travel, while the dealer paid the gas, and provided meal money. "We delivered it to a Ford dealer in El Segundo, California." The arrangement worked out good as Woodside was going to the *Argonne*, which happened to be with the *Astoria* in San Pedro.

With the car safely delivered, Alair reported for duty aboard the *Astoria*. Coming aboard as a deck line officer was quite different than boarding as an enlisted man as it did

Gene Alair had no idea where the *Astoria* was going after being briefed on the Guadalcanal operation. Like most of the sailors aboard the cruiser, he had never heard of the Solomon Islands (courtesy Gene Alair).

not involve immediate duty in the mess hall or engine room. Alair was assigned to the third division, which operated turret three. He was given a large technical manual and told to start reading. He was the third officer in the chain of command for the division behind Lieutenant Jack Gibson and Lieutenant (jg) Ike Blough. "Jack was a division officer; he had been on there probably a year. Ike was probably four or five months ahead of me." As a junior officer, Alair was positioned well below deck and was put in charge of the powder magazine.

After the war started, Alair moved to the 1.1-inch machine gun mounts. A fifth division had been created for the light anti-aircraft guns that were added to the cruiser. Lieutenant Art McLaughlin was the officer in charge. Alair remembered him as a good division officer. "He was a big, heavy set guy," Alair recalled. "Tougher than nails, but he was a caring sort of division officer. He wanted to make sure that you accounted for your men, that you made your reports. He was a disciplinarian, but he was a nice guy and capable." Alair was responsible for the two forward 1.1-inch guns that were located high on top of the superstructure. "We were above the searchlights," he said. In little more than a year the perch would give him a bird's eye view of events on the *Astoria's* final night.

Chapter 3

New Hands

As the *Chicago* and *Astoria* went about their peacetime duties, the United States and Japan were on a slow collision course towards war. The peace ended for good when the Japanese attacked Pearl Harbor on December 7, 1941. The cruiser sailors who had joined the navy to escape the Depression now found themselves at war.

Both the *Chicago* and *Astoria* had been moored in Pearl Harbor until just two days before the attack. On the morning of December 5 both ships departed with the aircraft carrier *Lexington*. The carrier was to deliver a marine bomber squadron to Midway Island. It was considered a routine reinforcement mission.[1] The ships were about 420 miles from Midway at the time of the attack.[2] Returning to Pearl Harbor six days later, the cruiser sailors were able to get a first hand view of the utter destruction. Don Yeamans was on duty topside just off the bridge when the *Astoria* entered the harbor. He quickly noticed an overturned plane on the shore. The ship suddenly seemed to be sailing in oil. "Oh, my God what a sight," he recalled of the scene. "It was just a hell of a mess. The *Nevada* was beached. The *Oklahoma* was completely upside down. There were people with torches trying to cut a hole in the bottom of the *Oklahoma,* trying to get people out."[3]

One *Astoria* sailor was not with the ship at the time of the attack. Ed Armes had enlisted in the navy in November 1940 from Brooklyn, New York. He was only seventeen at the time and wanted to change his life.[4] He boarded the cruiser in mid–1941 and became a member of the aviation group. About a month before the war started, Armes left the cruiser for temporary shore duty at Pearl Harbor. A directive had come out requiring cruisers to have aboard qualified parachute riggers. "So they kind of asked for volunteers to go to parachute school," he would later say. "I think I volunteered and was selected."[5] During the attack Armes fired at Japanese planes with a rifle and later assisted in ferrying wounded from Ford Island to the mainland.

* * *

In the aftermath of the attack, patriotic feelings overflowed all across the United States. Nowhere was it more evident than at the army and navy recruiting stations, which swelled with crowds. During the month of December alone, over 40,000 men enlisted in the navy, more than four times the normal monthly total.[6] The navy needed men fast. Some of the new sailors would end up with assignments to the *Chicago* or *Astoria*.

Less than a week after the Pearl Harbor attack, two young men had a chance meeting at a navy recruiting depot in Little Rock, Arkansas.[7] Bill Grady and Harry Blumhorst had never met before. The two soon became friends and began a journey together that ended almost a year later near Guadalcanal.

Bill Grady decided at a young age that he wanted to join the navy. He was just eleven years old when his foster parents took him from his hometown of Moss Point, Mississippi, to a Mardi Gras celebration in Mobile, Alabama. He picks up the story from there. "We went aboard a submarine, the U.S.S. *Perch,* and I saw this sailor drinking coffee out of this big bowl." Grady liked what he saw and began to think about his future. "That's what enticed me to join the navy. I didn't even drink coffee in the navy. I didn't like it."[8]

Years later, after moving to Arkansas, Grady spotted a newspaper coupon for the naval reserve. "At seventeen you could go for minority cruise until twenty-one. So I sent one in, unbeknownst to my mother of course. It just so happened that after Pearl Harbor the recruiting officer came to Camden, where I was working at the *Camden Daily News.*" The recruiter asked him if he was ready to join up. "Yes sir. I am ready," was Grady's reply. "I was seventeen years old, not even shaving. So I joined the navy on December Eighth." He first went to a recruiting substation in El Dorado, before going on to the larger city of Little Rock. "I planned to stay for twenty years," Grady later recalled of his decision.

In the years before the war, Harry Blumhorst wanted to join the navy but was unable to do so because of his age. He enlisted, but could not actually enter until he was seventeen, and then only with his parents' permission. Living in Stuttgart, Arkansas, he thought that the navy was a better opportunity than the farm work that he was doing. The work was paying one dollar and ten cents a day. The navy paid twenty-one dollars per month plus room & board, food, and medical. Blumhorst turned seventeen on December 8, 1941, and he entered the navy in Little Rock on December 13. It was the same day that Bill Grady arrived in Little Rock. Blumhorst and Grady, two seventeen-year-olds from Arkansas, became acquainted as they started out from Little Rock on the road to war. They became friends the very first night, ignoring the recruiter's recommendation not to make close friends.[9] They were soon boarding a train for San Diego and boot camp. "We were traveling in sleeper cars," Blumhorst remembered. "That's the way the navy was traveling at the time, just like civilians."[10]

The training that the two young sailors received was anything but normal and probably could not be called training at all. Since the navy needed men fast, basic training was largely abbreviated. "We had about two weeks," Blumhorst recalled. "We were there about long enough to get our shots." Bill Grady remembers the quick departure from San Diego. "We left and went down to the naval supply center and there was the U.S.S. *Harris.* I remember it just as plain as day, just waiting there. We went aboard it and went to Pearl Harbor."[11]

When the *Harris* arrived in Hawaii, the two apprentice seaman learned that they

Harry Blumhorst was one of many who joined the navy in the days after the attack on Pearl Harbor. The rush to get men aboard ships in the early days of the war often meant little or no basic training (courtesy Harry Blumhorst).

would be assigned to the cruiser *Chicago*. Neither knew much about the ship. Grady thought that all large navy ships were named after states, so he was somewhat confused about the city name. "So we went on the *Chicago*, and I didn't know an eight-inch gun from a forty-five pistol," he added.[12] They boarded around midnight and were fed a late meal. The two were soon given their initial assignments, both to main battery guns. Blumhorst was assigned to turret two, while Grady was given duty in turret three.

Shortly after Blumhorst arrived on the ship, he saw a group of men loading supplies aboard. They were formed into a line and were passing boxes of food and ammunition. He was immediately pressed into the service to help. Looking up he saw a group of men leaning on the rail looking down at the supply line. He recalled that they were "just looking down at us, not doing a thing." He asked someone what the men up there were doing and was told that they were part of the quartermaster group. "That is what I want to be," Blumhorst quickly concluded.[13] He thought it would be a good job and that he would learn a lot, but in reality he did not even know what the quartermaster job entailed. In the interim, he kept busy learning his duties and the inner workings of his new ship.

* * *

Among the cadres of young men who joined the navy in the days after the Pearl Harbor attack was Henry Juarez. Born and raised in Los Angeles, he was only seventeen years old when he left high school and went down to the recruiting office. It did not take long for Juarez to begin thinking about the navy after the attack on Pearl Harbor. "I had a friend of mine that was aboard the *Nevada*," he later recalled.[14] "I knew the family and they got all upset because the ship ... they said it was sunk." He decided to join the navy and look up his friend. "I enlisted. I volunteered." After both of his parents signed a permission form, he enlisted on December 18, 1941.

Henry Juarez was one of the youngest sailors aboard the *Astoria* at the time of the Guadalcanal operation. After the cruiser sustained serious battle damage, he stayed aboard to help in the salvage effort (courtesy Henry Juarez).

Juarez was soon on his way to what would be a very short period of basic training in San Diego. "We just marched one time," he remembered. "We had rifles for four hours and that was it. The thing I really didn't like was all them shots. They were just giving us shots after shots. Our arms ... boy it was sore." It seemed like he had just arrived when it was time to ship out. Juarez boarded the *Harris* for a voyage to Pearl Harbor. Six days later he learned that he would be transferred to the *Astoria*.

The *Harris* arrived at Pearl Harbor late in the evening of January 16, 1942. Juarez was in a group of almost one hundred men who were transferred to the cruiser. "We just got on dock and just marched through the dock. Then marched to this other motor launch and it took us to the *Astoria*, that quickly." The group was fed a late dinner and bunked down for the night.

The next morning all of the new hands assembled on the quarterdeck in the presence of the captain and a number of senior officers. After some welcoming words and a brief explanation of how the crew was organized into divisions, it was time for each division officer to introduce himself. One by one each officer gave a brief introduction, a description of his area, an overview of the required duties and concluded by asking for volunteers. The process continued until it came to the fifth division. Juarez continues the story. "And lo and behold, I was the only one left in the center of that quarterdeck. Just imagine me, seventeen years old, and here's all these ensigns, officers, and captains and everybody's watching me. Boy, you talk about feeling lonely. Then finally here comes this one tall officer; he was twice as tall as I was and he introduced himself." It was Lieutenant Art McLaughlin, the head officer of the fifth division. His division encompassed all of the light anti-aircraft guns, excluding the five-inch secondary batteries. He approached the young apprentice seaman and said, "Would you like to be in my division?" When Juarez replied that he would, McLaughlin continued, "Well, I think that I can find something for you to do."

Juarez remembers later being questioned by McLaughlin. "He called me twice to his office and questioned my age. I must have looked like a kid. I was little. I was one of the smallest aboard ship." Juarez was assigned to the number four 1.1-inch machine gun mount located on the main deck near the stern of the ship. As time progressed, he had further contact with McLaughlin. "We got pretty well acquainted. I was after a twenty millimeter gun. I wanted to handle one myself." McLaughlin told him that once the ship returned to the States that he could have one. The young sailor would soon be in the thick of action as the *Astoria* sailed off to war.

* * *

As the first Japanese bombs were falling on Pearl Harbor, over 4,000 miles away Matthew Bouterse was giving his Sunday sermon at the First Baptist Church in Carlisle, Kentucky. A native of Florida, the young minister, his wife, and infant son moved to Carlisle shortly after he completed his seminary work in Philadelphia. Returning home after the morning service, Bouterse heard the news of the attack and like the rest of America, listened to the radio. Almost eight months later to the day, the young minister would find himself aboard a sinking ship over 8,000 miles from home.

The chain of events started shortly after Bouterse arrived in Carlisle. A friend and seminary classmate had joined the navy as a chaplain. "He was assigned a ship in Hawaii," Bouterse later recalled, "and wrote glowing letters of his duty there."[15] When the draft was initiated in 1940, Bouterse was given a classification that meant that he could not be called up. He started to think about becoming a chaplain and soon his mind was made up. "All of these things conspired to cause me to offer myself to the navy as a chaplain."

After passing a basic physical, Bouterse was asked to travel to Washington, DC. "A trip like that on the train was a big expense for a country preacher in those days, but I felt I had to pursue what had been started and went." He was not alone in the travels. A group of sixty or seventy other religious men, all interested in joining the navy, were on hand to take a written test and undergo a thorough physical examination. Returning to Carlisle, it did not take long for Bouterse to receive a letter from the chief of chaplains. "I was accepted into the regular navy and would soon receive orders." However, only a week later he received a second letter requesting that he return to Washington due to irregularities in his physical exam. "There was just a perfunctory exam," he later wrote of the second trip, "and I have always suspected that someone forgot to get my signature on something or they had goofed in some other way and didn't want to admit it." One day after Pearl Harbor, Bouterse received a second letter. This time it was official; he was to become a navy chaplain.

Bouterse braved the frigid Chicago temperatures for a short stay at the Great Lakes Naval Base. After what amounted to only a brief introduction to the navy, he was assigned to the *Astoria*. He soon found himself kissing his wife goodbye as he boarded a troop train for California. Although he knew that he was going to a front line ship, he had no concept of what to expect. "I couldn't even imagine what a cruiser looked like," he later wrote. "I had never seen one." His wait to board the *Astoria* would not be a long one.

Chapter 4

Early Operations

The *Chicago* and *Astoria* followed different paths in the young war before reuniting almost eight months after Pearl Harbor for the voyage to Guadalcanal. The *Chicago* spent the rest of December 1941 and early January 1942 operating out of Pearl Harbor. Much of her time was spent participating in offensive sweeps in the Oahu-Johnston-Palmyra triangle.[1]

On January 17, 1942, Captain Howard Bode assumed command of the ship. A native of Cincinnati, Ohio, he graduated from the Naval Academy with the class of 1911.[2] After fulfilling his mandatory battleship duty aboard the *California*, he became qualified to command a submarine, which he did during World War I. He served in a variety of capacities during the 1920s before spending part of the next decade in Europe as a naval attaché at various embassies. The late 1930s found Bode working in Washington, D.C.

Bode assumed command of the battleship *Oklahoma* in November 1941. He was ashore at the time of the Pearl Harbor attack. Less than one month later, with his ship capsized and sunk, he spent a short time attached to Fourteenth Naval District before being assigned to the *Chicago*.

Captain Bode soon gained the reputation of being a strict disciplinarian. Often referred to as "King Bode," some crew members were downright afraid of him. "He was completely different than any captain that you could visualize. There was no other way than his way," recalled Ken Maysenhalder.[3] Some *Chicago* sailors felt that he was a good captain to be under during a war. "He wasn't afraid of nothing," said Bill Grady. "He was a ship-handling skipper. I am glad that he was my skipper in combat."[4]

Among the first to feel Bode's presence was Art King. Shortly after the ship returned to Pearl Harbor after the attack, the flag plotting room was converted into a radar control room. King was supervising the installation of the electrical circuits when he decided to take a quick break. He was leaning up against the main mast smoking a cigarette when someone yelled out, "Attention!" Into the room walked Bode. The captain walked right up to King, who was starting to tremble, and asked if he wanted a sandwich and coffee to go with his cigarette. King quickly replied no. Bode shot back, "If you are up here to work, get rid of the cigarette and start working."[5] The new captain then disappeared as quickly as he had arrived and King went back to work, at a somewhat stepped up pace.

On February 2, 1942, the *Chicago*, accompanied by the destroyer *Perkins*, left Pearl Harbor for the South Pacific. Arriving in Suva, Fiji, ten days later, the *Chicago* joined the Australian- New Zealand (Anzac) Force. She operated in the South Pacific for the next five months.

The cruiser briefly operated with the *Astoria* in early May as part of Task Force 17.[6]

The force participated in the Battle of the Coral Sea, the first ever sea battle fought entirely by airplanes. The *Chicago* detached from the main task force and proceeded with other ships to intercept a Japanese invasion force that was reported to be heading for Port Moresby on the southern coast of New Guinea. Instead of finding the invasion force, the ships were found by Japanese land-based bombers and had to fight off a fierce air attack. The *Chicago* survived with minor damage from strafing, although the Japanese reported sinking her.[7]

After the battle the cruiser headed for Sydney. Arriving on May 14 she entered a drydock for maintenance.[8] At the end of May she helped defend the harbor against a surprise attack by Japanese midget submarines. The *Chicago* spent the next month and a half operating between Brisbane and Noumea. During this time she conducted a variety of training exercises from range finding to both day and night target practice.

* * *

On December 15, 1941, Captain Francis W. Scanland boarded the *Astoria* and assumed command of the vessel, relieving Captain Haines.[9] The new captain had been the commanding officer of the battleship *Nevada*, another victim of the Japanese attack on Pearl Harbor. He immediately rushed the cruiser to sea to participate in an aborted relief operation for Wake Island.

In early 1942 the cruiser made her last trip to the Mare Island Naval Yard. She was fitted with additional anti-aircraft guns and a platform was added to the foremast in anticipation of a future radar installation. On February 16, 1942, the *Astoria* left Pearl Harbor for what would be a lengthy cruise in the South Pacific.[10] Most of the trip was spent operating as an escort for the carriers *Lexington* and *Yorktown*. After participating in the Battle of Coral Sea, the *Astoria* departed the area for Pearl Harbor making several quick stops along the way. The force arrived on May 27 for what would prove to be a very short stay.

* * *

After a short stay in San Francisco, Lieutenant (jg) Matthew Bouterse boarded the transport *Henderson* for the trip to Pearl Harbor and his assignment on the *Astoria*. At the time the cruiser was participating in the Battle of the Coral Sea. It was his first real time in distant open waters and a great learning experience. "I had learned practically nothing of the details of life at sea, especially in wartime, and I was overcome by it all," he remembered. "The *Henderson* was tailor made to gently break me into the navy I was going to soon join."[11] Although he had a great fear of becoming seasick, he survived the voyage without incident.

The trip to Hawaii ended with a brutal dose of reality. As the *Henderson* glided into Pearl Harbor, Bouterse stood on deck for a first hand view of the destruction. "Alongside the

The *Astoria* was the first ship assignment for Matthew Bouterse. The young chaplain entered the navy just after the attack on Pearl Harbor (courtesy David Bouterse).

great battlewagons that leaned forlornly against Ford Island resting on the bottom, the frantic actions of salvage crews still at work day and night seemed almost sacrilegious. This was a funeral for a fleet and no one but me was crying." Moving into a chaplain's office on Ford Island that overlooked the sunken *Arizona*, Bouterse waited for his ship to return.

His wait would not be long. Hearing the rumor that the ships from Coral Sea were about to arrive, Bouterse joined others waiting outside. "Finally I saw motion above the trees over toward the hospital, the masts of a ship!" He soon spotted the bow of a destroyer coming toward him. The first ship was followed by many others, including an aircraft carrier. Then the ship that Bouterse was waiting for came into view; the *Astoria* had arrived. "I think I knew her and loved her before the chief next to me identified her for me," he recalled. "That sleek, trim, graceful, proud looking lady was mine!"

Just moments after boarding the *Astoria* for the first time, Bouterse noticed another man getting ready to leave. It was Chaplain Walter Mahler. After spending almost a year and a half aboard the *Astoria*, the Roman Catholic priest received orders to transfer to the marine base in San Diego. Much to Bouterse's surprise, it proved nothing more than a brief encounter in passing. "His gear was on the way down to the waiting boat," Bouterse wrote, "as he shook my hand and wished me well, leaving me with mouth agape, and a thousand questions left unanswered."

It did not take long for the new chaplain to make friends. "The first enlisted man I met aboard was on my first attempt to find the wardroom." Approaching Bouterse in the passageway, Baker First Class Victor McAnney stuck out his hand and offered an introduction. "Naturally, I made it my business to visit the bake shop later that day and found Vic enveloped in the aroma of fresh baked bread." As it turned out, McAnney was the leader of a small Bible study group on the ship. He promptly invited Bouterse to meet the group that very night. "I almost shouted yes," the chaplain remembered. "This was healing for a young country preacher who had gotten away beyond his depth." The two quickly became good friends.

In the days that followed, Bouterse went about learning both the inner workings of the ship and his role as the chaplain. "There was so much I didn't know," he later recorded, "but I was headed for a crash course." Among the first things to be learned was the location of his battle station. The chaplain was assigned to the after battle dressing station in the chief petty officer's mess hall. Located near the stern of the ship, he soon discovered how long of a distance it was from his stateroom well forward in officer's country. Bouterse devised a plan to make it to his station before the watertight doors were slammed shut in his face. Racing out of his room at top speed he yelled, "Coming through and hold that door," as loudly as he could. "I usually made it, breathless and hoarse." Before long the new chaplain was a well liked member of the crew.

* * *

After only a few days in port, the *Astoria* rushed back to sea. In the days that followed, she helped defend the *Yorktown* against a series of air attacks during the Battle of Midway. Although the battle was a great American victory, the *Yorktown* was sunk by Japanese bombs and torpedoes.

The Battle of Midway was the first taste of combat for Matthew Bouterse. "Nobody was more surprised than I to find myself in the middle of a real sea battle so soon," he later wrote. "We didn't even have time to work up any anticipation or fear." He was able to listen in on parts of the battle through a speaker in his battle station that was hooked up to the radio circuit being used by some of the pilots. He later went topside in time to see the damaged and burning *Yorktown*. "Somehow we didn't feel safe anymore," he recalled of the moment.

The *Astoria* returned to Pearl Harbor on June 13. She remained there for a good part of the summer. During that time alterations and improvements were made to the ship and she frequently participated in drills and training. More than anything it was a period for the crew to recharge after months of continuous time at sea.

PART TWO

Going to Guadalcanal

"I didn't know how to spell it [Guadalcanal] let alone where it was. It was just a name on a map."[1]

Gene Alair
Ensign
U.S.S. *Astoria*

Chapter 5

Gathering Forces

Northeast of Australia lies a broad string of islands that separates the Coral Sea from the Pacific Ocean. Encompassing several named groups, the islands begin immediately adjacent to New Guinea and arch in a southeastward direction before turning straight south. Situated at the northwestern end of the arch, the Bismarck Archipelago is the home of the region's best harbor at Rabaul. The opposite end of the arch is anchored by the New Hebrides group of islands and the large island of New Caledonia. Stretching the almost 700 miles between the two ends are the Solomon Islands.

* * *

The Solomons lie between five and ten degrees south of the equator. The large island of Bougainville sits on the northwest terminus of the chain. The central part of the Solomons break into two almost parallel lines of islands with the inner waterway known as the slot. The chain rejoins at its southeastern end near the large islands of Guadalcanal, Malaita, and San Cristobal. The onset of World War II found the chain under British control and inhabited by a small number of Europeans and about 95,000 natives.[1]

Positioned between the advancing Japanese and Australia, the Solomon Islands took center stage early in the war. Japanese planners hoped to isolate Australia by seizing New Caledonia, American Samoa, and the Fiji Islands. By the middle of 1942, the Japanese were posing a serious threat to the Australian-American supply line. The Japanese had seized Rabaul in the first months of the war and immediately constructed a large naval base and network of airfields. Less than two months later troops went ashore at Lae and Salamaua on the northern coast of Papua New Guinea.

After the Midway defeat, the Japanese cancelled plans to occupy New Caledonia, the Fijis, and American Samoa and instead focused on establishing a defensive line across the lower Solomons. Tulagi, a small island near Guadalcanal, was seized in early May and deemed to have a good harbor. A seaplane base was quickly established on the island. About a month later a surveying party investigating Guadalcanal found an excellent site for an airfield. Construction began in early July.[2] A network of airbases in the lower Solomons would complete a strong defensive perimeter that would be difficult for Allied forces to penetrate.

The Solomon Islands did not even figure into American war plans at the time of Pearl Harbor.[3] It was the stunning naval victory in the Battle of Midway that paved the way for American offensive operations in the Pacific. Under the operational control of the navy, planning for the attack on Tulagi began immediately under the code name Operation Watchtower. The scope of the operation changed after aerial reconnaissance revealed the airfield site on Guadalcanal. The operation soon became the dual invasions of Tulagi and Guadalcanal.

The operation encompassed an expeditionary force under the command of Vice Admiral

Fletcher that was comprised of two large groups of ships. Built around the carriers *Saratoga, Enterprise,* and *Wasp,* Task Force 61 was to provide the carrier-based air support. Since the lower Solomons were beyond the range of most of the American land-based planes, the carriers would have to provide air support to cover the landing operation until the Guadalcanal airfield could be taken over and made operational. The South Pacific Amphibious Force, also known as Task Force 62, was the actual invasion group under the command of Rear Admiral Richmond Kelly Turner. You might remember that Turner had captained the *Astoria* on her pre-war trip to Japan in 1939. The First Marine Division, under the command of Major General Alexander Vandegrift, was called on for the amphibious portion of the operation.

Naval units scattered across the Pacific were marshaled for the sea attack. Groups of ships departed Pearl Harbor, San Diego, and Australia in early July bound for the South Pacific. Among the ships chosen to participate in the operation were the cruisers *Chicago* and *Astoria*. Both would arrive from different points of origin to ultimately end up part of Task Force 62.

* * *

When the strategic decision was made to move forward with the offensive in the Solomons, the *Chicago* was still operating out of Brisbane. During the early part of July 1942, she trained off the Australian coast with the *Salt Lake City* conducting target practice and rangefinder exercises. On July 14 the ships were ordered to sea. The *Chicago* departed in the afternoon making her way down the Brisbane River out to Moreton Bay. In addition to the *Salt Lake City*, the force contained the Australian cruisers *Australia, Canberra,* and *Hobart*. Seven American destroyers rounded out the small fleet. The force was under the command of British Rear Admiral Victor A. Crutchley who flew his flag aboard the heavy cruiser *Australia*.

Like many of the crew, Don Wallace did not know where the *Chicago* was going. "We were again on the move to an unknown destination," he wrote of the time. "Of course, we of the crew never did know where we were going, not that it made any difference; we had to go anyway."[4]

After five days of sailing, the ships arrived in Wellington, New Zealand. The *Chicago* sailors found Wellington bustling with activity. "The harbor was full of troop transports," recalled Don Wallace. "So we knew that something big was up." Being far south of the equator, the weather was cold with southern winds blowing up from the Antarctic. "It was the coldest place I ever was," remembered Bill Grady. "July and August, that's their winter."[5] The port had experienced rain in recent weeks making the weather conditions somewhat miserable for the soldiers and sailors getting ready for the Guadalcanal operation.

Task Force 62, less various ships and marine units that were still en route, pulled out of Wellington at 8:00 A.M. July 22.[6] The force contained twelve transports loaded with the Marines and their supplies. Crutchley's cruisers and destroyers provided the escort. Admiral Turner was in command of the force, flying his flag aboard the transport *McCawley*.

The force was headed for a meeting with other naval forces south of the Fiji Islands. The combined ships were to undertake a dress rehearsal of the landing operation. The task force initially traveled southeast before turning north and east, zig-zagging along the way. The ships started out in pleasant weather conditions, moving at a speed of fourteen knots. However, on July 24 speed was reduced to eleven knots after rough seas and poor visibility were encountered.[7] Moving north meant an end to the cold winter weather in New Zealand. It was back to the warm weather of the South Pacific. "Now back in the tropics the heat seemed almost unbearable, particularly below decks," wrote Don Wallace. "The sleeping compartments often remained at around 110 [degrees]." Although never quite adjusting, the crew learned to live with the heat.

* * *

One day after returning to Pearl Harbor from the Battle of Midway, the sailors of the *Astoria* received a new leader. After ably guiding his ship through the Coral Sea and Midway battles, it was time for Captain Scanland to move on to other duties. Late in the morning on June 14 Captain William Garrett Greenman assumed command of the cruiser.

Greenman was born on August 26, 1888, in Utica, New York.[8] He entered the navy in June 1909, just short of his twenty-first birthday, having been appointed a midshipman from his home state. He graduated from the Naval Academy with the class of 1912. His first assignment was to the battleship *North Dakota*.

World War I found Greenman rising to the rank of lieutenant commander as he spent time aboard the battleships *Nevada* and *Florida*. By the late 1920s Greenman was given his own ship, assuming command of the destroyer *Preston*. In April 1934, the same month that the *Astoria* was commissioned, Greenman was made a commander.[9]

The outbreak of World War II in Europe found Greenman, with the rank of captain, in command of a destroyer squadron. The ships were part of what was known as the Atlantic Squadron operating off America's East Coast. The destroyers became part of the Neutrality Patrol, whose purpose was to show the world that the United States Navy was ready and able to defend the Western Hemisphere.[10] Greenman later became chief of staff to Commander Destroyers, Atlantic Fleet. During his tenure he assisted in the transfer of fifty old destroyers to the British. On May 16, 1942, he received orders to report to the Pacific as the new commanding officer of the *Astoria*.[11]

Having a new commanding officer come aboard can cause a level of uneasiness among a ship's crew. No one for sure knows what to expect. By the time the Guadalcanal operation had begun, word spread around the *Astoria* that the new captain had a sense of humor. It was a boost to morale to know that Greenman was a so-called regular.[12]

During her post–Midway stay at Pearl Harbor, the *Astoria* also received a new executive officer. Commander Frank E. Shoup, Jr., was assigned to the cruiser in July. The Dallas, Texas, native graduated from the Naval Academy in 1923 and did his first duty aboard the battleship *Oklahoma*.[13] During the next fifteen years the young officer served in a variety of land and sea positions with most of his ship time being spent aboard destroyers. In 1940 Shoup became the engineering officer aboard the heavy cruiser *Minneapolis*.

Returning to Pearl Harbor from Midway, the crew of the *Astoria* knew that they had been part of a big victory. "We didn't know the details,

William Greenman took command of the *Astoria* shortly before the start of the Guadalcanal operation. He directed the valiant effort to save the ship in the aftermath of the Battle of Savo Island (courtesy Robert Greenman).

because we didn't know how many carriers were sunk," said Gene Alair.[14] The mood among the crew was good as rumors and scuttlebutt had the ship going back to the United States. "We didn't know where we were going." said Henry Juarez. "We were due to San Francisco for new guns and all that." Unknown to Juarez and his shipmates at the time, events would send the heavy cruiser back out into the Pacific. "We unloaded ... I thought we were going to come to the States. But then we started loading up, loading supplies."[15]

John Powell also remembered that the departure from Pearl Harbor was somewhat unexpected. The *Astoria* had been there for only about a month and had spent previous long stretches at sea. "We loaded up fuel," he remembered. "I guess everybody got ashore once and then we were gone."[16]

The cruiser went out for target practice in Hawaiian waters. "We went out for surface firing both day and night," Captain Greenman recalled. "When we returned to Pearl I felt that the battery was in good shape and had demonstrated the effect of long and careful training."[17]

On July 7, 1942, the *Astoria* departed Pearl Harbor as part of Task Force 11. Under the command of Admiral Fletcher, the force consisted of the carrier *Saratoga*, four cruisers, seven destroyers, four destroyer transports and three oilers. It appeared that the force was heading out on nothing more than a routine training cruise in Hawaiian waters. The next morning the force practiced covering a simulated amphibious landing on the southeastern coast of the island of Hawaii.

The cruisers lined up single file and opened fire on the beach with their big guns at a distance of 10,000 yards.[18] The simulated attack was later joined by the planes from the *Saratoga*. The cruisers then moved to within 4,000 yards of the beach and let loose with almost all their guns. The event created a mixture of small puffs and large explosions that caused pillars of smoke and dust.[19] Trees were uprooted and dirt was seen to be tossed upward.[20]

Instead of turning back toward Pearl Harbor in the afternoon, the task force headed southwest towards the South Pacific. Most of the men aboard the *Astoria* did not know where they were going. "No idea at all," added Henry Juarez.[21]

As the *Astoria* sailed south, Matthew Bouterse spent some time up in sky control watching with interest the launching and recovery of the ship's seaplanes. "I never tired of watching the teamwork of the crew who made it look so easy," he remembered.[22] When the ship crossed the equator he became a shellback, but only after going through the normal initiation process. A long standing tradition in nautical history, an initiation process typically took place every time a vessel crossed the Equator. All sailors aboard who were making their first crossing, dubbed pollywogs, were subjected a ceremony. The activities often included, but were not necessarily limited to: the shaving of heads, standing watch in a funny outfit, spending time in a dunk tank, and withstanding a mild electric shock. After completing the initiation, a sailor could then help administer it on the next crossing.

* * *

The second largest island of the chain, Guadalcanal anchors the lower portion of the Solomons. The island runs northwest to southeast and is about ninety-two miles long and thirty-three miles wide at its greatest point. The land mass encompasses almost 2,500 square miles.[23] Guadalcanal is home to a rugged mountain range and dense jungles. A broad coastal plain runs along the northern coast with sandy beaches and few coral reefs. The plain contained the Japanese airfield that was in the final stages of construction at the time of the invasion.

Positioned just off Guadalcanal's northwestern tip, Savo Island is a small circular land mass dominated by a rugged cone. Located approximately twenty miles across Sealark Channel from Guadalcanal is medium-sized Florida Island and a cluster of smaller islands, including Tulagi. The landing on Guadalcanal was planned for the northern coastal plain. Designated as Red Beach, the landing zone was a 1,600 yard stretch of sand located near the mouth of the Tenaru River. The northern portion of the amphibious operation was the assault on Tulagi. Expected to be the more difficult landing, it involved a direct assault on a small island. The landing area, located on the side facing Guadalcanal, was designated Blue Beach.

Outlining the details of the amphibious operation, Admiral Turner issued Operation Plan Number A3-42 to his task force on July 30.[24] At the conclusion of practice exercises in the Fijis, the carrier and amphibious groups would separate and proceed in close proximity to each other on a journey west and north to Guadalcanal.

The amphibious group, including the *Chicago* and *Astoria*, was to swing around the northwest tip of the island to arrive in the body of water surrounded by Guadalcanal, Florida, and Savo Islands. After disembarking the Marines and their supplies, the task force was to depart the area for bases to the south. The ships of Task Force 62 would divide into smaller groups during the final approach to the island.

Transport Group X-Ray, which included Turner's flagship *McCawley*, was responsible for the assault on Guadalcanal. A smaller force, designated as Yoke Group, focused on the Tulagi side of the operation. Each transport group had a fire support force composed of cruisers and destroyers to assist in the landing operation.

The *Chicago* was assigned to be part of the screening group, which consisted of the Australian cruisers *Australia*, *Canberra,* and *Hobart*, the latter being a light cruiser, and nine American destroyers. Operating from his flagship, *Australia,* Admiral Crutchley was in direct command of the force. The role of the screening group was to protect the amphibious convoy.[25] Just prior to the start of the operation, Crutchley distributed special instructions that outlined the operations of the group. Captain Bode of the *Chicago* received these instructions on July 31 along with Turner's operation plan.

The *Astoria* was part of a fire support group was responsible for the Guadalcanal side of the landings. In addition to the *Astoria*, the group consisted of the heavy cruisers *Quincy* and *Vincennes,* and some destroyers. The group was divided into sections of one ship each. The *Astoria* was responsible for providing fire support in the area 7,000 yards east of the Lunga River, essentially the area between Lunga Point and Red Beach. She was to "support landing by fire on enemy defenses and troops identified by own spotting plane or designated by shore fire control party."[26]

Ten minutes prior to the start of the landing operation, all of the fire support ships would participate in a five minute heavy barrage of Red Beach. The three heavy cruisers were to use both their eight-inch main battery guns and five-inch secondary batteries for the bombardment. The *Astoria* was to fire on the western third of Red Beach to a depth of 200 yards.

When not participating in bombardment operations, the *Astoria* would be temporarily assigned to the Screening Group. During these times, she operated under the same screening group instructions previously discussed. Like Bode of the *Chicago*, Captain Greenman received the details on July 31. Both cruisers were soon on route to an unknown place called Koro Island.

Chapter 6

Veterans

By the start of the Guadalcanal operation, both the *Chicago* and *Astoria* had seen a fair amount of combat, mostly defending against air attacks. Since starting the conflict together, at sea on the day of the Pearl Harbor attack, each had traveled a separate journey through the first months of war. The sailors who were aboard the ships during this timeframe surely had experienced the run of emotions from anguish to desperation, from defeat to victory. In the process, each sailor had learned how to proficiently do his specific job aboard the ship. The crewmen stood watches, longed for home, and spent many long hours at battle stations. Each had also earned the right to be called a combat veteran.

* * *

After transferring into the *Chicago's* aviation unit, Charles Germann began to learn the ropes of the yeoman's job. "All I had to do was to take care of the flight logs and the correspondence that came into the V Division," he explained. However, he really wanted to work on planes. "In the meantime I talked to Johnny Prast; he was one of the mechanics." Germann asked him if there was any possibility that he could learn how to work on the planes. Prast thought that the staff of mechanics could probably use some help. "So in my spare time I was out there working, cleaning airplanes and stuff like that."[1]

Before long, Germann had advanced to seaman second class. At the urging of one of the senior aviation officers, Lieutenant Anthony Kolonie, he took the test for seaman first class and passed. He then asked the lieutenant if he could transfer out of the yeoman's job. Kolonie agreed and Germann became an aviation machinist mate third class right after the start of the war.

Although the aviation men ate, bunked, and stood watch with the rest of the crew, they were exempt from many routine duties such as cleaning and painting. "The only separate area that we had was the hangar and two silos," remembered Germann. The silos were the large round bases that supported the catapults. On the starboard side the bottom of the silo was used by the radio crew for equipment storage. The upper area, reachable only by a ladder, was under the control of the aviation gang. Used to store records, the area had a small desk and typewriter. The aviation men had sole possession of the port silo. It was used primarily for storage. All of the ordinance used by the planes, such as bombs and ammunition, were safely stored in a magazine that was located well below deck near the bow of the ship. Germann was still an aviation machinist mate third class when the Guadalcanal operation started. His battle station was at the top of the port side ammunition hoist for the five-inch guns. During daylight hours he would also stand watch at the forward main battery director.

The standard secondary armament on all treaty cruisers at the start of World War II was the five-inch twenty-five caliber single barreled gun. Both the *Chicago* and *Astoria* were equipped with eight such weapons, four on each side of the ship. The guns were open air with each mount being protected by a thin gun tub or splinter shield. Against surface targets, the weapon's fifty-four pound shell could be hurled a distance of 14,500 yards.[2]

Aboard the *Chicago*, both Fred Tuccitto and Ken Maysenhalder were part of five-inch gun crews at the time of Guadalcanal. Tuccitto was positioned on the port side, while Maysenhalder was on the starboard. Tuccitto remembers that operating a five-inch gun required about seven or eight men. "I was the pointer," he explained. "I was the guy with the trigger. I elevated and depressed the gun." Tuccitto sat on a brass seat on the left side of the weapon. "The other guy on the other side of the gun, he moved it horizontally back and forth. I moved it vertically and we'd zero in on a target. Our gun sights were magnified and we had crosshairs in there and we could zero in on a target. The gun captain gave us the orders."[3]

Tuccitto was a qualified pointer, a status that was attained in training prior to the start of the war. "In order to be a qualified pointer, you have to get four hits in sixteen seconds on a tow sled. That we did, we got it." The event took place off Hawaii as the *Chicago* sailed parallel to another ship that was towing a target sled. More importantly for Tuccitto, being a qualified pointer meant an extra five dollars in monthly pay.

Ken Maysenhalder's first job at his starboard five-inch gun was as a shell catcher. In that position, he stood right behind the gun. Wearing large fireproof gloves, he would catch each hot shell casing when it was ejected from the gun barrel and toss it away from the gun mount. By the time Guadalcanal came about, Maysenhalder had moved up to a pointer.

Don Wallace had settled into the fourth division aboard the *Chicago*. "Life in the fourth division was a combination of hard work and boring watches," he wrote. The boat deck was among the areas that the division maintained. The area contained galley hatches, the paint locker, the sail-makers locker and the ship's dry garbage disposal. It meant extra work for Wallace and his comrades. "Despite the fact that we had so much extra foot traffic from the other divisions to use these facilities ... we were nevertheless required to keep our deck and paintwork as clean and shipshape as the rest of the ship that didn't have any of these extra problems to contend with."[4]

Also aboard the *Chicago*, Art King had transferred out of the fire room and into the E division, which was the electrical division. At the time the group had less than thirty people. It was headed up by a warrant officer named Larsen. An old salt with almost thirty years in the navy, "Wolf" Larsen proved to be a good teacher. King finally began to work in his area of specialty.

By the time the war started, King had made a rating and was an electrician's mate. His battle station was the searchlight platform. Located on the main mast, above and behind turret three, the platform mounted four large searchlights of three feet in diameter. "About the only thing above it," remembered King, "was they had a machine gun platform up at the top of the tripod mast."[5] During battle stations there were four electrician's mates and four searchlight operators crowded on the platform.

When the four electrician's mates were initially assigned to the station, they struck a deal. They agreed to set aside their money every payday. At sea during a war there was really no place to spend it. Each man would hold his own money, keeping it on himself at all times. If someone was killed the survivors would take his money and divide it up among themselves. No one knew if one of them was going to have to pay up during the upcoming journey to Guadalcanal.

Howard Fortney had successfully made electrician's mate second class aboard the *Chicago*. At the time of the Guadalcanal operation, his battle station was the interior communications room. "I was in the interior communications group," he said of his duties. "We took care of all the engine order telegraphs, telephones, and that type of communications."[6]

Located at the bottom of the ship approximately even with the foremast, the room housed the central switchboard for all of the ship's various communication circuits. Fortney remembers it being a pretty cramped room. "It was not very large at all. It was probably not more than fifteen feet long and six or eight feet wide." The room was one of three critical spaces that were clustered together. One central ladder led down to the area. Originating on deck two, it was enclosed within a trunk and led only to the central control room. A watertight door connected central control to the main battery plotting room on the starboard side and the interior communications room to port.

During battle stations the room was manned by two sailors. Both were electrician's mates, one being first class and the other second class. W.A. Litchfield joined Fortney in the room. Their role was to operate the switchboard, turning switches, and making adjustments as needed.

After boarding the *Chicago* as an apprentice seaman, Bill Grady had made seaman second class by the middle of 1942. He had spent a short amount of time working on a five-inch gun battery. However, he soon returned to work at his original assignment in the powder magazine below turret number three.

The eight-inch guns used what was known as semi-fixed ammunition. It meant that bags of gunpowder had to be loaded into each gun barrel in addition to the shell. In the case of the *Chicago*'s eight-inch guns, two powder bags were needed for each shell.

Below each of the cruiser's three main battery gun turrets was a complex network of rooms, positioned deep below the waterline, that stored the ammunition. For the purpose of safety, shells and powder bags were stored on racks in separate rooms known as magazines. Each shell or bag would have to be physically taken out of the magazine and moved to an adjacent handling room. From there it would be placed on a hoist to be sent up to the turret.

The bags of gunpowder were sent up to the turret on demand. "They said the word, pass powder and I started throwing powder at the powderman who put it into the hoist," said Grady.[7] Like shipmate Howard Fortney, Grady was well below deck and had little idea of what was going on above.

* * *

After finding an eager replacement for his job as bugler, Don Yeamans had settled into life as a part of the quartermaster gang aboard the *Astoria*. In addition to steering the ship and assisting with navigation, the quartermaster group also recorded weather conditions and kept the log book. It was a multi-faceted job that involved much learning. By the middle of 1942, Yeamans was a seaman second class but was striking for the quartermaster rating.

At the time of Guadalcanal, Yeamans' battle station was the port pelorus. The small lookout point was located just off the side of the bridge. Tuned into the JV circuit with a headset, he was responsible for relaying the captain's orders to the after steering compartment.

As pilots aboard the *Astoria*, Lieutenant Richard Tunnell and Ensign Bob Schiller had no other duties than flying planes. All pilots were not so lucky. "Some ships made the aviators stand deck watches." Schiller said. "I was fortunate to get on one that didn't."[8]

The Curtiss SOC Seagull first entered service toward the end of 1935.[9] By the start of World War II, the float biplane was the standard issue aboard U.S. heavy cruisers. The plane was manned by a pilot and back seat radioman that also operated the rear flexible thirty caliber machine gun. An attachment under each wing allowed for carrying a small bomb or depth charge. Essentially an aluminum frame covered with fabric, the SOC was very susceptible to damage from gunfire. The plane primarily served two purposes aboard the *Astoria*: reconnaissance and spotting for gunfire.

The *Astoria* normally carried four planes. A complement of eight pilots was usually aboard the ship. For the Guadalcanal operation, the cruiser carried five aircraft.[10]

After boarding the *Astoria* right after Pearl Harbor, Henry Juarez settled in to his duty as a crew member of a 1.1-inch gun mount. The close range anti-aircraft gun began to enter service in great quantities in 1940. The weapon had four parallel mounted seventy-five caliber gun barrels and a maximum range of 7,400 yards.[11] The *Astoria* carried four gun mounts of this type. Mounts one and two were above the bridge, while guns three and four were on the main deck near the back of the ship. Juarez was assigned to mount four on the port side of the fantail near the stern. He described the gun as being about fifty feet from the back of the ship. The location was his general quarters battle station.

In addition to a pointer and trainer, each gun had a group of first loaders. "They had four barrels," Juarez explains. "So that was four first loaders. They loaded the guns. It's a big heavy clip. They were pretty good size slugs." Each first loader was responsible for keeping one of the gun barrels continuously loaded with ammunition. The guns were fed with eight bullet clips and could fire at a rate of 150 rounds per minute.[12] "The first loaders would load the guns and each clip would go on the cradle on the gun and as the loaded cradle fires all off, the weight of the other one would drop in and dump the other one out," Juarez continueed. "And so the first loader would put another clip in there ... as fast as they put those clips in there was as fast as that gun shot."[13]

Each gun mount also had two second loaders. It was their job to keep the first loaders full of ammunition clips. "Here's where I come. I fed the second loaders. I kept the second loaders full of ammunition." Juarez remembers grabbing the ammunition clips from a hole in the deck, a type of chute. It was not an ammunition hoist as was used for some of the larger guns. Someone from below took the clips up from the magazine and put them in this area. Juarez took the ammunition from the deck and gave it to the second loaders, who in turn would give it to the first loaders. It was a strenuous job during the fury of an air attack.

Juarez remembers that a typical day for him aboard the *Astoria* was dominated by lookout duty. "We had to go on watch; you had to be out there watching ... day and night." He mostly stood watch at his gun mount. The day would begin with an early wake up. "Real early," he said. "Six o'clock. And the first thing we had to do was clean fore and aft. You know, hit the deck, clean fore and aft and then have chow."

Juarez felt that the quality of food was good as long as the ship's supply of fresh food held out. "Mess hall was good until we got on rations. It was pretty good, pretty good chow. Three meals a day right from the stove." However, the fresh food often ran out during long voyages and was replaced with rations. While at general quarters, food was brought up to the men at their battle stations. It was pretty much limited to sandwiches.

Unlike the mess hall, Juarez did not really like the sleeping arrangements. "I was assigned to a lower deck way below the waterline," he said. "As the ship was cruising, you could hear that water going by the side of the ship, and it sounded like a train on the railroad tracks. I didn't like that place. I didn't like it down there." The compartment had rows of bunk beds that were three levels high. "I always slept on the third bunk." Juarez was a seaman second class at the time the *Astoria* left for Guadalcanal.

Between the Coral Sea and Midway battles, John Powell had gained a great deal of combat experience as a fire controlman. By the time the Guadalcanal operation began, he had attained the rating of fire controlman first class. Powell's battle station was the forward Mk 28 director. Used to control the four starboard five-inch guns, it was located up high on the superstructure above the bridge. "To be properly manned you had sixteen people," he told me. "The anti-aircraft director was sitting up on a post." The crew entered the director from the bottom. "Once you got on top of that shed at the bottom, there's a ladder that goes up underneath and there's a hatch. There is a hatch on both sides that you can go up into it."[14]

A range finder and range keeper were two key pieces of equipment on the director. "The range finder was strictly a visual type thing," Powell explained. "I operated the range keeper." He had to keep track of a target after it had already been sighted. "When we got on the target you had to coach the people who were on the telescopes. The trainer, the pointer, and the range finder operator all had to see this thing [target] before we could do anything. We would stand there and just hold our hands up pointing in the right direction. They would look around and eventually somebody would see [the target]. We had a cracker jack for a range finder operator and he could get a range on that thing in two seconds." As one might imagine, the operation of the director required a great deal of training and many individuals working together.

Once all of the information on a target was obtained, it was transmitted down to the five-inch guns, which could be set to automatic control. The guns were then director controlled and would turn automatically towards the target. Once all of the information was in the director, a crewman yelled "Set!" Anytime after that the director control officer yelled, "Commence firing on the gun batteries!"

Powell's director had a special radio receiver. He remembers having to fight to get it installed. "We had a radio speaker up in our director on the fighter circuit," Powell explained. "It was on a fighter director circuit off the carrier. He was telling the airplanes what to do. This was an air war and we were in an anti-aircraft battery, so we wanted to know what the hell was going on. That was the only way you'd know what was going on. By the time we got the word up from the bridge it was ancient history." The first wartime captain of the *Astoria* denied the request for the radio. However, Captain Scanland, who had already lost a ship to an air attack at Pearl Harbor, approved it. "It wasn't too long before the radiomen were up there," Powell remembered. The radio later proved to be a handy addition in the waters off Guadalcanal.

Chapter 7

Rendezvous at Koro

On July 26 the naval forces involved in Operation Watchtower rendezvoused about 350 miles south of the Fiji Islands. The *Chicago* had arrived from the southwest with Task Force 62 after traveling about 1,000 miles. The *Astoria* and Task Force 11 came almost 3,100 miles across the Pacific from Pearl Harbor. Also arriving from Hawaii was Task Force 16 with the carrier *Enterprise*. Several smaller groups of ships came from various points of origin.

Seventy-six ships were involved in the meeting, with seventy-two arriving on time.[1] Few of the ships had previously operated together. The ships maneuvered around the area in a confusing mess in a bid to change positions. Eventually, all of the ships present joined one of the two groups of the expeditionary group.

At 8:10 A.M. on July 27, the *Astoria* reported for duty with Task Force 62.[2] "They said we're going to have a rendezvous ... out in the Pacific, going to meet some ships," remembered Henry Juarez. "Ships start popping up all over. There were ships from one side of the ocean to the other side. Then I knew something is going on."[3] Matthew Bouterse watched the scene in amazement. "Early one morning in July I came on deck," he recalled, "and was amazed to see a huge convoy of ships of all kinds that had joined us in the night. I had never seen so many naval ships in one place before and was fascinated by the conversations that were going on by flashing lights and signal flags."[4]

The armada, an awesome site this early in the war, proceeded north to a point one hundred miles south of the Fijis. The first order of business was a meeting of senior commanders to review operational procedures. It took place aboard the *Saratoga*. By many accounts the meeting was a series of heated discussions with disagreements over how long the aircraft carriers should stay in the Guadalcanal area. When the stormy meeting ended, it was time to start the rehearsal exercise.

Located roughly in the center of the Fijis, tiny Koro Island was the site of the rehearsal exercise code named Operation Dovetail. The location was partly chosen for the isolated nature of the area, ideal to hide a large gathering of warships. To ensure the secrecy of the operation, communications between nearby islands were temporarily halted and about half of the native population was moved to the opposite side of the island.[5]

The practice operation was scheduled to take place between July 28 and 31. It was planned that all 19,000 Marines would twice go ashore on three beaches along the northern coast of the island to simulate the conditions that were expected in the Solomons.[6] Cruisers, destroyers, and carrier planes conducted both simulated and actual bombardments. For the practice run, the *Chicago* became part of the escort group, which was comprised mostly of the cruisers from the former Task Force 44. Missing was the *Salt Lake City*, detached for carrier escort duty. The *Astoria* assumed a position in the fire support group.

On the early morning of July 28, the armada gathered off the northern coast of Koro Island. The sky was overcast, the sea smooth, and visibility extended to almost fifteen miles. The rehearsal exercise began as planned at 9:00 A.M. However, the results were anything but satisfactory. Coral near the beaches resulted in an early cancellation of the landing operation. If damaged during the practice run, the landing boats could not be replaced in time for the actual operation. Troops that were not already ashore were sent back to the transports. Only about one-third of the Marines actually made it onto the island. *Chicago* sailor Art King summed up the rehearsal exercise in plain terms: "It was all screwed up."[7]

"We went to the Fiji Islands and we kind of did a dress rehearsal of the landing operation," recalled *Astoria* pilot Richard Tunnell, who participated in the exercise. "It was pretty limited, and there was nobody with any experience to do any of this stuff. We just had to make it up as we went along. We flew in the Fiji area, and we tried to figure out how many smoke flares we could put in the rear cockpit and whether we would carry hundred pound bombs or depth charges. It was pretty low key."[8]

The rehearsal exercise did provide some benefits. The cruisers and aircraft were able to practice the pre-landing bombardment, while the Marines practiced debarkation procedures from the transports. Training was also conducted on large scale landing boat operations.

Before departing the area, the *Astoria* needed to restock her magazines for the coming voyage. The supply ship *Rainier* was on hand to replenish ammunition stocks. The cruiser, along with her sister ships *Quincy* and *Vincennes*, formed a triangle around the supply ship. Then the hard work began. Hours were spent loading shells and powder bags. The arduous work continued into the early evening with searchlights providing the required illumination.

* * *

In addition to the normal crew, both the *Chicago* and *Astoria* took aboard visitors during the stay off Koro Island. Beyond her duties within the Screening Group, the *Chicago* would play an important role within the amphibious force. She would be the temporary home of a fighter director officer who would assist in coordinating the fighter coverage during the landing operation. Lieutenant Robert Bruning, Jr., boarded the cruiser from the *Saratoga* while ships were in the Fijis area. He was to operate under the code name Black Base. Bruning chose not to go aboard the flagship *Australia* over concerns about unfamiliar Australian plotting methods and communication techniques.[9]

Just prior to the start of the rehearsal exercise, a trio of marine aviators boarded the *Astoria*. Captain William "Soupy" Campbell, Second Lieutenants Roy Spurlock, and Robert Todd Whitten were all members of Marine Observation Squadron 251. The three, along with two others assigned to the *Vincennes*, had made their way to the Fijis from New Caledonia aboard the destroyer transport *Calhoun*.

Spurlock was a member of the National Guard while attending the University of Kentucky in 1940. He decided to leave school to enlist in the Marine Corps as an air cadet in 1940. Flight school quickly followed. Upon the completion of training, the young airman received a commission. At the time he was only twenty years old.

Boarding the cruiser, Spurlock seemed quite surprised as to the size of the ship. "This ship looked like a city compared to the little *Calhoun* from which we had come," he later wrote.[10] The aviators were assigned quarters in the captain's outer cabin. The area was normally used for meetings, and in peacetime, entertainment. The room contained a large conference table that could accommodate as many as twenty people. On the mahogany sideboard, Spurlock noticed silver flatware. It had been a gift to the ship from the City of Astoria. Folding cots were set up for the three guests.

It did not take long for the aviators to learn why they were put aboard the ship. "We found that we were on board for the purpose of flying as rear seat observers in the cruiser's scout planes," Spurlock recounted. It was our job to observe the battle area from the back seat of the cruiser scout planes and report any enemy activity back to the commanding general on the [command] ship during the initial stages."[11]

It would be several days before the hazy picture of where the *Astoria* was going started to become clearer for the crewmen aboard. It began with the officers. "We didn't know the destination," said Gene Alair. "At least at my level we didn't know the destination. We had left. We were probably three or four days before we got there [Guadalcanal] before we knew the destination. They put a chart up in the wardroom and told the officers what we were doing."[12] The junior officers were given a briefing of the upcoming operation by Executive Officer Shoup. Since most of the *Astoria*'s crew had never heard of the Solomon Islands, they really had no idea as to where they were going. Like many of the others, Alair did not really know the location of Guadalcanal. It was not long before information started to be disseminated down to the enlisted men by various officers. "Finally, they said what we're going to do," said Henry Juarez. "We're going to go make a landing in Guadalcanal. It was just that we were going to some islands to get back at the Japs."[13]

Sailors aboard the *Chicago* also learned of their destination. Like the crew of the *Astoria*, they did not know much about their target. "Nobody knew where we were going," said Fred Tuccitto. "We had been at sea for maybe a day or two before they even told us. Then we kept going north and it got hot. Then they told us that we were going to land in Guadalcanal. Well, that didn't mean anything us. None of us had maps or anything. We didn't know where we were going."[14] Bill Grady recalled hearing the news over the ship's loudspeaker directly from Captain Bode. "The captain came on and told us where we were going to go and what was going to happen, that we would have casualties."[15]

When the rehearsal exercise concluded on July 31, it was time to leave Koro Island behind. Late in the afternoon the ships weighed anchor. The voyage to Guadalcanal had begun.

Chapter 8

The Voyage

As the rehearsal exercise drifted to a close on July 31, Task Force 62 made ready for the almost 1,100 mile voyage to Guadalcanal. In the vicinity of Koro Island, the sky was blue except for a few broken clouds. The sea was calm and in places the visibility stretched out as far as twenty-five miles. In preparation for the voyage, some of the ships refueled from the tankers *Kanawha* and *Platte*. Admirals Turner and Crutchley conferred with regards to operational orders. The final preparations had been completed.

At 4:30 P.M. the ships of Task Force 62 weighed anchor and began their departure.[1] The *Astoria, Quincy, Vincennes,* and seven destroyers detached from the task force to complete fueling. Koro Island soon became a distant memory. The task force initially traveled south and west to arrive in the general vicinity of the carriers. The flattops had been milling around the waters south of the Fijis for several days as their planes participated in the rehearsal exercises.

By 8:00 A.M. on August 1, the task force was located just southwest of the Fijis. The ships were traveling west and slightly north at an average speed of seven knots using various courses to clear the island group.[2] The weather was good and ideal for cruising with moderate wind and calm seas. The carriers were located north of the transports traveling on an almost parallel course.

By midday a number of ships of Task Force 62 had departed on various duties, all ordered to return upon the completion of their assignments. The destroyer *Hull* departed to deliver messages and mail to the carrier task force. The *Kanawha, Platte,* and *Rainier* were sent away under the escort of two destroyers. The *Astoria* and others that had detached for fueling arrived back with the force in the morning. The speed of the group soon increased to fourteen knots. At one point the force sighted the carrier group off in the distance and briefly exchanged signals.

Two ships assigned to the task force that did not make the rendezvous south of the Fijis had missed the practice exercise and were not en route to Guadalcanal. The transports *Zeilin* and *Betelgeuse* had departed from Pearl Harbor as part of a small convoy on July 21. The ships were loaded with a battalion of Marines.

Strict radio silence made finding the transports a difficult endeavor. To ascertain the whereabouts of the missing ships, Admiral Turner directed Captain Bode of the *Chicago* to send two of his scout planes to the port city of Suva, Fiji. The planes carried a letter from Turner to the port director instructing the transports to rendezvous with two destroyers that were left behind. The return of the planes brought good news. Having arrived at Koro after the task force departed, the stragglers had gone to Suva. The two transports were soon on their way to the task force under the careful escort of the *Dewey* and *Mugford*.

8. The Voyage

* * *

The voyage to Guadalcanal was fraught with peril. A critical factor in the success of the landing operation was the ability to take the Japanese by surprise. If the invasion force were to be discovered while on route to the Solomons, the Japanese might have time to plan a nasty reception. In addition to the large naval and air facilities at Rabaul, an even larger naval base stood directly north at Truk. The hazards were many and varied. American commanders and sailors alike had plenty to worry about as their ships moved northwest.

Among the first sources of worry was that the large gathering of American ships in the Fijis was somehow noticed. Perhaps a neutral agent or one sympathetic to the Japanese would be in a position to report the information. The isolated nature of the area around Koro Island and steps previously discussed seemed to ease those concerns.

Once the voyage began, concern quickly shifted to the possibility of detection by submarine. In spite of the best efforts of the escorting destroyers, it seemed entirely possible that an enemy demon lurking just below the waves could sound the alarm of the approaching ships. During the late July and early August time frame, the Japanese actually had only two submarines operating in this general area of the South Pacific, with three additional vessels in the waters off Sydney.[3] However, submarine *I-169* sank a Dutch ship near New Caledonia on July 27.[4] In light of this information, unknown to Admiral Turner at the time, the submarine threat was real. To counter the threat the task forces followed a zig-zag pattern during daylight hours.

As the ships moved closer to the Solomons, the submarine threat was supplemented by a menace from the air. Intelligence indicated that the Japanese habitually sent one, possibly two, seaplanes daily from Tulagi south to the New Hebrides area. Additionally, on alternating days a scout was sent to the open waters northwest of the Fijis.[5] The route of the voyage was carefully planned to avoid these areas. However, there was no guarantee that the Japanese would not change or add to their normal patrol routes.

As Task Force 62 plodded toward the Solomons, the men of each branch of the service did what they could to pass the time and ease the anxiety. The Marines made the most of their cramped conditions aboard the transports. Officers reviewed and re-reviewed the assault plans. Some enlisted men passed the time away playing cards, while others spent time cleaning their guns or sharpening bayonets. One marine officer had his men write letters home, lamenting "that for some of them it would probably be the last letters they would write."[6]

As for the navy men, the sailors aboard the *Chicago* and *Astoria* were not alone in wondering about what the future might hold. It is not difficult to imagine what questions they might have been asking during this time. *Would our ships be discovered? What would be the Japanese response? Will we have to fight our way to Guadalcanal? Would we participate in a sea battle?* Nobody knew for sure, but it likely made for hot conversation in the galleys, mess halls, and wardrooms of each ship of the task force. Roy Spurlock later reflected on the time. "The night before the attack on Guadalcanal was not a restful one for anybody."[7]

* * *

While the ships of Task Force 62 headed for Guadalcanal, the Army Air Corps began its vital operations in advance of the landing. Beginning on July 31 Army heavy bombers began to hit Guadalcanal and Tulagi. Operating from bases in the New Hebrides, B-17s were scheduled to bomb the islands for seven straight days with the airfield on Guadalcanal being a prime target. Supply depots and gun emplacements were also targeted on both islands.[8]

* * *

A transport and destroyer are seen off the bow of the *Chicago* on July 30, 1942. After a very unsatisfactory rehearsal exercise off Koro Island, the ships began the perilous voyage to Guadalcanal (U.S. Navy / National Archives).

Once away from the Fijis, the fifty-one ships of Task Force 62 assumed a cruising formation that they would follow for a good part of the remaining voyage. The disposition was an arrangement in a series of circles. At the center were the nineteen transports, including Turner's flagship *McCawley*, positioned in five columns. The columns stood 1,000 yards apart and each transport stood 600 yards ahead of the one behind. Arrayed ahead of the cluster of transports were the four converted destroyer transports.

The cruisers were clustered in three locations forming somewhat of a triangle around the inner circle. The *Chicago* was second behind the light cruiser *San Juan* off the port bow of the transports. Opposite the two cruisers off the starboard bow was the *Australia* followed by the *Hobart* and *Vincennes*. The remaining three cruisers were positioned directly behind the transports with the *Astoria* and *Canberra* running parallel ahead of the *Quincy*. The remaining destroyers and minesweepers provided an anti-submarine screen forming a wide outer circle.

The formation provided for good protection against an attack by either submarine or aircraft. Every type of precaution was taken to ensure that the presence of the ships would not be discovered. Strict radio silence was to be maintained by all ships. Visual signals were to be used only during the daytime hours with no use of blinker lights at night.

Aboard the *Astoria* the cruiser's searchlights were turned inward. Each had a three foot wide glass lens that could easily reflect the moonlight on a dark night. In anticipation of battle, her crew had scraped off much of the paint off the bulkheads prior to the start of the voyage.[9] Unknown at the time, it would add precious hours to the life of the ship during the critical situation that lay ahead.

* * *

As the *Astoria* began the journey to Guadalcanal, Chaplain Bouterse's Bible study group was growing. The group met almost every night in the mess hall with as many as fifty men in attendance. "It was a new and rewarding experience for me," Bouterse later wrote. "At the heart of it all was the little group of men led by Vic McAnney, who had been praying for a chaplain that they didn't yet know and hadn't seen."[10]

As dawn broke on Sunday August 2, Bouterse was getting ready for his weekly worship service. The chaplain had somewhat of a restless night, waking up to write out his planned sermon. "Only in seminary had I ever written a sermon," he later recalled, "but I was writing a sermon as if someone were dictating it to me."[11] With a potential big battle looming only days away, Bouterse knew that this service would be an important one. "I took the notes for the message I had said I was going to use and walked into a compartment filled with churchgoers." In attendance among the full crowd were Captain Greenman and a large contingent of officers.

When it came time for the sermon, the chaplain decided to be impromptu. "I took my page of notes from my Bible and before a startled congregation I tore them into shreds," he later wrote. "Then I began to speak from my heart." Bouterse delivered a powerful sermon talking to the men about the realities of life and death. "I went to my room trembling because I had never had such an experience before. It was as though someone else had preached and I had just listened." The message was a good prelude to the test that many of the men would face in the upcoming days off Guadalcanal.

* * *

August 2 proved to be another good day for sailing with a blue sky, broken clouds, calm seas, and light winds. At 11:00 A.M. six destroyers left the task force for a fuel stop at Efate. Located in the southern part of the New Hebrides, the port stood directly ahead of the task force. The Australian light cruiser *Hobart* and the minesweeper group left for the same destination later in the day.

The missing transports finally joined the task force on the third day of August. At 5:55 A.M. a ship was sighted on the horizon that turned out to be the *Zeilin*, arriving for duty with the *Mugford*. The *Betelgeuse* along with her escorting destroyer arrived later in the morning, having been delayed with engine trouble.

At 9:05 A.M. the *Chicago* signaled a submarine contact off the port beam. It was the first sub scare since leaving the Fijis. The task force immediately changed course to avoid the contact area with all of the ships simultaneously turning forty degrees to the right. Upon further investigation, no submarine was found and the contact was thought to be nothing more than a large fish.[12]

During August 3 and 4 the task force continued traveling in a west-northwesterly direction and passed directly below the New Hebrides Islands. The large island of New Caledonia lay almost 500 miles to the southwest. During this time the ships entered what American intelligence considered to be the extreme search range of the Japanese seaplanes based at Tulagi. The ships continued to move in the same direction to avoid the previously observed reconnaissance routes flown by Japanese search planes. Starting at 8:00 A.M. all twenty-four destroyers of Task Force 62 refueled from either the transports or from the tanker *Cimarron*. Refueling was completed by late afternoon. It was the last topping off for the smaller ships. The larger storage bunkers of the cruisers allowed for enough fuel for the entire voyage.

While traveling below the New Hebrides, the carriers of Task Force 61 shifted to the south of the amphibious force and continued to follow a roughly parallel course. During the early afternoon hours of August 4, four Wildcat fighters from the *Saratoga* conducted a search for a bogey that had appeared on radar. No enemy planes were found, and there was no evidence to suggest that the invasion fleet had been sighted by the enemy.

Blue sky became increasingly scarce during the day of August 5. Scattered clouds in the morning increased to a complete overcast by afternoon. The calm sea turned moderate and the winds began to pick up. The amphibious force was passing directly south of the Solomons. The carrier task force was once again sighted at 7:30 A.M. Later in the morning Task Force 62 turned to the northwest. Eventually the ships were pointed straight north. During the day a report reached the task forces that land based reconnaissance planes saw no enemy aircraft on the airfield at Guadalcanal. As daylight faded the invasion force was less than 500 miles from the Solomons.

The sailors and Marines of Task Force 62 awoke on the morning of Thursday, August 6, to different weather conditions. The day was to be the most critical of the voyage. Closing in on Guadalcanal and Tulagi from the south, detection by enemy search planes seemed almost unavoidable. However, the weather had come to the rescue. Gone were the mostly blue sky and calm seas that marked the early days of the voyage. Dawn broke to reveal a completely overcast sky and a thick heavy haze in the air. Visibility was as low as four miles, ideal conditions to hide a large group of ships.

Tricky currents and hazy weather conditions made it difficult for the navigators to get a good positional fix. Guadalcanal was beyond the range of radar and the sun could not be seen though the thick haze. It was of major concern to American commanders given the narrow passages and shoals that lay ahead. Zig-zagging was discontinued due to the difficult conditions. At noon the destroyer *Selfridge* departed the task force with orders to fix a navigational position on Bellona Island. The small mass of land, located directly below Guadalcanal, was about sixty miles northeast of the task force. The destroyer returned with the critical information late in the afternoon allowing the force to forge ahead with less worry, at least about the navigational issues.

The invasion force once again suffered a scare during the early afternoon. Wildcat fighters from the *Saratoga* searched for reported radar contacts, in this case four bogeys. No enemy planes were sighted, likely due to poor visibility. Monitoring of known enemy radio frequencies yielded no frantic warning messages. It appeared that the invasion force had once again escaped detection. As history would later show, three Japanese search planes took off from Tulagi that morning to scour the waters south of the Solomons. Evidence suggests that at least one of the planes may have passed close enough to sight Task Force 61, but was unable to do so owing to the poor weather conditions.[13]

Late in the afternoon the carrier group began to move away from the amphibious force. The flattops would mill around in the waters between Guadalcanal and Rennell Island to support the landing. The amphibious force continued to move north at twelve knots. The final approach to Guadalcanal lay ahead.

Chapter 9

Approach and Landing

For the final leg of the voyage to Guadalcanal, Task Force 62 assumed a different formation, one that would present a narrow front to the target island and any potential Japanese lookouts. The arrangement placed many of the cruisers in front of the transports in case it became necessary to fight through Japanese surface forces to get to Guadalcanal.[1] At about 4:00 P.M. on August 6, the ships switched to the approach disposition as outlined in the operation plan.

The new formation required the ships to separate into two groups on the basis of their target destination. The ships bound for Tulagi were to swing around the northern side of Savo Island and proceed directly to their target. The second group would navigate the narrow channel that separated Guadalcanal from adjacent Savo Island. Arriving off the northern coast of Guadalcanal, the transports would disembark their troops in landing craft toward Red Beach.

Bound for Tulagi, Squadron Yoke assumed the lead when its four transports and four destroyer transports formed a single column with the latter in the lead. The *Chicago* was positioned 1,000 yards ahead of the lead destroyer transport. Leading the entire procession directly in front of the *Chicago* was the light cruiser *San Juan*. The destroyers *Bagley* and *Henley* stood off the cruiser's port and starboard bow, respectively. The *Canberra* trailed behind the last transport. Destroyers and minesweepers flanked both sides of the single column. Harry Blumhorst remembered a rumor going around the *Chicago* that Captain Bode had requested that the cruiser be the first ship in the formation.[2] As the rumor went the request was denied and Bode had to settle for being number two behind the *San Juan*.

Almost six miles behind the Yoke Squadron were the ships of Squadron X-Ray. The fifteen transports were arranged in two parallel columns spaced about 1,500 yards apart. Centered between the columns and positioned 1,000 yards ahead were the cruisers *Australia*, *Hobart*, and *Vincennes*, with Admiral Crutchley's flagship in the lead position. Almost 1,000 yards behind the transports, also spaced between the two columns, the *Astoria* led her sister ship *Quincy*. A similar arrangement of destroyers flanked both sides of the cruisers and transports.[3]

At 8:00 P.M. Task Force 62 was located just over sixty miles southwest of Guadalcanal.[4] Near the end of the day, Admiral Turner distributed a final message of encouragement to all of the ships under his command. It was to be read over the loudspeaker of each vessel for all hands to hear.

The final hours of the day found the ships of the amphibious force plodding along at twelve knots bound for the almost twenty mile wide channel that separated the northwest tip of Guadalcanal from the Russell Islands. As midnight passed, the sky remained overcast blotting out the moon and keeping the visibility poor. Conditions, however, began to get better during the early morning hours. Visibility began to improve shortly after midnight. From their forward positions and through the dark of night, the destroyers *Bagley* and *Henley* led the task force into the waters off Guadalcanal. At 1:33 A.M. the *Henley* sighted a dark mass off on the horizon. Guadalcanal was now in sight.

From her position right behind the *San Juan*, lookouts aboard the *Chicago* quickly sighted the coast of Guadalcanal. The cruiser was steaming at twelve knots with six of her eight boilers in use.[5] The crew was at condition of readiness two. Under the semi-alert arrangement, 50 percent of the crew was at their battle stations, while the other half rested off duty. The two groups of the crew rotated every four hours.

The stroke of midnight brought a change of watch aboard the *Astoria*. Commander William H. Truesdell climbed into position at sky control. The thirty-nine-year-old officer had graduated with the Annapolis class of 1925. He had been promoted to commander right after the Battle of Midway.[6] As gunnery officer he was responsible for just about everything related to the ships armament.

Located near the forward main battery director, sky control was high up on the superstructure. It was the control center for the cruiser's guns. From his vantage point, Truesdell

In what may be the last photograph of the *Astoria*, the cruiser is seen during the voyage to the Guadalcanal area. The photograph was taken from the Chicago (U.S. Navy / National Archives).

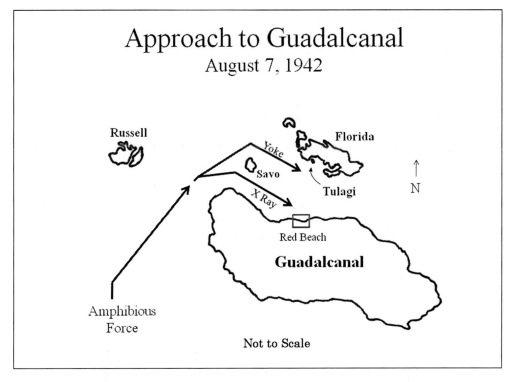

Adapted from Leonard Ware, *The Landing in the Solomons* (Washington, DC: Office of Naval Intelligence, United States Navy, 1943). *Note:* Map is not to scale and represents approximate movements.

would direct the pre-invasion bombardment later in the morning. At the particular time the area was filled with a crowd of men busily going about their duties. Lookouts manned the outdoor areas, carefully scanning the horizon with their binoculars.

By way of headphones Truesdell was connected to various key parts of the ship. He quickly was brought up to speed on the latest information. There was no word from the Japanese. Apparently the task force had not been sighted. On the outside some stars could now be seen. It was not long before men aboard the *Astoria* also sighted Guadalcanal. The land mass was dark and it seemed as if the island was sleeping.

At about 3:00 A.M. the task force was located just off the northwestern tip of Guadalcanal. It was time for the two squadrons to split.[7] The Yoke Squadron turned slightly to the northeast and began to venture around the north side of Savo Island. The *Chicago* maintained her position behind the *San Juan*. The *Chicago* went to general quarters at about 3:30 A.M.[8] The X-Ray Squadron and the *Astoria* turned to the east and entered the narrow passage between Savo and Guadalcanal. The distance between the islands was only about seven and a half miles. The ships were truly entering the unknown.

Aboard the *Astoria* Captain Greenman wanted to make sure his ship was ready for action early. "I decided that 2:00 A.M. would be the right time to go to general quarters," he recalled, "but I had no instructions at that time or any other time."[9] It was time for every sailor to report to his battle station. Every lookout had to be extra alert.

It was very possible that Japanese patrols could be lurking in the vicinity of Savo Island. The water was calm and could be heard slapping against the ships. The waves could be heard breaking against the shore in the distance. A quarter moon had risen in the northeast, silhouetting the islands.[10] The partial moon provided just enough light for good visibility. As fate would have it, no Japanese were encountered. The ships peacefully cruised past Savo Island unmolested.

During the last hours before dawn, the final pre-invasion preparations were completed. Aboard the transports heading for Guadalcanal, the Marines were up early at 4:30 A.M. and calmly ate a heavy breakfast.[11] Many would soon be nervously loitering on deck, lining the rails to get a good look at the distant island.[12] Before long the Marines, loaded with rifles and packs, would be waiting on deck to board the landing craft.

Aboard the aircraft carriers of Task Force 61, sailing in the waters southwest of Guadalcanal, the flight decks were loaded with planes. The pilots aboard the *Saratoga* had gathered one last time the night before for a final review of the maps. They had been studying their impending missions nightly during the voyage north.[13] Blue exhaust streaked from engines of planes that were warming up on the flight deck in the pre-dawn hours. At about 5:35 A.M. the first plane, a Wildcat fighter, rose from the flight deck of the *Enterprise*.[14] A total of ninety-three planes were soon airborne and on the way to the Guadalcanal area.

* * *

The early morning light revealed Guadalcanal and Tulagi for the first time in full color. The weather was generally clear except for a few scattered clouds. Some light mist or fog was hovering in the area but seemed to be burning off.

As the *Chicago* passed Guadalcanal bound for Tulagi, Fred Tuccitto was among the sailors who wondered what the next day would hold. "[The Japanese] knew what it was like to be in a war. We didn't," he recalled. "We had no inkling of what we were getting into. I don't think anybody knew."[15]

For the men who were on deck it was a chance to see the islands that they had heard so much about. Ken Maysenhalder was at his battle station, a five-inch gun mount on the starboard side. "Approaching the island of Guadalcanal, I could smell the aroma of tropical plants as the wind blew the smell out to sea. All was quiet as we approached the island." Maysenhalder recalled the calmness. "It was very eerie."[16]

Charles Germann was also topside during the approach. "I was on the flight deck for some reason," he remembered. At first he had trouble seeing the islands off in the distance, but not later. "I could see everything."[17]

Fred Tuccitto recalled the first time that he saw the island. "It was sort of covered with a lot of clouds," he said. "It was sort of mysterious. As we approached the island we could see land on the horizon. And then you don't see it. And then you see it. Finally we got pretty close to the island. You could smell it. It smells different than being out in the ocean." After arriving off Tulagi as part of the Yoke group, the *Chicago* stayed with the transports as she did not have a specific gunfire assignment.

Gene Alair was at his battle station on the forward 1.1-inch gun mounts as the *Astoria* nudged closer to Guadalcanal. "You could smell it. We knew we were getting near land," remembered Alair. "We knew what we were doing, but it was new to us. We had never gone into an amphibious operation."[18] Also topside was Henry Juarez. He was manning the 1.1-inch guns near the stern of the ship. "We knew we were going into something," he said. "Early in dawn in the morning we could see the islands. It was dead quiet."[19] Like many others pilot Richard Tunnell simply remembered the approach to Guadalcanal as being quiet. "It was spooky," he said. "It was an eerie sensation."[20]

Off the coast of Guadalcanal, the *Astoria* was following the *Quincy* and *Vincennes* toward the fire support position. The three heavy cruisers were joined by four destroyers. There appeared to be no activity on land as the seven ships quietly approached the island.

Intelligence made available to the *Astoria* as part of the operation plan suggested that supplies, motor vehicles, and anti-aircraft guns were likely in her assigned bombardment area.[21] In the days leading up to the invasion, B-17s had reported the existence of twelve anti-aircraft guns at various locations on the island.

At exactly 6:13 A.M. the silence of the morning was shattered by the tremendous blast of the *Quincy*'s eight-inch guns. Directed to the west of Lunga Point, her shots soon started a large fire.[22] The *Vincennes* then spoke with an eight-inch salvo of her own. Finally, it was the *Astoria*'s turn. Her three turrets trained out to the starboard side, and she opened fire with a full nine gun main battery salvo directed at the area east of the Lunga River. A flash of light coming from the eight-inch guns was quickly followed by thin streaks of red heading in the direction of land. A flash ashore indicated the approximate point of the impact.

When the *Astoria* opened fire, Matthew Bouterse was below deck at his battle station. His location did not stop the chaplain from wanting to see the action. "I managed to snatch a few quick glimpses through a hatch that we had loosened in the huge watertight door that led topside from the chief's quarters," he later recalled.[23] He soon paid the price when the concussion of an eight-inch salvo sent the hatch crashing down on his head. He later returned to the viewing point wearing his steel helmet for protection. With the firing of the eight-inch guns, he saw red streaks reaching out to the beach area. "I can still remember the way the concussion of those blasts felt in my gut. And this was the sending end!"

As Guadalcanal shook from the rumble of explosions, coconut trees became uprooted and fell to the ground as debris flew through the air. By many accounts it was a spectacular show of force. Shortly after the bombardment began, a flare or series of small rockets shot up from the island in the direction of Tulagi. Perhaps it was some type of belated warning.

In what seemed like only a matter of a few minutes since the bombardment started, the carrier planes suddenly appeared overhead roaring past the *Astoria* to begin the attack from the air. Fighter planes swooped down near Tulagi shooting up the Japanese seaplanes that bobbed on the water. All seven of the large four engine flying boats, as well as the nine floatplane fighters were destroyed on the water. No Japanese planes made it airborne.[24] From his gun mount on the *Chicago*, Ken Maysenhalder saw the planes coming in for the attack. "After only a few minutes," he recalled, "all hell erupted. Overhead our carrier planes approached and dropped bombs. When these bombs hit the target you could feel the explosion and the impact that they made."[25] Additional fighters and dive bombers hit targets on Tanambogo, Florida, and Guadalcanal.

At sea the naval bombardment continued. Each time the *Astoria* fired her eight-inch guns the entire ship shook from the concussion. There was a slight pause between salvos, just enough time for minor adjustments to be made to the bearings. The *Astoria* poured salvo after salvo onto Guadalcanal with no return fire coming from the island.

Action was suddenly taking place at sea off the *Astoria*'s port bow. The destroyers *Dewey* and *Selfridge* were firing at some type of small craft. An observer aboard the *Astoria* believed that the target was a Japanese patrol boat. However, it was actually a small schooner loaded with gasoline that had initially been set aflame by the carrier planes. The destroyers finished off the boat, which burned furiously before going under. It was now time for the Marines to get into the action.

* * *

Exactly eight months to the day since the attack on Pearl Harbor, the first full scale American amphibious operation since 1898 was about to begin.[26] As the sea and air bombardment drew to a close, the transports moved toward the assigned beach. On both sides of the sound, the decks of the transports were crowded with Marines, each carrying a rifle and loaded down with various packs. Davits swung outward and slowly lowered landing craft down into the water, each of which carried a small American flag perched on the back. Marines then descended down rope ladders into the waiting craft below.

Off Guadalcanal the transports slowly glided to a stop at a debarkation point that was four and a half miles directly north of the beach area. The final step before the Marines could go ashore was a thorough blasting of the beach. As the first wave of fully loaded landing craft began to move away from the transports, the bombardment force moved into position.

A total of seven ships was assigned to fire away at the landing zone. The *Astoria* and four destroyers covered the actual beach.[27] The bombardment was to cover the entire beach plus an additional 800 yards on each side.[28] The ships had been instructed to fire from the water's edge to a depth of 200 yards inland and to avoid hitting wharves, jetties, and bridges that did not appear to be threats.

The bombardment commenced at 9:03 A.M. with the thundering roar of gunfire.[29] The combined fire of the seven ships provided a tremendous display of firepower. Gun crews aboard the *Astoria* worked at a feverish pace to keep up the bombardment. Five-inch guns cracked out single shells as the main batteries shot out sheets of flame. As the shell fire continued, the landing boats sped toward the beach maneuvering in a 1,600 yard wide channel that was marked by a destroyer on each side.[30] Directly in front of the small boats, the beach area was a mass of explosions. As the landing craft came to within 1,300 yards from the beach, the guns fell silent. The bombardment was over, having lasted only about six minutes. In the short time the *Astoria* had expended forty-five rounds of eight-inch and two hundred five-inch shells.[31]

From his vantage point in the forward anti-aircraft director, John Powell had a bird's eye view of the bombardment. "Before the troops went ashore, we bombarded all the area where they were going to land; knocked down a lot of coconut trees," he said. "It didn't hurt anything, just shook up a couple of natives over there."[32]

In the aftermath of the bombardment, a thick haze of dirty smoke floated in the air over the beach. [33] Just four minutes after the firing stopped the first troops landed without opposition. The first Marines ashore quickly advanced inland about 600 yards to establish a beachhead. No Japanese were encountered. Word quickly reached Admiral Turner that things ashore were going better than expected.

* * *

The *Astoria*'s scout planes were called on to participate at the very start of the landing operation. As the senior aviator aboard the *Astoria*, Lieutenant Allan Edmands flew the first flight off the cruiser.[34] Most of the initial missions were related to fire support, with the intention that the planes would act as spotters for the ship's gunfire. However, with no opposition reported ashore, the air patrols later shifted to anti-submarine flights.

Richard Tunnell was one of the pilots assigned to fly a morning mission over Guadalcanal. His specific mission was to over fly Red Beach repeatedly dropping smoke flares at each end and then to act as a forward spotter. His rear seat passenger for the flight was Marine major Campbell. Just prior to departure, Tunnell reported to Captain Greenman for final instructions. The captain warned him of Japanese float fighter planes reported to be at Tulagi. The thought crossed the pilot's mind that Greenman believed that he was not coming back. "When he said goodbye," recalled Tunnell, "I think he meant it."

Just after launching, Tunnell spotted two planes diving down close to his position. He felt a bit unnerved, but was relieved when it turned out to be American fighters. A short time later he caught a glimpse of tracer bullets passing below the plane on the right side. Believing to be under fire, Tunnell immediately began evasive maneuvers. He yelled back to check on the well-being of Major Campbell. "I was just test firing the machine gun," the marine replied. The mission continued, although with a somewhat irritated pilot.

At the appointed time, Tunnell guided his plane over the beach. The bombardment of the landing zone had just been completed. Campbell dropped the smoke flares, replacing earlier ones that were on the verge of burning out. Emerging from the beach area, Tunnell banked his plane and headed over the island, swooping in low for a close look at the Japanese airfield that was under construction. Flying over a nearby camp, he noticed smoke gently wafting up from some cooking grills. There was no sign of the Japanese. Tunnell soon noticed some type of warehouse that the Japanese had constructed under a cluster of coconut trees and decided to attack it. Climbing back up to 2,000 feet, the plane dived down and

Smoke from a fire on Tulagi is seen almost directly off the bow of the *Chicago*. Little gunfire support was needed after the initial landing on Guadalcanal due to lack of resistance, but that was not the case of the Tulagi side of the operation (U.S. Navy / National Archives).

unleashed two small 100 pound bombs on the structure. After pulling up, Tunnell yelled back to Major Campbell to see if he had observed any hits. There was no reply. Turning around, he soon noticed that the major was out cold. The observer had not properly secured the rear machine gun after his earlier surprise test firing. During the dive, the gun swung around striking the marine in the head.

Additional searches of the immediate area yielded no sign of the Japanese. "We could see the Marines getting ashore," Tunnell said. "Everything was quiet." With the mission completed, the pilot and passenger headed back to the *Astoria* after having been in the air for almost five hours.

* * *

By midmorning, the Marines began to advance west, moving along the coast towards the Lunga River. The *Astoria* was assigned to follow the westward progress of the troops along the beach. She was to stand by to provide gunfire support as needed. However, since no Japanese opposition was encountered, the fire support was not necessary.

While the *Astoria* was fulfilling her duties as part of the bombardment group, the *Chicago* continued to operate with the screening group. The ship cruised at various speeds near the transport area off Tulagi. The operation plan called for the *Chicago* to stay underway just outside of the 100 fathom curve in close proximity to the transports.[35] The screening force was now operating without the four cruisers and six destroyers who had departed to shell the beaches. Just after 8:00 A.M. the *Chicago* launched two seaplanes for inner air antisubmarine patrol. Twenty minutes later an additional plane was launched for the same duty.[36] The original two planes were recovered after spending about an hour in the air. The alternating process of launching and recovering planes continued throughout the late morning hours. However, the *Chicago*'s role of hosting the fighter director officer would soon be taking center stage.

Chapter 10

Air Attacks

Japanese naval leaders believed that the Solomon Islands would be the scene of an American counterattack. However, such a move was not expected until sometime late in 1943.[1] The first indication of trouble in the Guadalcanal area on the morning of August 7 came to Rabaul in the form of a of plain language emergency radio message. The commanding officer of the Tulagi Communication Base reported, "Enemy surface force of twenty ships has entered Tulagi. While making landing preparations, the enemy is bombarding the shore."[2] A later message reported one battleship, three cruisers, fifteen destroyers, and various transports in the waters offshore. The final message was received just short of two hours after the initial warning. "Enemy troop strength is overwhelming. We will defend to the last man. We pray for the continuance of military fortune." [3] A short time after the last message was sent, gunfire from the *San Juan* knocked out the radio station silencing the Tulagi garrison forever.[4]

The Japanese commanders at Rabaul wasted no time in preparing a response to the American intrusion into their empire. The initial task fell on Rear Admiral Sadayoshi Yamada, commander of the 25th Air Flotilla. On the airfields around Rabaul, he had at his disposal an assortment of bombers and fighters. As it turned out, the Japanese already had an attack force ready. Only a few days earlier the Japanese discovered the existence of a small Allied airfield at Rabi on the far eastern end of New Guinea. In the hours before dawn, ground crews had prepared twenty-seven bombers and nine fighters for an attack.

The stunning news from Tulagi suddenly changed the mission. Admiral Yamada quickly issued new orders for the planes to instead attack Tulagi. Additionally, he directed nine dive bombers to take off and attack as soon as ready. The transports were to be the main target unless the American carriers assumed to be part of the operation could be located.

The Japanese bombers that set out to attack the invaders were no strangers to American sailors. The Mitsubishi G4M1 entered service in April 1941.[5] Officially named the Navy Type 1 Attack Bomber, the plane was known to the allies as the Betty. The twin engine land-based bomber had a long and thin cigar-like fuselage. The plane was fast and had a long range, but it lacked armor protection for the crew of seven. An internal bomb bay could carry four small bombs, two larger bombs or could be modified to carry a torpedo.

The *Chicago* had survived an attack in the Coral Sea by Japanese twin engine bombers of a similar type nearly three months earlier. Bill Grady remembered how Captain Bode's seamanship helped the cruiser survive the attack. "He wasn't afraid of nothing," Grady said. "In the Battle of Coral Sea he was at the helm and he saved us. If one [torpedo] was at starboard, he would swing the helm to port. It would lean to starboard and it would bring the keel up out of the water and the torpedo would go under us."[6]

The twenty-seven Bettys took to the air at about 10:00 A.M. Since there was no time to switch to torpedoes, the planes contained the same payload of bombs intended for the Rabi mission. The escort was increased to eighteen Zero fighters as American carrier planes were expected to be in the area. Scout planes scurried out just ahead of the bombers in hopes of locating the carriers. After departing Rabaul, the planes traveled southeast over Bougainville.

About an hour after the main attack group departed, a second group of Japanese planes took flight. Nine Aichi D3A "Val" dive bombers comprised the second wave of the air attack. Normally a carrier based plane, Vals had delivered punishing blows to American ships in Pearl Harbor and British vessels in the Indian Ocean. Flying without the benefit of a fighter escort, the single engine planes did not have the range to make the round trip. After attacking the American ships, the pilots were instructed to ditch their planes off the southern coast of Bougainville where a flying boat and seaplane tender would be waiting.

From a perch on top a hill in southern Bougainville, coastwatcher Paul Mason took note of the first group of passing planes. As the planes roared past his jungle hideout, he quickly counted the bombers and transmitted a radio message using an emergency frequency.[7] The message was picked up by Pearl Harbor and was quickly re-sent to the invasion fleet.

With the word that enemy planes were on the way, the task force sprang into action. A simple message, hoisted from the flagship read, "Repel air attack."[8] The transports ceased unloading operations and made ready to get underway. In the event of an air attack, the ships of the screening force were to form a tight ring around the transports, which were assumed to be the target.

At 10:40 A.M. the *Chicago* received the warning that enemy planes were on the way. At the time she was patrolling with the *Australia* and destroyers *Henley* and *Helm* near the Yoke transports.[9] Lieutenant Bruning, the guest fighter director officer from the *Saratoga* who was stationed aboard the cruiser, would have his work cut out over the next day and a half. Bruning and his small staff controlled the fighters that were providing a protective cap over the transport area.

The Japanese attack force winged its way south reaching the approximate halfway point over the island of Vella Lavella in the Central Solomons. The jagged mountains of Guadalcanal came into view when the planes reached the Russell Islands. The target was only about fifty miles ahead. Scattered clouds hung at about 13,000 feet with clear sky above and below.[10]

Approaching the target area, Japanese pilots were astonished at what they saw. The wakes of the ships below appeared as hundreds of white lines in the waters off the northern coast of Guadalcanal. The warships, transports, and landing craft were too numerous to count.[11] The twenty-seven Japanese bombers flew in three tight formations of nine planes each. The attackers approached the waters between Guadalcanal and Tulagi from the northwest passing over Savo Island.

At 1:14 P.M. the enemy planes appeared on the *Chicago's* CXAM radar set at a distance of forty-three miles. Just then twelve Wildcat fighters from the *Saratoga* tore into the attacking Japanese planes. Some of the fighters were able to make a clean pass at the bombers, but others were jumped by the escorting Zeros.

Less than ten minutes after the radar sighting, lookouts aboard the *Chicago* visually sighted twenty-five bombers and three escorting fighters. Two minutes later the lookouts reported that one bomber dropped out of formation and was falling toward the water in flames. There appeared to be at least some type of an air battle in progress. It looked as if the enemy planes were headed toward the X-Ray transports. The bombers were outside of the effective range of the cruiser's anti-aircraft guns but in range of the ships that were off the beach. Dots of anti-aircraft fire soon began to appear in the sky.

All of the bombers dropped their deadly payloads in unison from an altitude of almost 12,000 feet.[12] The mass of bombs curved slightly during the long drop to the sea before exploding harmlessly in the water between some of the cruisers and the X-Ray transports. Upon hitting the water, the bombs exploded in tremendous fashion throwing up large geysers. The formation of bombers banked to the left for the journey back to Rabaul.

At the time of the air attack, John Powell was on duty in his director when he received the word that enemy planes were on the way. He remembers the *Astoria* being about five miles from the transports. "I heard it on the radio," he recalled. "We were off of a big plantation area on the west end of the island between Lunga Point and Cape Esperance."[13] As the bombers moved closer to the *Astoria*, Powell's director started tracking the incoming planes. "We tracked them just to find out how fast and how far they were going," he said. "They were making 165 knots." The young fire controlman remembered the high altitude and tight formation of the approaching planes. Then he saw the bombs fall. "We could see the bombs coming down. Everybody dropped their bombs at once." Powell felt that the planes were too high for effective anti-aircraft fire.

As a marine aviator, Roy Spurlock was not accustomed to seeing air attacks from a ship. "I shall never forget the silver of those Betty bombers directly overhead in formation," he recalled of his position aboard the *Astoria*, "silhouetted against the blue sky over Guadalcanal. This attack was quickly over and the invasion continued."[14]

At 1:35 P.M. lookouts on the *Chicago* sighted a Zero fighter about 5,000 yards off the port beam. The port side five-inch gun batteries quickly opened fire, but the target disappeared behind a cloud. Fire resumed when the plane reappeared a short time later, and then ceased all together as the Zero again disappeared into another cloud bank. The guns expended twenty-six rounds of ammunition in the futile effort.

From his battle station on the *Chicago*, Art King gazed out into the distance and saw a group of American dive bombers tangling with a Japanese fighter. "I saw three of our dive bombers flying low in formation," he said. "All of a sudden I could see this little plane way behind them, but catching up in a hurry and of course it was a Zero. As it got into range the three SBDs started firing at it, and the little old fighter did a ninety degree turn going straight up and disappeared. So the three dive bombers went ahead to their target and did what they were supposed to do."[15] It was just one of the many air battles that took place on that particular day above Task Force 62.

One of the American planes to be shot down during the air battles was piloted by Ensign Joseph Daly of the *Saratoga*. His Wildcat was caught from behind by Zeros as he was readying to make another pass at the bombers. A twenty-millimeter shell exploded somewhere under his cockpit and suddenly everything around the young pilot, including his clothes, was on fire. Managing to open the canopy and unfasten his belt, Daly jumped out of his stricken plane barely clearing the tail. A Japanese Zero streaked by as he began to fall toward the water almost 13,000 feet below. Pulling the rip cord at about 6,000 feet he landed in the water some two miles from Guadalcanal. He could see ships far off on the horizon and began to swim in that direction.[16]

With the attacking planes gone from the area, the *Chicago* resumed her position in the screening force near the Yoke transports. Just after 2:00 P.M. the cruiser catapulted off two seaplanes for anti-submarine patrol. The planes flew low to scour the area for any sign of enemy submarine activity. The task force had received a message from Pearl Harbor earlier in the day warning that enemy submarines were on route to the area.[17]

Ensign Daly was not making much headway swimming towards the distant ships. Several destroyers had passed near his position, but had not noticed the downed aviator. After being in the water for about two hours, he heard the sound of a plane coming up from behind. It was one of the *Chicago*'s seaplanes. The pilot, Ensign John Baker, noticed the downed flier waving and splashing in the water. He circled his seaplane around and came in for a landing. Baker drew his handgun as he pulled up, not sure if the darkened face in the water was American or Japanese. Daly believed that there was a good chance that he was going to be shot.[18] However, the *Chicago* pilot quickly learned that the downed aviator was an American. His left leg wounded, Daly struggled to get aboard the plane. He was soon airborne riding on the lap of the back seat radioman. Baker initially wanted to drop off his wounded passenger at the first heavy cruiser he came upon, the *Vincennes*. However, he decided to continue on to the *Chicago*.[19]

The second wave of the Japanese air attack arrived in the Guadalcanal area just before 3:00 P.M. The nine Val dive bombers had flown down the north side of the Solomon chain, keeping out of view from the watchful eyes of the coastwatchers as well as off the radar sets of American ships. Entering the sound over Florida Island, cloud cover blocked out the ships of the Yoke squadron below and the planes continued on toward Guadalcanal. Appearing unannounced near the ships of the X-Ray squadron, the attackers were quickly jumped by as many as fifteen American fighters. Five of the bombers were shot down, but not before one successfully planted a bomb on the *Mugford*. The destroyer was the first American ship to be damaged in the Guadalcanal campaign. The four remaining Vals splashed near Shortland Island, just south of Bougainville. The surviving crewmen claimed to have damaged two light cruisers.[20]

At 4:35 P.M. the *Chicago* recovered both of her seaplanes. Joseph Daly was quickly hoisted aboard and was immediately sent down to the sick bay for treatment by the ship's doctor. The fighter pilot was soon diagnosed as having second degree burns and a gunshot wound to the left leg. His prognosis was recorded as favorable, and he was to be retained on board until he could be transferred off at the first opportunity.[21]

* * *

While the ships were fending off the air attacks, operations on land had continued throughout the day and into the early evening hours. The Marines on Guadalcanal advanced steadily outward from the beachhead. The 2,500 laborers and 150 Japanese troops on the island had disappeared into the hills soon after the opening bombardment had begun.[22]

The initial landing on Tulagi had been relatively uneventful. However, heavy fighting erupted in the afternoon as the Marines advanced toward the southeastern end of the island. The small Japanese garrison was well entrenched in this area and was prepared to fight to the death. Reports of heavy American casualties soon reached Admiral Turner aboard the *McCawley*. By the end of the day the Japanese were still clinging to positions on the southeastern tip of Tulagi.

* * *

The night of August 7–8 was uneventful for the sailors aboard the *Chicago* and *Astoria*. Both cruisers patrolled the waters around Guadalcanal and Tulagi as part of the screening force. As the night progressed the *Chicago* went off general quarters and set condition two. It was time for some of the weary sailors to get much needed rest. Just after 8:00 P.M. two boilers were cut, but were put on fifteen minute notice in case an emergency developed.[23]

As the night progressed, the junior officer of the watch made two inspections of the lookout stations to make sure that the lookouts were alert and had received proper instructions.

On the *Astoria's* first night off Guadalcanal, John Powell stood watch at his director. He alternated duties with Chief Fire Controlman Henry Henryson. "He was an old China hand, as nervous as anything," recalled Powell. Each worked a six hour shift, two hours longer than the normal condition two shifts. Some of the men aboard the *Astoria* had received piecemeal reports of the day's operations ashore, learning there had been no opposition on Guadalcanal but fighting on Tulagi. Looking at Guadalcanal through a set of binoculars, an observer aboard the cruiser saw men, trucks and tanks on the beach with some tents nearby.[24] It had been a long and exhausting day, and no one knew what tomorrow would hold.

Chapter 11

August Eighth

Dawn brought the start of a new day to the sailors plying the waters off Guadalcanal. The morning of August 8 featured blue skies, light winds, and a calm sea. At 5:10 A.M. the *Chicago* left her evening patrol position and headed to the Yoke transport area off Tulagi. Almost ninety minutes later she launched two seaplanes for anti-submarine patrol. She continued to alternate between launching and recovering planes throughout the morning hours.

After spending the night patrolling with the *Quincy* and *Vincennes*, the *Astoria* headed off to resume her duty with the bombardment group. Given the lack of resistance reported on Guadalcanal, it soon became apparent that additional fire support would not be needed. Captain Greenman was then directed to rejoin the screening group and the *Astoria* returned to the X-Ray transport area off Guadalcanal.

* * *

Not pleased with the results of the previous air attacks, Admiral Yamada was ready to try again. He knew that American carriers were lurking in the area around Guadalcanal, but he still did not know where. Intent on locating the American flattops, he dispatched five search planes from the Rabaul area during the early morning hours. All of the available bombers took off a short time later, this time armed with torpedoes. The planes were under orders to attack the carriers and were to target the transports if the former could not be located. With fifteen long-range Zeros providing the fighter escort, twenty-three bombers headed southeast flying at a low altitude.

The invaluable coastwatchers again gave Task Force 62 an early warning of the impending attack. From his jungle hideout in northern Bougainville, Jack Reed heard the distant drone of airplanes. The noise kept getting closer until the Japanese bombers were rumbling only a few hundred feet overhead. Reed tried unsuccessfully to raise Port Moresby by radio. However, another coastwatcher picked up his message and relayed it down to the invasion force.[1] The task force received the message at 10:37 A.M.[2] Admiral Turner immediately ordered all of the transports to move away from the debarkation areas.[3]

When the *Chicago* received the warning message, she and the nearby Yoke transports distanced themselves from the coast. The small escort group was bolstered by the arrival of the *San Juan* and two destroyers. The *Astoria* also moved out to more open waters to better screen the X-Ray ships.

As the Japanese planes approached the area from the north side of Santa Isabel Island, the strike leader was hoping to get a last minute sighting report on the American carriers. When none was forthcoming, the bombers instead headed for Tulagi.

Aboard the *Chicago*, Lieutenant Bruning was hoping that the ship's radar would get a fix on the approaching enemy planes. However, he had no such luck. The Japanese approach route, behind several mountainous islands, shielded their detection by the CXAM radar set. The bombers swung around the eastern end of Florida Island and turned west toward the ships below. At 11:50 A.M. lookouts aboard the *Chicago* sighted a large formation of enemy planes over Florida Island that appeared to be flying low and slow at an estimated range of fifteen miles.[4] At the time of the sighting the *Chicago* was located east of Tulagi and was heading in a southwesterly direction.

When the bombers arrived overhead, only three American fighters were in a position to intercept. Nine more scrambled from the *Wasp*, but could not arrive in time to disrupt the attack. Unlike the day before, the ships of Task Force 62 would have little help from the air in fending off this attack.

Flying just above the water, the Japanese planes raced toward the Yoke transports as all of the ships on the Tulagi side put up a wall of anti-aircraft fire. The planes finally appeared on the *Chicago's* radar scope at 11:58 A.M. Two minutes later, the starboard five-inch gun batteries opened fire on a lone plane that was about 11,000 yards off the cruiser's starboard quarter. Fearing a torpedo run, Captain Bode started evasive maneuvers turning the ship to starboard and eventually bringing the cruiser to within eight miles of the Florida Island coast. As the plane closed range, the twenty-millimeter and 1.1-inch starboard batteries opened fire, quickly followed by the rattle of thirty caliber machine guns. The plane sped by and continued on into the distance without dropping its torpedo.

From his exposed position on the searchlight platform, Art King witnessed the action as at least one plane raked the *Chicago* with machine gun fire. "That's when one of my guys got hit," King recounted. Although he stayed upright as the planes flew by, some of the others on the platform hit the deck. "I didn't know whether they were hurt or staying out of trouble. Actually they were pretty smart; by being flat they were less of a target." One of the men lying down was Bobby Grier. The Texan had survived the sinking of the *California*

A Japanese bomber is seen from the *Chicago* off Guadalcanal in August 1942. Although undamaged by air attacks in the days after the initial landing, the cruiser was later sunk by aerial torpedoes near Rennell Island (U.S. Navy / National Archives).

at Pearl Harbor before transferring to the *Chicago*. "I went over to see if he was okay," King continues. "When I went over to Bobby Grier, he was lying there face down and I just went over there to turn him over so I could talk to him and see how badly he was hurt. As soon as I touched him to roll him over, he looked up at me and he says, 'Go away from here you son of a bitch, I ain't dead yet!'"[5] Given the deal in place between the electrician's mate on the searchlight platform, he wanted to make sure that his wad of money stayed in his own pocket. "I remember telling Bobby Grier to go down to the sick bay," King said. "He wasn't hurt all that bad. I really didn't look at the side of the wound. He said he was all right." Grier eventually went down to the sick bay right after the battle only to find the area overcrowded. He did not want to wait and had the wound treated at a later date.

Ken Maysenhalder was manning one of the five-inch anti-aircraft guns during the attack. "It was spellbinding to look up and see these big planes," he later wrote. "I could see the face of the enemy plane crew shooting at us from their plane. It seemed like a slow motion movie. Here was real danger. One could get killed, but the scene was so real one was almost hypnotized in what was taking place: guns firing, black smoke puffs made by our shells exploding on their way to targets."[6] Maysenhalder was so caught up in the action that he did his duty in spite of the danger that was all around him.

During the attack Maysenhalder's gun was firing at any target that could be found. In some instances the five-inch gun was operating under director control, while at other times the crew was working in local control. During the height of the action, he remembers seeing a plane hit the water off in the distance, but he did not know which ship had shot it down. As one enemy plane approached, Maysenhalder was able to get a fleeting glimpse of the pilot. "I could see the pilot and co-pilot," he remembered. "It was like a fascinating movie."

A short time later the *Chicago*'s five-inch guns on the port side briefly opened fire towards two planes far off the port bow. Fred Tuccitto was on a port-side gun during the attacks. "They flew real low and they were fast," he said. "They were good. They were putting on a show for us and we shelled 'em."[7] At 12:05 P.M. the cruiser ceased firing as the enemy planes had moved out of range.

Reflecting on the day's air attack in his official report, Captain Bode noted how low the Japanese planes were flying. "Planes generally flew lower than in the Coral Sea action and several were observed to climb at steep angles to increase altitude when encountering flak." The captain reported that several planes released torpedoes at some distance from the *Chicago* and made the assumption that they were aiming for the transports. Bode did note that a number of planes were seen to go down. "Eight planes were observed to be shot down," he wrote. "It cannot be stated positively that this ship shot down any planes since many ships were concentrating on the same targets." He did, however, report that witnesses supported the contention that three planes seemed to go down based on shots fired from the *Chicago*.

After racing past the transports off the Tulagi side, the planes banked and headed towards Guadalcanal and the *Astoria* with at least one plane veering off to machine-gun Red Beach. The X-Ray transports and escorts were now steaming at full speed well away from the landing zone. Under the direction of Admiral Turner, the transports made several thirty degree turns to move away from the approaching planes.[8] As the bombers headed toward the transports, the ships put up a thick wall of anti-aircraft fire, with some of the cruisers firing their eight-inch guns hoping to knock down the low flying intruders.

The bombers seemed to break into smaller groups during the final approach to the transports. A few of the attackers roared directly over the ships, while others passed between or on either side. Every possible shipboard gun, on the screening ships and transports alike, was being aimed at the incoming bombers. Observers counted only three planes making it through or around the transport area.[9] During the height of the action, several planes raced past the *Astoria*. Early in the action at least two bombers approached the cruiser's stern coming in low and fast. The *Astoria*'s anti-aircraft guns hammered away with red tracer bullets seeming to hit one of the planes. The bombers passed so close to the ship that sailors could clearly see the big red circles on the wings and fuselage. The tail gunner on one bomber sprayed the cruiser with bullets as his plane zoomed past.

From his vantage point in the forward anti-aircraft director, John Powell was in a good position to see the attack. He remembers hearing the coastwatcher's warning being passed on to the ships off Guadalcanal. "We heard his message over the radio," he said. "It was time for these damn planes to show up and we couldn't see 'em. Then all of a sudden somebody says, 'There they are!' They came over Florida Island right on the water. They were twenty miles away."[10] The director initially had trouble tracking the planes and almost lost sight of the targets over the horizon. However, the crew was soon able to get a good fix on the enemy.

Powell remembers the planes splitting up in a somewhat disorganized attack. "They went in every direction," he said. "[The planes] all started turning ... disorganized, no formation at all." The bombers seemed to be flying by the cruisers and destroyers in an effort to get to the transports. "We were banging away with 'em like crazy," Powell continues, "but you know, they're making 180, 200 knots. They're passing by a mile away; you can't turn the guns that fast. The director will turn, but the guns couldn't keep up." Powell believed that one bomber was taking aim at the *Astoria* and watched as it headed towards the ship. The plane banked as if to get into position for a torpedo run. "Well that was his mistake," Powell said, "when he started turning he was duck soup then because he had no motion over the ground." Just as the plane was making the turn, the starboard five-inch guns opened fire. "We must have got twenty rounds out and he hit the water with a bang."

Far from Powell's perch in the director, young Henry Juarez witnessed the attacks from deck level at the number four 1.1-inch gun mount near the stern of the ship. The gun crews had been alerted that the enemy was on the way, but no one knew for sure what to expect. "We got word that more horizontal bombers are coming over from Rabaul," recalled Juarez. "So we were waiting for them. They said they were twin engine bombers, so they figured it was these high altitude bombers." Juarez remembers seeing the planes coming from off in the distance, flying much lower than he expected. The low altitude made the planes look huge compared to the high altitude attack of the previous day. A small cluster of planes seemed to be heading directly towards his gun. "Three of them came right toward our gun and you could see the pilots," he said. Juarez's gun took aim at one of the planes. "It got so low that our gun couldn't reach it ... couldn't hit 'em because they were so low." Being at deck level the 1.1-inch guns could not depress low enough to hit the water-skimming attackers. Instead, the guns sprayed bullets right over the bombers. Suddenly, one of the planes touched the water and jumped up right into the stream of bullets. "As soon as they bounced up, boy our shells would just go right inside of them," he said. After the attack ended, Juarez walked back to the fantail and saw a line of bullet holes in the deck from the attacking planes. The holes were right behind his gun mount. It was a close call to say the least.

Not in the air himself at the time of the attack, pilot Richard Tunnell helped defend the *Astoria* in a different manner. He positioned himself behind one of the light anti-aircraft guns and assisted the gun crew by pointing out the best and most productive targets.[11] An extra set of eyes always helped in the hectic situation.

Japanese bombers dodge anti-aircraft fire while approaching American ships off Guadalcanal on August 8, 1942. A series of air attacks over two days failed to stop the surprise invasion (U.S. Navy / National Archives).

Captain Greenman decided to send the seaplanes that were on the catapults away from the area after hearing that another attack was on the way. It happened to be Roy Spurlock's turn to fly in the rear seat as an observer when the order was given. "We were catapulted when the ship came into the wind," he later wrote. "We found that other ships' captains were of like mind, for there were five cruiser float planes up there milling around."[12] Forming into a group the planes flew near Tulagi before flying over to the Guadalcanal side of the sound.

Looking out over the rudder, Spurlock suddenly spotted the formation of Japanese planes coming over Florida Island. Counting the individual planes, he noted a mix of Bettys and Zeros. "They were streaming across our stern, and I fully expected to see one or more of the Zeros detach themselves to come over and take care of us sitting ducks," he wrote of the moment. He did not have to wait very long. "Suddenly I saw a lone plane headed right at us from where they were." As Spurlock uncovered the single thirty caliber machine gun, he noticed the lack of armor plating to protect him. Much to his great surprise and relief, the plane heading toward him turned out to be American. The lone dive bomber was also running from the Japanese formation. The enemy planes completely ignored the seaplanes and continued on towards the ships below.

The attack was over quickly, having lasted only about ten minutes. After racing past the ships, the remaining Japanese planes fled to the northwest. Seventeen of the Japanese bombers failed to return, most falling victim to the heavy curtain of anti-aircraft fire.[13] In two days of attacks, the Japanese planes had failed to dislodge the American invaders.

At least one bomber, and possibly several, hit the water in the general vicinity of the *Astoria*. One observer recalled seeing a bomber cart wheeling across the water during the height of the attack.[14] John Powell distinctly remembered seeing a bomber go down. "When those things would hit the water," he said, "the engines would fall off and the tail would break off, but the center section with the wings would float because it had these gas tanks in it. We counted about eight of them [planes] at one time on the water." Richard Tunnell also spotted a downed Japanese plane on the water. As it began to slowly sink, the wing raised up into the air to reveal a large red circle. Tunnel remembers it as being a symbolic moment. He watched for a brief time as the Japanese insignia slowly disappeared beneath the waves.

In the minutes immediately following the attack, the *Astoria* cautiously approached one of the downed Japanese planes. From his battle station near the bridge, Don Yeamans could clearly see five survivors clinging to the wreckage of their plane. "Our ship was going toward the direction of where the airplane went down and we just kept on course," he said. "We were coming up on them and the captain got on the speaker." Yeamans remembers Captain Greenman issuing a stern warning that no one was to fire at the Japanese in the

Wreckage from a downed Japanese bomber lingers on the water off Guadalcanal on August 8, 1942. Although seen from the destroyer *Ellet*, the *Astoria* passed similar wreckage on the same day (U.S. Navy / National Archives).

water. The *Astoria* quietly sailed right past. "They were just floating in the water," Yeamans recalled the odd moment. "They were just looking up at us and we were just looking down at 'em."[15]

John Powell also remembered seeing the Japanese aviators in the water clinging to wreckage. "It still had both wings on, but only one engine fell off," he said of the wrecked plane. "The whole crew was sitting on top of the fuselage. There were five people up there." Powell remembers hearing that the *Astoria* was going to put a boat in the water to capture the airmen. "Unfortunately, one of the destroyers was steaming up at a pretty good clip and they got in about as half as close. They had a boat in the water before we did." Powell carefully watched the events that followed. "We watched this whale boat come over and they had one kid in the bow with a Thompson submachine gun." The boat cautiously approached to within a hundred feet of the survivors. "I was watching through a set of binoculars. The rangefinder operator was watching ... I heard him holler, 'watch out!'" Powell saw a small puff of smoke near the Japanese. "One of the guys in the plane shot the other ones and then shot himself. They weren't going to be captured."

Chaplain Matthew Bouterse scanned the surroundings as he came topside after the air attack. He had ridden out the battle in the after battle dressing area. "It was almost like a surrealist painting," he recalled as he noted the extreme array of colors. "The deep blue sky mirrored in the equally blue sea, the varied shades of green and brown on the mountains of Guadalcanal, and the palm trees that were left along the shore somehow didn't quite accept the flotsam in the water and the smoking, damaged ships."[16]

Astoria pilot Bob Schiller was airborne during the attack. He had flown an uneventful observation flight late in the previous day. On this day he was flying a midday mission in the vicinity of Lunga Point when a warning message was sent out directing all scout planes to move out of the immediate area. "We were told to retire to a point south of the main beaches," recounted Schiller. "Everybody that got the word went down to this point south. I didn't get the word so I was still up north."[17] Although unable to see the Japanese planes' initial approach, Schiller did see smoke in the distance from the attack on the transports. After their attack, some of the bombers headed in his direction. "The Japanese bombers flew right toward me," he said. When some of the bombers flew under him, he dropped two small bombs in the hopes of getting a chance hit. Both missed. "[The bombers] were too fast for me," he said. "They pulled away too fast." Schiller fortunately did not attract the attention of any of the Zero fighters.

Task Force 62 sustained some damage during the attack. The *Vincennes* narrowly escaped major damage when a bomber crashed into the water just off the cruiser's stern. Gunners on the transport *George Elliott* poured fire into a plane that was approaching off the starboard beam, but the flaming bomber crashed into the ship, hitting a midship and spreading fire in all directions. The vintage 1918 transport was soon burning out of control.[18] One unlucky American warship was hit by a torpedo. The destroyer *Jarvis* was between an attacking plane and the *Vincennes* when a torpedo slammed into her starboard side opening a fifty foot gash.

At 1:55 P.M. the task force received another warning that enemy planes were once again headed for the area. Admiral Turner quickly ordered the transports away from the landing areas. However, this time it was a false alarm and no enemy planes appeared. All ships returned to the screening position or debarkation areas, and the transports resumed unloading just before 5:00 P.M.[19]

* * *

The conclusion of the air attack marked the end of action for the day. When efforts to control the fires on the *Elliot* seemed to be failing, the order was given to scuttle the ship. The destroyer *Dewey* put three torpedoes into her, but she refused to go down. The old transport instead drifted along eventually grounding herself in shallow water. The damaged *Jarvis* was towed to shallow water off Lunga Point where wounded sailors were transferred off and emergency repair work began. Deemed to be seaworthy, the battered destroyer was ordered to proceed to New Caledonia for emergency repairs.

The situation on land was proceeding well. The Marines on Guadalcanal continued to advance inland, capturing the airfield by late afternoon. Organized Japanese resistance on Tulagi ended. However, the Marines would continue to skirmish with stragglers over the next few days.

While the Marines attacked the small island Tanambogo, the *Chicago* continued to cruise with the screening force on the Tulagi side. Some of the men aboard were able to catch brief glimpses of the fighting ashore. Looking through the periscope of a turret, one junior officer spied an American tank advancing alone on the beach. Suddenly a swarm of Japanese soldiers seemingly came out of nowhere to attack and set the tank aflame with gasoline. One crewman emerged from a hatch and was quickly subdued by the mob.[20] Marine infantrymen ended the attack with a hail of gunfire. Over forty dead Japanese were found littered around the tank the next day.[21]

* * *

Just after 6:00 P.M. Admiral Fletcher sent a dispatch to Admiral Ghormley's New Caledonia headquarters recommending the withdrawal of his carrier force. Fletcher specifically raised concerns over the loss of twenty-one fighters in the two days of air battles, the fuel supply of the carriers and the safety of his ships given the large number of Japanese land-based planes in the area. Fletcher had lost the *Lexington* and *Yorktown* under his watch and did not want to risk losing a third carrier. Unaware of the exact situation off Guadalcanal, Ghormley approved the request.[22] It is important to note that the Japanese had not yet discovered the location of the American carriers.

The *Enterprise, Saratoga,* and *Wasp* that had been operating in the waters south and southeast of Guadalcanal, now moved away from the battle. Fletcher did not notify Admiral Turner of his impending withdrawal. However, Turner's flagship intercepted Fletcher's original message. The commander of Task Force 62 was furious.[23] Air cover was still needed as the transports were nowhere near being fully unloaded.

As the sunlight faded the sailors of the *Chicago* and *Astoria* settled in for their second night off Guadalcanal. They had been through two very busy days of action, but events seemed to be going in their favor. *Astoria* sailor Ed Armes summed up the feelings of many. "Everyone was optimistic," he said. "Everything had gone along very smoothly."[24] The previous night had been relatively peaceful. However, the impending evening hours would be very different.

PART THREE

A Night off Savo Island

"I can still hear [Captain Greenman's] voice saying, 'Turn around, men, and watch your ship go down.'"[1]

Abe Santos
Machinist's Mate Second Class
U.S.S. *Astoria*

Chapter 12

Unheeded Warnings

Japanese admiral Gunichi Mikawa arrived in Rabaul on July 30, 1942, to assume a new command. By this stage of the war, the fifty-three-year-old admiral was a seasoned veteran having participated in the Pearl Harbor attack and the Battle of Midway. A mild and soft-spoken individual, he was recognized by his superiors as being both competent and aggressive.

After the Midway defeat, the Japanese Navy established the Eight Fleet to support the defensive build-up in New Guinea and the Solomon Islands. Given the command, Mikawa's mission was to defend the area south of the equator and east of New Guinea.[1]

Headquartered in Rabaul, Mikawa was assigned the heavy cruiser *Chokai* as his flagship. Captain Toshikazu Ohmae, assigned to be the new fleet's operations officer, met with Mikawa to review the general situation in the command area. Operations in the New Guinea area seemed to be the top priority.

Mikawa had just settled into his new role when the calm of his command was shattered in the early morning hours of August 7 by the stunning news of the American attack on the Solomons. Even while listening to the radio reports from the beleaguered Tulagi defenders, Mikawa was formulating a plan. He quickly accessed the situation and decided that the American attack was not a diversion.[2] Others were organizing air attacks on the invaders, so Mikawa decided to strike by sea. Within an hour Mikawa decided "to put the fleet into action immediately to destroy the enemy."[3] All available ships were to be organized into an attack force that would proceed to the Guadalcanal area. Although initially viewed with some reluctance, the bold plan was approved by his superiors. As the most experienced flag officer in the area, Mikawa decided to personally lead the operation.[4]

The hastily assembled force consisted of eight ships. Four heavy cruisers of Cruiser Division Six, the *Aoba*, *Kinugasa*, *Furutaka*, and *Kako*, provided the real firepower. The older light cruisers *Tenryu* and *Yubari*, the flagship *Chokai*, and the destroyer *Yunagi* rounded out the small fleet.

Although confident of success, Mikawa's concerns were many. Most of his ships had neither operated nor trained together. Only imperfect charts existed for the area of travel, which meant that navigational hazards would be a concern.[5] As more information became available, it was clear that American carriers were supporting the invasion, but the flattops had not yet been located. The attack itself would have to take place at night. Mikawa knew that he would have to arrive and leave the Guadalcanal area in darkness before the American carrier planes could descend on his ships.

It appeared that Mikawa was about to grab onto something that had eluded him at both Pearl Harbor and Midway: a chance to battle with the American fleet in a surface fight. The Japanese had been preparing for such a duel for more than a decade, having focused heavily on night fighting tactics and training. The development of advanced optical equipment began in earnest in the early 1930s. With the exception of radar, by the eve of World War II the Japanese Navy possessed the best night fighting equipment available.[6]

The concept of surprise attack weighed heavily in Japanese naval doctrine before the war.[7] Considered a third party behind the United States and Britain in the various interwar naval treaties, Japanese strategists saw surprise as a way to level the playing field. In executing the bold attack, Mikawa would have to rely on just such a principle.

Wasting no time, Mikawa and his staff quickly boarded the *Chokai*. The admiral's red and white striped flag was hoisted up. As preparations were made to get under way, the admiral waited for updated information. By 3:30 P.M. Mikawa had what he was lacking, a new intelligence report. Compiled from both attacking planes and those sent for reconnaissance, the report gave him a general idea of the situation around Guadalcanal. The summary reported warships and transports off Guadalcanal and Tulagi as well as a large number of enemy planes in the air.[8] The information confirmed the admiral's original belief that the attack was not a diversion or armed reconnaissance, but rather that the Americans had arrived in force and were intending to stay.

By 6:00 P.M. Mikawa's force was under way cruising in a single column led by the *Chokai*. Once the force departed Rabaul it had to adhere to strict radio silence. Known from this point forward as the Japanese Cruiser Force, the eight ships moved forth into the fading daylight. By midnight the force was twenty miles from Buka Island, just northwest of Bougainville.

* * *

It did not take long for Mikawa's small fleet to be sighted by the Allies. A portion of the cruiser force was sighted by a B-17 just outside of Rabaul. The contact report sent by the plane warned of Japanese ships heading southeast, but lacked key details. Just before 8:00 P.M. on August 7, the ships crossed paths with submarine *S-38* near Cape St. George. The Japanese ships passed so close that the sub was unable to attack. Lieutenant Commander Henry Munson instead radioed a contact report of five ships heading southeast at a high rate of speed.[9] On the morning of August 8, the Japanese ships were twice spotted by Australian reconnaissance planes operating from New Guinea. Knowing that he had been sighted, Mikawa worried that American carrier planes could be on the way. For various reasons the news of both contact reports was slow in getting to American leaders around Guadalcanal and the warnings of the approaching Japanese force went unheeded.

Close to noon a scout plane from the *Aoba* returned from the Guadalcanal area with detailed information. It reported that one battleship, four cruisers, seven destroyers, and fifteen transports were in the waters off Guadalcanal. Also in the area was a ship that looked to be an escort carrier. Off Tulagi the pilot reported seeing two heavy cruisers, twelve destroyers, and three transports.[10] Short of the battleship and escort carrier, the report gave a reasonably accurate assessment of the actual situation. Totaling up the reported enemy warships, Admiral Mikawa knew that he would be outnumbered. However, if the enemy ships were to be divided while his force stayed together, then the advantage would be his.

Mikawa along with his staff took stock of the situation. The cruiser force had been sighted. American leaders must have been alerted to his presence and surely would respond. After weighing all the risks he decided to continue with his plan. The force increased speed to twenty-four knots. At 4:00 P.M. on August 8, the ships passed southeast of Bougainville, entered the Slot and were now headed directly for Guadalcanal. At 4:40 P.M. Admiral Mikawa signaled his battle plan to all units of the cruiser force. It was simple and straightforward, relying on the element of surprise. On final approach to the area, the ships would form a single column. The force would first maneuver south of Savo Island to attack the enemy ships off Guadalcanal and then proceed toward Tulagi. The admiral added, "Each commanding officer will operate independently as regards to gun and torpedo firings."[11] In accordance with normal Japanese naval protocol, no ship would fire before the flagship except in the case of an emergency. In the aftermath of the battle, the force planned to withdraw north of Savo Island.

As the cruiser force plodded along, radio operators listened in on American traffic. The frequencies used to direct carrier planes were coming in loud and clear. It appeared that the American carriers were winding down flight operations for the day. Apparently, there was no air attack headed for the cruiser force.

At 9:00 P.M. Mikawa received a report detailing the day's air attack on Guadalcanal. The report stated that two heavy cruisers, one large cruiser, and nine transports had been sunk. Three other ships had been damaged and were left on fire. This was good news, the admiral reasoned. Burning ships at night could serve as a great beacon to guide his force to the transports. However, there was still no word on the location of the American carriers.

A key aspect of the Japanese night fighting strategy was illumination. The ability to hit a target in the dark of night was largely based on the ability to see the target. The previously discussed advances in optical equipment certainly gave the Japanese a great advantage. However, more was needed. Up to World War I the Japanese Navy solely relied on ship-mounted searchlights for this task.[12] Although effective at illuminating the target, the light beam also gave away the location of the attacking ship. In the interwar years emphasis was placed on developing new ways to illuminate targets that did not jeopardize the attackers. The outcome was two effective ways of illuminating targets from above: star shells and aircraft flares. Although the use of searchlights would still play a role, Japanese naval units had trained heavily in the use of the new illumination techniques prior to the start of the war. It was the latter that Admiral Mikawa chose to use in the opening round of his impending attack.

In the last hour of August 8, Mikawa directed that cruiser scout planes be launched to form an illumination unit. The mission of the planes was specific: fly ahead to the Guadalcanal anchorage to report the dispositions of the American ships and to illuminate the transport area when the cruiser force was within striking distance.[13] Additionally, the scouts were to leave markers to guide the cruiser force into the area. Accordingly, one plane each from the *Aoba* and *Kako* were catapulted off at 11:13 P.M. A third plane, launched from the *Chokai*, was later added to the mission.[14] Upon completion of the mission, all of the scout planes were to fly northwest to Shortland Island.[15]

At 11:35 P.M. the cruiser force sighted a navigational marker that had been left by one of the scout planes. The floating flare was some thirty miles from Cape Esperance near the northwest tip of Guadalcanal. It had been carefully placed to avoid detection by American eyes.

Just before midnight Mikawa observed a distant light in the general direction of Tulagi. A short time later lookouts aboard the *Kako* spotted land fires in the same area. At 11:55 P.M. another ship reported seeing the reflection in the sky of a large fire. Japanese officers wondered if this could this be one of the three ships reported to be set on fire during the air attack. As midnight neared the ships were approaching Savo Island from the northwest. The southern passage between Savo and Guadalcanal lay just thirty-seven miles ahead. Only the dark of night now stood between the Japanese Cruiser Force and the American ships.

* * *

Aboard the *Astoria* Captain Greenman recalled receiving a contact report of enemy ships on the afternoon of August 8. "The report was made to me sometime after an air attack we had that morning," he later remembered. "The report was made either in the morning or sometime before the afternoon action. It was earlier than 3:00 o'clock in the afternoon."[16] He recalled it being a message that was intercepted from a coastwatcher on Bougainville. The captain concluded that addition information would be forthcoming if the ships posed a threat to the Guadalcanal area. "I knew that they could get there somewhere around from 2:00 [A.M.] on, but it never occurred to me that we would not hear further information about it," Greenman continued. "I had every expectation that our airplanes would pick them up and advise us. For some reason they didn't get it."

* * *

In the waters off Guadalcanal, Admiral Turner had nothing more than several pieces of a puzzle that suggested Japanese ships were at sea between Rabaul and Guadalcanal. He did not have available to him the most up to date radio intelligence reports.[17] American analysts had gleaned a small, but critical piece of information: the commander of the Japanese Eighth Fleet was at sea. Such information could have easily been interpreted to suggest that a major operation was about to start or was already under way.

Based on the information he had available, Turner concluded that the Japanese ships were seaplane tenders and escorts, as the ship types had been misidentified in one of the sighting reports. He suspected that the tenders were planning to set up operations near Santa Isabel Island northwest of Guadalcanal. Information that a scout plane from the carrier *Wasp* earlier in the day had shot down an enemy seaplane in that same area supported this conclusion. Just before 10:00 P.M. Turner sent a dispatch to the land-based air commander recommending an attack on Rekata Bay the next day.[18] He was certain that his ships would now be facing two air attacks per day and felt that a surface attack was unlikely.[19] As the sailors aboard the *Chicago* and *Astoria* went about their routine evening duties, the setup for the impending Allied naval disaster was now complete.

Chapter 13

Night Dispositions

Admiral Turner's plan for the Guadalcanal invasion had appointed Admiral Crutchley as second in command of the operation. Although Crutchley would have no role in the actual amphibious landing, he commanded the screening group and had the important job of escorting the assault convoy. The objective of the group was both clear and straightforward: "to protect the convoy against surface, air, and submarine attack by the enemy."[1] Crutchley had at his disposal six heavy cruisers, two light cruisers, and fifteen destroyers.

To effectively deal with the potential of a surface attack, likely to take place at night due to the American air cover, Crutchley decided to divide the ships of the screening force. The waters between Guadalcanal, Tulagi, and Florida were divided into three patrol areas. A small force was assigned to cover the eastern area to guard Sealark Channel, the least likely Japanese approach route.

The area to the west was further subdivided. It was here that Crutchley decided to put his heavy cruisers divided into two groups. Operating south of the dividing line were the *Australia*, *Canberra*, and *Chicago* along with the destroyers *Bagley* and *Patterson*. Known as the southern force, the ships were under Crutchley's direct command in the *Australia* and would block the entryway between Guadalcanal and Savo. The southern force patrolled back and forth along a straight line that ran somewhat parallel to the Guadalcanal coast, reversing course about every hour.

The area north of the dividing line was covered by the remaining three American cruisers, the *Astoria*, *Vincennes,* and *Quincy*. The destroyers *Helm* and *Jarvis* provided the antisubmarine screen. The northern force was under the command of Captain Frederick Riefkohl of the *Vincennes*. The group was charged with blocking the approach route between Savo and Florida islands.

Due to the extensive aerial reconnaissance being conducted as part of the operation, Crutchley believed that he would have an advance warning of any approaching Japanese ships.[2] As an additional precaution against both surface and submarine attack, the disposition plan called for having two radar-equipped destroyers positioned to the northwest of Savo Island. In the event of a surface contact, the destroyers were to make an immediate report and then shadow the enemy.[3]

Crutchley was comfortable with his night plan. Admiral Turner had reviewed the plan at Koro Island and again studied it while off Guadalcanal. He thought the orders were excellent.[4]

* * *

As the day of August 8 passed into the early evening hours, the transport *George Elliott* slowly drifted eastward away from the landing area. A victim of the afternoon's air attack, the effort to subdue the fire on board had failed.[5] The destroyer *Hull* took off her crew for transfer to the *Hunter Liggett*. At 5:30 P.M. Admiral Turner gave the order to sink her.[6] The destroyer *Dewey* fired three torpedoes into the burning hulk to no avail. The *Hull* fired off four more around 11:00 P.M. Still the transport would not sink. As the destroyers left the area, the transport continued to burn and drift into the night.

At about 6:30 P.M. Crutchley ordered the ships of his screening force to assume night dispositions. The sun had set just fifteen minutes earlier.[7] With the onset of darkness, the calm weather of the daylight hours faded away. The sky became overcast with heavy clouds. Intermittent storms were moving into the area, especially around Savo Island. Visibility was poor in some places with rain squalls and patches of fog.

The *Chicago* recovered her last seaplane of the day at 6:25 P.M. and then made her way toward the evening patrol position in the company of the *Canberra* and *Bagley*. Speed was reduced to ten knots when the ships arrived in position at 6:40 P.M. Forty minutes later Admiral Crutchley arrived in his flagship. The *Australia* took the lead position among the cruisers. The *Bagley* stood 1,300 yards off the starboard bow of the column, while the *Patterson* screened the same distance to port. Everything seemed normal as the southern force slowly steamed back and forth along a patrol line.

The *Astoria* arrived slightly late to her assigned position in the northern force. "Just before dark I got orders from Admiral Turner," Captain Greenman later explained, "to send a plane out to see if I could locate an aviator that landed on the surface from the *Saratoga*."[8] The aviator could not be found and the plane did not return until after dark.

Upon reaching the northern force, the *Astoria* took the last position in the cruiser column about 600 yards astern of the *Quincy*. With the *Vincennes* in the lead position, the group patrolled in a five mile square box directly east of Savo Island. Moving at a speed of ten knots, the course was changed every thirty minutes. The destroyers *Helm* and *Wilson* provided the anti-submarine screen. The latter ship replacing the damaged *Jarvis*.

* * *

At about this time Admiral Turner decided it was necessary to call a meeting of his two key commanders. The amphibious force was losing its air cover as a result of Fletcher's decision to remove his carriers. Turner had tentatively decided to withdraw the transports at first light on August 9.[9] He needed to know Crutchley's thoughts on fending off additional air attacks without fighter cover and General Vandegrift's assessment of the supply situation for the Marines ashore. At 8:45 P.M. Turner notified his subordinates of the meeting. It would take place late in the evening aboard the *McCawley*, which was off the Lunga Beach landing zone.

Upon receiving Turner's summons for the meeting, Crutchley sensed a level of urgency. At 8:55 P.M. he directed Captain Bode of the *Chicago* to take command of the southern force. "Take charge of patrol. I am closing [Commander Task Force 62] and I may or may not rejoin you later."[10] With that he began the twenty mile journey to the *McCawley*. As the *Australia* slipped away into the night, Crutchley neglected to notify Captain Riefkohl of the *Vincennes* that he was leaving the area.

After the departure of the *Australia*, Captain Bode decided not to move the *Chicago* into the lead position of the southern force. He may have been under the belief that the *Australia* would be retuning or that shifting positions in the column was too dangerous at night. He had conferred with Captain Getting of the *Canberra* and decided that it would be less of a disruption to the column when the *Australia* returned if the *Chicago* simply stayed in the rear.[11] Bode directed the *Canberra* to follow the same course and patrol route as previously planned.

***

The fatigue was beginning to show on the sailors aboard the *Chicago* and *Astoria*. The crews had been at an almost constant state of readiness in the two days since arriving off Guadalcanal. The men with topside battle stations had been exposed to the sun and heat. For the crew below decks, the ships must have seemed like a steaming pressure cooker. While the blowers helped circulate some air, the equipment was certainly not capable of fanning out all of the heat and humidity that had built up during the day. "The stress level on the ship's crew mounted," observed *Astoria* passenger Roy Spurlock, "and more hours went by without sleep."[12] The night offered the hope of a shower and some rest. However, there was something else circulating in the air of the two cruisers that night, rumors of an impending battle.

The *Chicago* secured from general quarters at 7:31 P.M. and assumed condition two.[13] "We had been at battle stations for almost seventy-two hours," recalled Bill Grady. "That is when I drank coffee. They'd bring it around to battle stations." Coming off duty later in the evening, he decided to get some rest and made his way out of the powder magazine below turret three. "I walked through the mess hall and went underneath the blower and I just dropped there. I was asleep before I hit the deck. I fell right there instead of going to my bunk."[14]

Also off duty during the first hour of August 9 was Howard Fortney. He had left the interior communications room and was soon asleep in his bunk. His job kept him well below the waterline and unable to see what was going on above. He was not especially fond of the situation. "It wasn't too comfortable," Fortney said of being near the bottom of the ship. "I'd rather been up where you could see what was going on ... it was just something that had to be done."[15]

Art King did not often sleep at his battle station. He preferred to go below deck to the bunk area. He was not a big fan of condition two, because of the short time off in between duty periods. "We were always on that from the time the war started and there was a lot of criticism later on about that," King said. "Everybody was worn out all the time. So nobody was getting enough sleep."[16] He had heard the word that Japanese ships were on the way. The scuttlebutt going around the *Chicago* was that the enemy would arrive sometime before dawn. "At the very worst [the *Chicago*'s officers] though that they would get there at about six in the morning." He added, "Most of us didn't go to bed." King was at his battle station on the searchlight platform as the new day began.

Other *Chicago* sailors did not like the idea of going below decks for sleep. Charles Germann was one of them. "I liked the outside," he remembered. "I stayed out on deck as much as I could." It was not uncommon for Germann to sleep on deck near turret three. However, since transferring into the aviation division, he changed locations. "When I got into the V division we'd slept in the hangars ... out on the quarter deck or in the hangars."[17] However, on this particular night Germann did decide to go below decks. He had completed standing watch at the forward main battery director. "I got relieved to go below and take my time off," he continued. "I went down to where my bunk was, but it was so hot." Germann decided not to sleep there after all. Instead he found a comfortable place to rest near an air blower that was not too far from his battle station at an ammunition hoist.

The crewmen of the *Astoria* also relished the evening hours. "All men were at their battle stations," recalled Greenman of the first two days off Guadalcanal. "Meals were served at battle stations. When a man left his battle station, he had to get permission from his local officer in charge."[18] The ship also secured from general quarters and people began to slowly move about. The fantail area was soon crowded with sailors breathing in the fresh ocean air and relaxing.[19] Some were looking forward to a meal, while others just wanted rest.

Don Yeamans was scheduled to be on duty from midnight to 4 A.M. He did not like to sleep below deck owing to the long journey from his battle station down to the bunk area, a trip that included a mandatory detour around officer's country. "You didn't have too much time to sleep," he lamented. "In that four hours off you have to eat, you have to take a bath; you have to brush your teeth, and everything else. And that's on your four hours, not on four hours duty. So I wanted to get as much sleep as possible. I wasn't going to take all the time to go clear back down to the bottom of the damn ship to quarters."[20] Instead of going below, Yeamans often slept near his battle station. Early in the war a platform was added just off his battle station to house a twenty-millimeter gun. "The platform was maybe eighteen inches off the ground ... it was extended out about three feet." Being on the skinny side, Yeamans just slid right in when it was time to sleep. He was always careful to notify others of his whereabouts. "So when it was time to come to relieve, they just kick me in the butt and get me up and then I'd get back on duty. That was my personal place." Come midnight he was back on watch.

Since Henry Juarez had pulled the 8 P.M. to midnight watch, it was time for him to get some rest. Although he does not recall how he specifically heard, he also knew of the rumors that the Japanese were coming. "We heard rumors earlier that there [were] some ships coming down," he remembered.[21] "We were going to get ready for them, early in the morning. We all knew all the scuttlebutt ... there's somebody's coming, so we're going to get into it tomorrow. We'd be ready for 'em because we were going to get up early in the morning too." Juarez was unsettled by the rumors of battle. "When I heard that rumor it kind of spooked me a little bit," he continued. "I went down below decks, I grabbed my blanket and I come back to my gun." Juarez asked his gun captain to wake him up at about 2:00 A.M. so that he would have time to take a shower. With that he went to sleep close to his gun, just outside of the gun shield. He had on both his life jacket and helmet.

Rest for Seaman First Class Theodore Torsch would also have to wait. The Louisville, Kentucky, native was part of a group rotating duties between the forward five-inch magazine and the after anti-aircraft director. On this particular evening he was on duty at the latter station. The director crew that night consisted of four men: a pointer, trainer, additional crewman, and a lieutenant as the leader. Torsch was the trainer. The leader, Lieutenant (jg) Vincent Healey, was connected to other parts of the ship via talker headset. Torsch recalled of the watch, "Everyone was kind of sleepy and drowsy."[22]

As the night progressed aviators Bob Schiller and Richard Tunnell retired to their cabins. Both seemed to have an idea that the Japanese were coming. Tunnell remembered hearing talk in the wardroom among the officers. The Japanese ships were expected to arrive at 8 A.M.[23] "Aviators did not have any watches to stand," Schiller said.[24] When general quarters sounded, the pilots divided into two groups. The four senior aviators, which included both Schiller and Tunnell, were to report to the navigation bridge to await the possibility of launch orders. The remaining pilots went to the hangar area to assist in any plane launching that might occur.

Another member of the aviation crew also heard that the Japanese were coming. Ed Armes remembered hearing the news from lead pilot Lieutenant Allan Edmands. "We heard that they [the Japanese] were coming down. Then we heard that they turned back and then I think we heard they turned around again." The final scuttlebutt of the night was to be prepared for battle at dawn. "No one was expecting them until dawn," Armes continued, "about 6 A.M."[25]

John Powell was on duty at the forward anti-aircraft director from 6 P.M. to midnight. Fire controlmen in his group often worked six hour shifts to allow for a longer rest period. When his shift ended he went to sleep. "I never went below decks," said Powell. "I didn't want to be down there when the ship sank. I only went down there when we were in port."[26] The fire controlmen had a small workshop located just above the bridge in the forward battle lookout station. It was nothing fancy, but it was where Powell liked to sleep. "I just went down and slept on the work bench. I had a locker and everything up in the forward battle lookout where I slept."

Gene Alair relieved Ensign William Hagerty for the midnight to 4:00 A.M. watch at the forward 1.1-inch machine guns. The two gun mounts were located above the navigation bridge on the battle lookout platform. Each gun was positioned on a small wing that protruded out from a center area that housed the ammunition clipping room. Inside the small room crewmen loaded bullets, supplied from a magazine below, into clips to be used by the nearby guns. The area served as a base for the forward battle control station that was directly above. The thin metal half circle wall that surrounded each gun offered only minimal protection against shell fire. Directly above each of the 1.1-inch guns was a small director that was shrouded in a circular tub.

Taking his position, he asked Hagerty if he knew which ships comprised the destroyer screen. He did not. A short time later Alair asked the same question of battle control two, but was unable to get an answer. "It was dark and quiet," Alair later wrote of the time. "Men in both gun crews were tired and the gun captains, while alert, were casual."[27] The beginning of the shift was anything but eventful.

In the late evening hours, Roy Spurlock heard the news that a Japanese fleet was on the way to Guadalcanal. "We expected attack at daybreak," he recalled. He remembered being told that the ship would go to general quarters at 2:30 A.M. "This would give about us four hours before daybreak to get ready." As a guest passenger, he had no assigned battle station. Expecting to awake to sound of the alarm at 2:30 A.M., he went to sleep in his cot in the sitting room of the captain's cabin.

During the evening hours, Matthew Bouterse was again gathering thoughts for his Sunday sermon. While in the wardroom he noticed a copy of a message stating that Japanese ships were reported to be heading towards Guadalcanal. "Estimated time of arrival at current speed was 7:00 A.M.," he recalled. "Church tomorrow looked a little dubious."[28] Planning to get up to walk the ship during the early morning hours, Bouterse returned to his cabin and went to sleep wearing his uniform.

The enlisted men were not the only tired ones aboard the two cruisers. The senior officers were in just as bad of shape. Aboard the *Chicago* Captain Bode had earlier in the evening noted how tired his executive officer looked and suggested that he get some rest.[29] Commander Cecil Adell took Bode's recommendation and went to his stateroom late in the evening. Thoroughly exhausted, Bode decided to retire as well. However, he did not go below to his cabin. Instead he went to the emergency cabin on the bridge level.

Equally exhausted was Captain Greenman of the *Astoria*. Expecting some type of action in the morning, he too decided to rest. He noted that the night was very dark and overcast with an occasional light rain and made his way to the emergency cabin. The doors of the sparsely equipped room opened directly to the navigation bridge, which was right behind the pilot house. The doors remained opened at all times. Greenman remained fully dressed and could be up on the scene at a moment's notice. Neither captain knew that what would later become known as the Battle of Savo Island was about to begin.

Chapter 14

The Enemy Arrives

The Japanese heavy cruiser *Chokai* was a foreboding sight. Her 632 foot length was dominated by a massive pagoda-type superstructure. A tall mast stood just forward of a large funnel that was tilted back on an angle. The combination of the pagoda-looking structure and the angled funnel made for a strange look to American eyes.

For the Japanese, the cruiser was a contemporary design that was authorized under the 1927 construction program and launched in 1931.[1] With a displacement of over 13,000 tons, the *Chokai* was larger than either the *Chicago* or *Astoria* and her weapons packed a vicious punch. The main battery armament consisted of ten eight-inch guns mounted in five double turrets. Unlike most American cruisers, the vessel also carried torpedoes. Eight torpedo tubes carried a twenty-four-inch torpedo perfected by the Japanese before the war specifically for night fighting. With such a powerful array of armament, the ship was more than a match for any American treaty cruiser.

* * *

The night sky was dark and the sea was extremely calm as the Japanese Cruiser Force approached Savo Island from the northwest.[2] At exactly midnight the ships increased speed to twenty-six knots and assumed battle formation in accordance with the operation plan. As the flagship, the *Chokai* maintained the lead position. She was followed directly by the heavy cruisers *Aoba*, *Kako*, *Kinugasa*, and *Furutaka*. The *Tenryu*, *Yubari*, and *Yunagi* completed the column.

Twenty-five minutes after midnight, Mikawa signaled his ships with the latest intelligence information that had just come in from one of the scout planes. "Three heavy cruisers south of Savo Island," was passed to every ship of the force.[3] The ships that the plane had sighted were clearly those of the south force, which at the time was actually composed of two heavy cruisers and two destroyers. A short time later the same scout plane reported that there were about twenty transports off Guadalcanal along with a second group of cruisers and destroyers. Mikawa now knew that he would be facing a divided enemy and one that was not expecting an attack.

Long white sleeves were hoisted up on each side of the bridge on all of the Japanese ships. The banners served as recognition symbols to help lookouts identify friend from foe. At 12:40 A.M. the flagship *Chokai* signaled, "Prepare for attack."[4] All men were alert and at their battle stations. The cruiser force was now only minutes away from sighting its first enemy ship.

Northwest of Savo Island the *Blue* and *Ralph Talbot* methodically went about their patrols. Each destroyer was equipped with SC radar, a newer type of equipment that was used for long range searches. The radar was thought to provide a reliable range of up to ten miles.[5] Admiral Crutchley had placed great faith in the radar pickets and felt the destroyers

Order of Battle
The Battle of Savo Island

Japanese Cruiser Force		Allied Screening Force	
Vice Admiral Gunichi Mikawa		**Southern Force** Rear Admiral Victor Crutchley	
Heavy Cruisers:	*Chokai (Flag)* *Aoba* *Kako* *Kinugasa* *Furutaka*	Heavy Cruisers: Destroyers:	*Australia (Flag)* *Canberra* *Chicago* *Bagley* *Patterson*
Light Cruisers:	*Tenryu* *Yubari*	**Northern Force** Captain Fredrick Riefkohl	
Destroyer:	*Yunagi*	Heavy Cruisers: Destroyers:	*Vincennes (Flag)* *Quincy* *Astoria* *Helm* *Wilson*

would surely detect any approaching enemy ships. On this particular night the radar equipment may not have been functioning properly or the operators were not well trained. In any case, neither destroyer was destined to discover the approaching Japanese ships.

Just before midnight the large rain squall that had been hanging over Savo Island moved slowly to the southeast obscuring visibility between the northern and southern cruiser forces. It was about this time that a lookout aboard the *Ralph Talbot* sighted one of Mikawa's scout planes flying low over Savo Island toward Tulagi. He was specifically able to identify it as a cruiser-type float plane. Fifteen minutes before midnight a warning rang out from the destroyer's T.B.S. (Talk Between Ships) radio. "Warning. Warning. Plane over Savo headed east."[6] Strangely the warning did not mention the type of plane.

The message never made it to Admiral Turner. However, several other ships did receive the warning, but it was not acted upon for various reasons. At least one recipient of the message dismissed it as being a friendly plane. There is no record of the message being picked up by the *Astoria*. The *Chicago* could not have received it as the cruiser did not have T.B.S.

American ears below could not have understood the reports that the float planes were sending back to Mikawa. None of the Allied ships in the area had the capability of interpreting Japanese radio transmissions. Admiral Turner had declined the opportunity to have a mobile radio intelligence unit stationed aboard his flagship.[7]

With alert crews, the Japanese Cruiser Force continued on through the dark night. The ships were heading southeast towards the southern passage around Savo Island. At about 12:53 A.M. a lookout aboard the *Chokai* made a sudden discovery, a ship was approaching from the starboard side.[8] It appeared to be a destroyer about 10,900 yards off the starboard bow. A minute later the next ship in the Japanese column, the heavy cruiser *Aoba*, made the same sighting. The ship that the Japanese were eyeing was the destroyer *Blue* on radar patrol almost directly west of Savo Island. The report took Admiral Mikawa by surprise as his scout planes had not reported any ships outside of the sound. He feared that his surprise entry might soon be spoiled.

Upon considering his alternatives, Mikawa decided that it would be best if he avoided the destroyer and entered the sound through the north passage around Savo Island. Just before 1:00 A.M. he notified the other ships of his intention and changed course accordingly. To lessen the telltale wakes of his ships, the Japanese slowed to twenty-two knots as their guns quickly trained on the new target. Mikawa was relieved when the *Blue* showed no signs of having sighted his approaching ships. As his ships slipped past the unknowing destroyer, Mikawa commented to his staff about the sleeping Americans.[9]

Less than five minutes later, the Japanese sighted a second destroyer off the port bow. The ship was at the considerable range of almost 16,000 yards and seemed to be moving away from the cruiser force. It was the *Ralph Talbot*. Reversing course at the far end of her patrol line, she did not notice the Japanese ships. A short time later the first destroyer suddenly turned away from the cruiser force. The *Blue* had reached the northeastern end of her patrol line and was reversing course. Much to Mikawa's surprise, neither destroyer seemed to be aware of his presence, so he decided to revert back to the original plan. At 1:08 A.M. he angled right, sped up, and signaled his ships, "Enter from the south passage!"[10] The cruiser force was now headed southeast directly toward the gap between Savo Island and Guadalcanal. Sighted by neither radar equipment nor human eyes, Mikawa's ships had slipped pass the pickets and were now heading directly towards the southern force.

* * *

The meeting of senior American commanders aboard the *McCawley* concluded just before midnight. As an outcome of the discussions, Turner was still planning to depart with the transports the next day, but he agreed to postpone setting a time until General Vandegrift

Adapted from *The Battle of Savo Island, August 9, 1942: Strategical and Technical Analysis*.
Note: Map is not to scale and represents approximate movements.

could determine how many more supplies were needed for the Marines on Tulagi. As the meeting concluded the idea of a night attack did not seem to be on anyone's mind.[11]

It was a gloomy night off Guadalcanal. Low clouds hung overhead in the waters off Lunga Point, while rain clouds stood off in the direction of Savo Island. An occasional flash of lighting lit up the night sky to make for an eerie scene. The glow of the burning *George Elliott* was noticeable off the in the distance.[12] After arriving back aboard the *Australia*, Admiral Crutchley decided not to rejoin the southern force. With warnings of enemy submarines plentiful, he decided not to risk the night maneuvers that would be necessary for him to return to his force. He instead decided to remain within the protective screen of the Guadalcanal transport area and rejoin his force in the morning when it again resumed daylight positions. He retired for the night without telling anyone of his location.[13]

* * *

A thick bank of clouds was located southeast of Savo Island as the Japanese Cruiser Force entered the south passageway. Shortly after 1:30 A.M. Admiral Mikawa signaled his ships to attack. At about this time the last ship in the Japanese column, the destroyer *Yunagi*, moved out of formation to guard the rear of the force by keeping a watchful eye on the American destroyers.

At 1:36 A.M. the Japanese sighted the *Canberra* and *Chicago* at a range of 12,500 yards. The *Chokai* quickly changed course with the ships of the column following suit. The opposing forces were now heading directly toward each other. An alert lookout on the *Chokai* then sighted a cruiser of the northern force. Seen at an extreme range of almost 18,000 yards, the ship was the *Vincennes*.[14] There now was no doubt in Mikawa's mind, he had two groups of enemy cruisers to contend with.

The *Chokai* was the first Japanese ship to fire, as planned. She opened the battle by sending four torpedoes in the direction of the *Canberra* and *Chicago*. Other Japanese ships quickly followed suit with their torpedo tubes issuing a brief orange flicker as the deadly weapons hit the water with a splash and disappeared out into the night. After firing her torpedoes the *Chokai* turned to unmask her main battery guns.

None of the Allied ships had yet sighted the Japanese, but that was about to change. The destroyer *Patterson* was the one ship in the southern force that was awake and alert. Cruising off the port bow of the *Canberra*, the destroyer's captain had not retired for the night. Commander Frank Walker was on the bridge as the southern force was nearing the northwestern end of their patrol line. A lookout suddenly cried out that a ship was dead ahead. It was about 5,000 yards away traveling to the southeast. Walker quickly sounded general quarters and ordered the *Patterson* to unmask her gun and torpedo batteries. Trying to send a warning to the *Chicago* and *Canberra* by blinker light, he readied a radio message that was immediately sent out via the T.B.S. "Warning. Warning. Strange ships entering the harbor!"[15] With the issuance of this warning, the area south of Savo Island exploded into battle with a rapid sequence of events. It was about 1:45 A.M.

High above the area the Japanese scout planes, having already provided Mikawa with timely and effective intelligence, now turned to illumination. The planes unleashed a series of parachute flares that suddenly dropped down through the clouds. Brilliant in color and intensity, the blossoming flares were spaced about a mile apart.[16] Strung out over the Lunga Point area, the flares quickly revealed the *Chicago* and *Canberra* silhouetted against the backdrop of light.

Just before the flares dropped out of the sky, sailors aboard the *Canberra* heard an explosion off the starboard bow. Apparently one of the Japanese torpedoes exploded prematurely.[17]

It was all that was needed for the Australian ship to jump into action. The captain was immediately called to the bridge. A lookout soon spotted a ship off the port side. Bridge personnel initially struggled to make out the sighting but soon identified three Japanese cruisers. The general alarm sounded as torpedoes were seen passing on both sides of the ship. Just then Captain Frank Getting arrived on the bridge, immediately ordered full speed, and started a turn to port to unmask the main batteries. However, Getting quickly changed his mind and instead swung the *Canberra* to the starboard. The turn blocked the Japanese line of approach to the transport area and caused Mikawa to turn his force to the left. Sending a yeoman running off to the radio room, an officer on the bridge ordered a contact report be sent to the *Chicago*.

By this time the *Chokai* had closed to within 4,500 yards of the *Canberra*. The Japanese had now also sighted the other ships of the southern force. Without further delay the *Chokai* opened fire on the Australian cruiser with her eight-inch guns. The *Aoba*, *Furutaka*, and others followed the lead of the flagship.

When the first shells crashed into the *Canberra*, the general alarm was still sounding and the cruisers eight-inch guns were not yet trained out. The hail of gunfire that followed was deadly in terms of accuracy and intensity. An early hit killed the gunnery officer and mortally wounded Captain Getting.[18] Both boiler rooms were hit resulting in all power being lost. Intense fires broke out topside, especially in the middle part of the ship. The *Canberra* may have fired off a few four-inch shots in her defense, but the main battery never had the chance to open fire.

In the span of about five minutes the *Canberra* was hit twenty-four times.[19] The ship was listing badly, on fire, and barely alive as she drifted to a stop. The battle was over for the Australian cruiser. The intended message to the *Chicago* never made it off the ship; amid the carnage the yeoman arrived at the radio room only to find the transmitters destroyed.[20]

After sending out the warning message, Commander Walker ordered the *Patterson* to turn left to unmask her torpedo and gun batteries. But his order to fire torpedoes was drowned out by the sound of the five-inch guns, which opened fire with two spreads of starshells in an attempt to illuminate the Japanese cruisers, and the torpedoes never left the ship. Before long the *Patterson* was locked in a gunfight with the *Tenryu* and *Yubari*. The light cruisers were the last ships in the Japanese column. During the height of the action, the *Patterson* was hit on the number four turret. She was able to continue the vicious gun battle until the Japanese moved out of range.

When the battle started the destroyer *Bagley* was in position off the starboard bow of the *Canberra*. Just moments after the *Patterson*, she sighted the enemy ships about 3,000 yards off the port bow.[21] Swinging hard to the left to unmask her starboard torpedo batteries, the *Bagley* increased speed to twenty-five knots. However, before the torpedo primers could be inserted, the destroyer had moved past the safe firing bearing.

The destroyer kept turning in order to fire from the port side. The Japanese ships were barely visible through the haze. Four torpedoes jumped out of the port battery as soon as a safe bearing was reached. As the torpedoes sped through the water, the Japanese ships disappeared from sight altogether. A soundman aboard the *Bagley* followed the track of the torpedoes and reported hearing an explosion about two minutes later.[22] However, it was not to be. No American torpedoes were to find Japanese hulls on this particular night. Having received no orders from anyone, the *Bagley* moved northwest through the south passageway finding nothing. The only ship left in the southern force that had not felt the Japanese wrath was the *Chicago*. Her turn was now at hand.

Chapter 15

A Torpedo Finds the *Chicago*

For the officers and men aboard the *Chicago*, the events of the battle started suddenly and soon overtook them. At 1:42 A.M. a lookout saw two small orange flashes near the surface of the water very close to Savo Island. It appeared to be a small fire on the island.[1] It is very possible that the flashes were actually the *Furutaka* firing torpedoes.[2] Just a minute later, flares began to appear off the *Chicago's* stern. Seen in the direction of the transports, the glowing lights were immediately identified as the type of flares used by aircraft for illumination purposes. Lookouts soon reported a total of five flares hanging in the air.

No sooner had these two events occurred then at 1:45 A.M., the *Canberra* suddenly turned out of formation to the right. No course change was planned at this time. The movement of the *Canberra* revealed two dark objects in between the Australian cruiser and the *Patterson*. A third object was quickly identified to the right of the *Canberra*.

Lieutenant Commander George Holley, the *Chicago's* officer of the deck at the time, ordered the general alarm to be sounded. Rushing to the bridge from his emergency cabin, Captain Bode arrived at almost the same time as the initial sighting report. The forward five-inch gun director trained out to get a fix on the object to the right of the *Canberra*.[3] Bode quickly ordered a spread of starshells to be fired.

Sailors all across the *Chicago* sprang into action when the general alarm sounded. Howard Fortney bolted out of his bunk, put on his clothes and ran for his battle station. His path took him through mess hall number three, which was adjacent to his bunk area. Standing right in the middle of the mess was Chief Boatswain's Mate Steve Balint, who was telling sailors to get moving to their battle stations as a few were trying to stop for a quick drink of water.

Before much else could be done, a lookout on the bridge cried out that a torpedo wake was on the starboard side. Bode ordered the rudder hard to starboard. Only seconds later the main battery control officer reported that two torpedoes were approaching the port bow. By ordering a full left rudder the captain hoped to thread the needle. He soon steadied the ship on a course that was about parallel to the wakes. At that instance what appeared to be a destroyer in a position to fire torpedoes was spotted to port. It was actually the *Furutaka*, which at the time was about 4,000 yards away. Of the two approaching torpedoes, one crossed the bow at a distance of about seventy yards, while a second missed by just twenty yards.[4]

At 1:47 A.M. a talker in the forward main battery control station abruptly reported another torpedo approaching the port bow.[5] At the same moment the report arrived on the bridge, the *Chicago* shuddered from an explosion well forward. A torpedo had slammed into the bow. The blast sent a towering column of water rising up as high as the top of the foremast. When it came down, the water drenched the forward half of the ship.

The torpedo blast mangled the lower tip of the bow just under the waterline. The concussion damaged various pieces of equipment, including both of the ship's gyrocompasses.[6] The force of the blast also bent the upper portion of the foremast, restricting the operation of the forward main battery director.

Unknown at the time to those aboard the *Chicago*, torpedoes from no fewer than three Japanese cruisers had been fired at her. The initial wake on the starboard side came from one of four torpedoes that the *Chokai* had earlier unleashed. The torpedo passed by the *Canberra* and was likely spotted after it had already missed the *Chicago*. The bubbling wakes seen on the port side were the torpedoes fired by the *Furutaka*. However, the torpedo that hit the bow actually came from starboard and was fired by the *Kako*.[7] In addition to the hit on the bow a second torpedo struck the cruiser in the engineering spaces on the starboard side, but did not detonate. It may have been the only luck that was with the *Chicago* that night.

Still running towards his battle station, Howard Fortney had made it to the ladder that led down to the interior communication room. He had just started going down in the trunk when the torpedo hit, shaking everything. "I really had to hold on," he remembered. Fortney knew that the ship had been hit by a torpedo, but he did not know the location or the extent of the damage. He paused and momentarily thought about not continuing down. "I sure felt like I'd like to go back up rather than go down," he said. "I kept on going down. I knew I had to go down." Once down in the interior communication room, curiosity got the best of him. "I remember pouring some water out on the deck to see which way the water would run. I didn't know whether we were down in the bow or just what was going on."[8] Fortney stayed on station for the rest of the night. He only went topside after daybreak.

The abrupt start of action woke up more than one sleeping sailor. Bill Grady did not get to enjoy his resting place in the mess hall for very long. "I no sooner hit that deck when, pardon my French, all hell broke loose," he said.[9] He knew that he had to get to his battle station quickly and followed the normal routine for moving about the ship. "The general alarm went," he continued, "and you are supposed to go down and aft on the port side, up and forward on the starboard side. There was some guy coming through the hatch the wrong way and I stiff armed him. I don't know whether he got hurt or not. I was headed for my battle station. I stiff armed him good."

Grady made it to the powder magazine below turret three just as the torpedo hit the bow. "It shook the ship from stem to stern," he said. "Of course we were back there; we didn't hear the explosion, we just got the shaking from it." For a brief moment he thought the superstructure was collapsing. However, he soon realized that it was actually meat falling in the cooler that was a couple of decks up and forward from his position. His turret saw no action that night.

Sleeping under a blower, Charles Germann woke up and sprang into action. "I don't think I got to sleep and general quarters went again," he said.[10] He ran onto the quarterdeck to a ladder that was on the port side of the hangar near the base of the catapult. "Just as I got up on the ladder going up to the flight deck, the torpedo hit the bow." He was more than halfway up when the ship shook from the hit. "I went up in the air," he recalled. Losing his grip, Germann fell almost twenty feet down, hurting his ankle. "I ended up on the quarterdeck," he recalled. "I got up, got back up my ladder and went to my battle station." The ammunition hoist was still closed when he arrived. "I opened up the hoist and the ammunition started coming up." By now he could hear shooting as the five-inch batteries opened fire. He worked quickly, feeding the ammunition to the guns. "I saw the *Canberra* get hit, catch on fire," he continued. "I saw guys jumping off of it. We picked up one or two guys ourselves next morning ... burned pretty bad." Germann never left the ammunition hoist. "We stayed up there the whole night."

Ensign Joseph Daly also awoke to the sound of the general alarm. The clanging sound was followed by the noise of closing hatches and firing guns. It had been less than two days since the *Chicago*'s seaplane had plucked the wounded *Saratoga* pilot from the sea. He was not necessarily fond of being trapped below deck and wondered if he would be able to make it out if the ship were to sink.[11] Daly bounced in his bunk as the *Chicago* shook from being hit, but made it through the battle. By the end of the night he must have certainly been glad that he was not dropped off on the *Vincennes* as originally planned.

Not long after the torpedo hit, a single shell struck the starboard leg of the foremast and exploded about even with the top of the forward funnel. Shrapnel showered over a wide area including portions of the communications platform, well deck, and boat deck. Many sailors in the area were hit by the fragments. Steve Balint, now on the way to his battle station, was struck and fell to the deck. Executive Officer Adell, running right behind him, stumbled after being hit.[12] Seaman First Class Howard Hatch was killed after being hit in the face and head. Commander Adell had been hit in the neck and right forearm. A piece of shrapnel had passed close to his jugular vein. Seriously injured, he crawled along the deck to reach a repair station. Once there the ship's dentist, Lieutenant Commander Benjamin Oesterling, was able to administer lifesaving first aid.[13]

Balint was wounded badly in the stomach. Art King remembers hearing the story of his fight for life. "It must have been a pretty good size piece [of shrapnel]," he recalled. "It just ripped his stomach off. The fleshy part of it ... just ripped it off so that the inside just

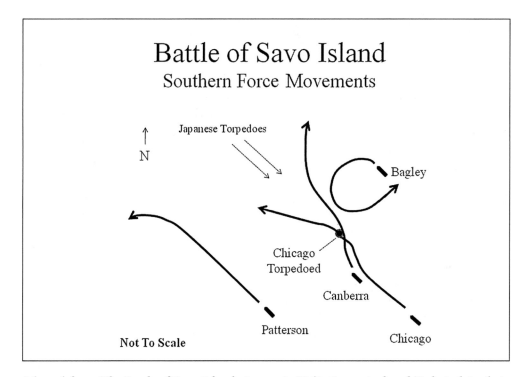

Adapted from *The Battle of Savo Island, August 9, 1942: Strategical and Technical Analysis*. *Note:* Map is not to scale and represents approximate movements.

bulged out and he was holding 'em in his hands." Balint made it down below under his own power and walked into the midship battle dressing station that was located in the wardroom. "He died later on," King continued. "I don't know how much later, but I was told that he died of shock. That was too much damage to his midsection."[14]

The port battery of five-inch guns now fired two four-gun salvos of star shells set for 9,200 yards off the port bow.[15] At almost the same time, the starboard guns fired off an equal number of star shells. The spreads were fired 5,000 yards off the port bow with the intention of illuminating a ship that was beyond the *Canberra*. At the time the Australian cruiser was only about 1,200 yards off the port bow of the *Chicago*. The two dark objects that had been seen to the left of the Australian cruiser were thought to be enemy destroyers. However, these ships were actually the heavy cruisers *Kinugasa* and *Kako*. The third object, seen to the right of the *Canberra*, was the heavy cruiser *Aoba*.[16]

Up to this point all attempts by the *Chicago* to get a fix on a target failed. "All star shells fired on the first two spreads failed to ignite," recorded Captain Bode, "apparently because of the failure of candles to ignite." The main battery director fared no better. It had been trying to locate the target off the starboard bow, but failed due to poor visibility.

At about this time the *Patterson* was seen off in the distance dueling with two ships. Observers aboard the *Chicago* incorrectly believed that the destroyer was using her searchlight to illuminate the Japanese ships. It was actually searchlights from the *Tenryu* and *Yubari* that were illuminating the *Patterson*. The *Chicago* joined the fray when a port five-inch gun opened fire on one of the enemy vessels at a range of 7,200 yards. Twenty-five rounds were fired before the director lost track of the target. Lookouts saw one shell hit and burst on the target, most likely the *Tenryu*.[17]

Still unable to get a fix on a target, the main battery did not join the action. With star shells not working, Captain Bode ordered the searchlights into action to search for a target. At 1:51 A.M. two searchlights briefly snapped on and scanned the area on the port side finding nothing. A preliminary damage assessment now reached the captain. Holes in deck platforms one and two existed forward of frames fifteen and ten respectively. There was some flooding. Damage control parties were in the process of shoring up bulkheads and hatches. A maximum speed of twenty-five knots was believed to be safe. As the battle now moved to the northeast, the *Chicago* remained on a westward heading with no targets in sight.

* * *

From his vantage point on the searchlight platform, Art King had a bird's eye view of the battle. "I knew we were hit," he recalled of the moment that the torpedo exploded forward, "and I knew that we were going too fast. When the word got up there that the bow had been blown off, I figured somebody's got to get word to the captain to slow down otherwise those forward bulkheads were going to collapse one by one. I guess somebody did get the word up there and [Bode] did slow down."[18] With the battle just beginning, King did not want to attract attention to his position. He was hoping that he would not have to turn on his searchlight, but the order soon came to strike an arc, meaning that the lights were to be turned on with the shutters remaining closed. "So they were all ready to go," he added. "Then we finally did get an order to open the shutters and oh I dreaded that. We opened shutters and in a matter of seconds we got another order to close shutters and I was happy to hear that." King stayed on the searchlight platform until well after the battle ended and the ship was secured from general quarters.

Don Wallace was on the bridge during the height of the battle. "There was mass confusion on the bridge as nobody had any idea what was happening," he recalled. "Suddenly the ship was rocked by a heavy explosion and we knew immediately that we had taken a torpedo hit forward and were in bad shape."[19] Looking out into the distance, Wallace could see another ship on fire. It almost certainly was the *Canberra*.

Wallace was probably not the only sailor aboard the *Chicago* that was afraid. "To my utter chagrin I felt my knees shaking," he wrote. "I tried to convince myself that I wasn't scared, although if the truth were to be known I was most likely terrified." He instead tried to focus on his duties as a talker on the JW phone circuit. In that capacity, Wallace was able to overhear an argument between Captain Bode and his gunnery officer. The two were squabbling about which one was going to control the radar. "It was with great relief that the morning sun finally came up," Wallace continued, "and I was relieved to know that everyone on the bridge had been so busy that no one else had witnessed me trying to keep my knees from shaking." He was probably not the only one who was scared that night on the bridge of the *Chicago*.

Also on duty when the battle started was George Pursley. He was on watch at the forward anti-aircraft director and remembers the battle being close and confusing. "Everything was dark," he said. "Everything happened so quickly. Nobody knew what was going on."[20] Pursley stayed on station all through the night.

Ken Maysenhalder and Fred Tuccitto were both on duty manning five-inch guns on opposite sides of the ship when the battle started. On the starboard side, Maysenhalder had been at his gun mount for almost the whole day. Most of his recent meals had been eaten on station. In the opening minutes of the battle, he remembered hearing the sound of a plane just moments before the first flares appeared in the sky. Almost immediately he saw the *Canberra* get hit and start on fire. "The next thing I remember was seeing a torpedo wake coming at us from the starboard side," he said. "I felt the ship turning." Before long he also felt the shock and concussion of the *Chicago* being struck by the torpedo. "It was like a kitchen full of pots and pans," he related. "You knew you were hit."[21] After the torpedo hit, he felt an immediate drop off in speed. As the battle continued, Maysenhalder's gun never fired on a target. "We could not find a target," he recalled.

One of Maysenhalder's mates was off duty when the battle started and rushed to get to his station. Running to the gun mount, Seaman First Class John Hayes was hit in the back with shrapnel when the shell struck the foremast.[22] Known by his shipmates as "Red," he made it to the station and quickly fell under the gun. Buddy Gannon, the gun captain, was known to have a comic side. He remembered an incident that took place off Pearl Harbor shortly after the war started. The ship's doctor happened to stop by the gun mount. He told the men that if someone were to die while a battle is raging, then the body should be thrown over the side to prevent problems in rotating the gun. Maysenhalder remembers the gun crew being pretty shaken up after hearing this recommendation. Seeing that Hayes was not hurt badly, Gannon yelled that it was time to throw him over the side. Hayes quickly bolted up from under the gun and ran down a nearby ladder to go below for first aid. Red Hayes was destined to catch a lot of ribbing over the incident in the coming days. It was a brief light moment in the heat of battle. Maysenhalder stayed at his gun all night and did not participate in any damage control efforts. "We didn't know how bad the damage was," he said. "We really did not know what was taking place."

On the port side of the ship, Fred Tuccitto was acting as a fuse setter for his five-inch gun. Normally a pointer, he was temporarily serving in this capacity so that other crewmen could be trained. He remembered the battle starting with no warning. Early on he saw the Australian cruiser ahead of him being hit. "I can still see them shooting at the *Canberra*," he said. "One event I can't get rid of is seeing the *Canberra* taking hit after hit. How could anyone live through such an ordeal?"[23]

Tuccitto remembered the torpedo hit as simply being a large boom. For a brief moment the whole ship seemed to shudder and rise up out of the water. Losing his balance, he struggled to keep from falling to the deck. His gun soon received orders to fire star shells, all of which failed to work. When the gun began to run low on ammunition, the gun captain ordered some of the crew to help the ammo handlers. Tuccitto continues the story: "I ran around to the rear of the gun, and an ammo handler rammed the nose of a five-inch shell into my face. All of my front teeth were knocked loose, one tooth was broken off, and my upper lip was cut." Although grimacing in pain, Tuccitto stayed on duty all night. "We had never been in [a surface] battle before," he would later relate of the night. "It was a big mess. We had no idea that the Japanese were so good. They were good at night battles. Even our officers didn't know what to do."

Captain Bode's conduct can be called into question as the battle unfolded. Despite his being an experienced naval officer, he inexplicably made no attempt to warn others that enemy ships had entered the sound. At minimum, he should have at least tried to warn Captain Riefkohl of the *Vincennes*. He also should have tried to get word of the battle to Admiral Turner. While the *Canberra* was being pummeled by heavy Japanese gunfire, Bode offered no direction to his two screening destroyers. His actions remain as much of a mystery today as they were the night of the battle. By 1:50 A.M. the southern force had been shattered. Admiral Mikawa already had his sights set on the northern force, which still did not know he was coming.

Chapter 16

The Battle Moves North

Ignorant of the events befalling the ships of the southern force, the cruisers of the northern force continued to patrol at a speed of ten knots. The sky in the area was overcast and the sea was smooth. An occasional squall of light rain mixed with intermittent pockets of mist. Savo Island and the adjacent area to the south were shrouded in heavy clouds making visibility about 10,000 yards.[1]

Last in the column of the northern force, the *Astoria* was steaming on four boilers. Sufficient steam pressure was being maintained in the remaining boilers to allow the ship to increase speed to twenty-four knots on a moment's notice. Power was also likely to be available for two additional knots if necessary.[2] The crew was at condition of readiness two. Some of the off-duty sailors were sleeping at or near their battle stations. The ship was maintaining a general state of watertight integrity with most of the doors and hatches above the second deck closed. A few watertight doors were left open to permit limited traffic. Hatches leading to central station and the after steering compartment were open, but could be closed instantly as there were two men being stationed at each. About half of the repair parties were on duty and alert.

Captain Greenman had a practice of rotating his key officers for watch duty. "My practice was to put heads of departments on supervisory watch," he later said. "When things quieted down I would go in and lie down and turn the watch over to the supervisor."[3] The emergency sea cabin was located just off the bridge. "I had a little bunk and wash-stand in a section of the chart house just off the bridge where I slept," Greenman added. "The doors opened directly on the bridge and were open at this time."

Lieutenant Commander James Topper began his watch as supervisory officer of the deck just before midnight when he relieved Lieutenant Commander John Hayes. The engineering officer, Hayes left the bridge to go down to his cabin for some sleep. Before departing, he told Topper that all of the lookouts were on top alert for submarines and that Captain Greenman wanted the *Astoria* to be kept as close up to the other ships in the formation as possible in order to get the maximum anti-submarine protection of the destroyers.[4] Hayes also noted that the *Astoria* had picked up a message on the T.B.S. from the *San Juan* to the *Vincennes* that a plane was sighted over Savo Island going east. The captain had been notified of the development. Topper also knew that Greenman was sleeping in the nearby emergency cabin and could be called at a moment's notice.

Joining Topper on duty was Lieutenant (jg) Noel Burkey. As officer of the deck, he was responsible for overseeing the bridge watch. Among others coming on duty was a pair of enlisted men. Quartermaster Second Class Roy Radke was the lead quartermaster of the watch. Yeoman Second Class Walter Putnam manned the JL circuit. It was just one of many communication networks that linked different parts of the ship.

Also coming on watch at midnight was Lieutenant Commander William Truesdell. As part of the fire control group, John Powell had the occasion to observe the gunnery officer. "He never wore a set of phones," Powell remembered.[5] Since Truesdell would have to be in constant communication with others he usually had a talker standing nearby who had on a headset, or he would occasionally talk on the battle phone. "Most of the times he would tell the talker to tell the people what to do," Powell continued. He noticed that the gunnery officer always seemed to take things in stride.

As a junior officer in the gunnery division, Gene Alair had plenty of time to view Truesdell close up. "Truesdell was an argumentative sort of a guy," Alair remembered, "but he was no damn fool. He was a good gunnery officer. Guys either liked him or disliked him, but he was no problem to me."[6]

After arriving at the forward main battery control station, Truesdell quickly took stock of the readiness of his department. Two of the guns in each of the eight-inch main battery turrets were manned. All nine of the guns were loaded with shells, having been readied the day before during the threatened air attacks. Powder bags were in position but not yet loaded in the guns. The five-inch secondary batteries were each fully manned with seven or eight men at each gun.[7] One man stood ready at each of the twenty-millimeter anti-aircraft guns. All four of the 1.1-inch machine gun mounts were half manned, but the guns were ready to fire.

Located high on the superstructure near the directors, the forward main battery control station was alert and fully manned. All of the fire control equipment at the station appeared to be operating properly. Deep in the recesses of the ship, the main battery plotting room was half manned. If battle conditions developed, Truesdell felt that there were enough men in the plotting room to keep things moving until the rest arrived.[8]

As the plotting officer on duty, Lieutenant (jg) Dante Marzetta was the individual responsible for keeping the room functioning. The main battery plotting room was the linchpin of the fire control system for the *Astoria*'s eight-inch guns. The area contained the main battery switchboard and firing computer. The room served as a central clearinghouse of information on targets that was gathered by lookouts and various types of fire control equipment. The information was inputted into a rudimentary fire control computer with the result being a firing solution that was transmitted to the turrets.[9]

Early in his watch, Truesdell noticed that the forward fire control radar did not seem to be functioning properly. It was not the first time on the trip that the *Astoria* had experienced radar troubles. The after fire control radar had already gone out shortly after departing from Pearl Harbor, a victim of a shorted transformer. Since no replacement part was available at sea, the set had been out of service for some time.

Truesdell sent a radar striker down to get Chief Radioman John Datko. Off duty at the time, Datko had already tinkered with the forward radar that night. He had repaired the set between 10 and 11 P.M. In his final inspection he noticed a defect in the control indicator. The equipment seemed to be properly functioning except that the pattern on the screen was depressed to about half of its horizontal size.[10] Deciding that he could not effectively dig into the problem during the blacked out conditions, Datko left a note for the radar officer before departing. It would be better to fix it during daylight hours.

Seaman Second Class George Barker awoke Datko from a sound sleep at about 1:10 A.M. He told him that Truesdell wanted the forward fire control radar fixed at once. En route to the set, Datko first met up with the radar officer, Ensign Raymond Herzberger. The two went to the half deck below the signal bridge to find some replacement tubes. By

16. The Battle Move North

1:45 A.M. they had started work on the set. It took two attempts to locate the problem, but by 2:00 A.M. the set was back in working order.

For a critical five minute span of time near the start of the battle, the *Astoria* was without working radar. However, even had it been working it is uncertain if the set would have been able to pick up anything. Ensign William Cramer had stood watch at the radar plot from 8 P.M. to midnight. He reported that the radar was operating with continuous three-hundred and sixty degree sweeps. However, there was interference on all sides from nearby land. Only a small slice of the scope was clear, the position of which varied with the direction of the ship.[11] About an hour before midnight a report had circulated around the ship that a radar contact had been made bearing north at a distance of thirty-four miles. Although no action seems to have been taken from the report, it may have been a plane since the timing was close to the T.B.S. report made by the *San Juan* to the *Vincennes*.[12]

In recalling the events leading up to the battle, Captain Greenman felt that his radar offered no help. "What we got only lent to confusion," he later said. "The officer on watch in radar frequently reported to me early in the evening that he was picking up strange objects in the area where these ships were supposed to be." The captain concluded that the objects were other ships of the screening force.[13]

Right at midnight the *Vincennes* changed course turning northeast on the patrol box. Last in the formation, the *Astoria* made the turn about four minutes later. Glancing out into the distance, Lieutenant Commander Topper noticed some firing off in the vicinity of Tulagi. "The Marines were not having much of a picnic over there tonight," he remarked.[14] Some twenty minutes later word came from the *Vincennes* over the T.B.S. that the group would continue on the current leg of the patrol box for an extra ten minutes. The lead cruiser was able to get a fix on Savo Island and determined that the formation was slightly off the assigned patrol route.[15]

* * *

Entering the engagement with the southern force, Admiral Mikawa had his flagship pointed east. He was well into the southern passageway roughly halfway between Savo Island and Cape Esperance. It was an ideal heading to get him to his intended target, the transports. Up until now the cruiser force had been moving in a single column. Whether it was the brief sighting of the northern cruisers or the *Canberra*'s hard turn barring his original path, Mikawa turned the *Chokai* to the northeast. The new direction put him on a direct course to attack the northern cruisers, but away from the transports off Lunga Point. Like loyal soldiers the cruisers *Aoba*, *Kako*, and *Kinugasa* followed the flagship.

The *Furutaka* also turned northeast, but in a somewhat abrupt and radical fashion that may have been in response to the *Canberra*'s turn.[16] The light cruisers *Tenryu* and *Yubari* also made the turn following the *Furutaka*. As a result of these various maneuvers, the Japanese Cruiser Force became divided into two distinct groups, both of which were headed toward the northern force. The main group of heavy cruisers, led by the *Chokai*, was on a route to pass on the eastern side of the northern force. The *Furutaka*, *Tenryu*, and *Yubari* took a western path much closer to Savo Island. Both groups were now southeast of Savo Island heading towards the American cruisers.

Even before the long distance sighting of the *Vincennes*, Mikawa was aware of the northern force. An additional message from one of his scout planes reported cruisers east of Savo Island. As he moved northeast, he must have initially assumed that this second force of cruisers would be ready for him. It was not to be the case. As the *Chokai* approached the northern force from the southwest, an alert lookout noticed an important fact regarding the last ship in the American column, the *Astoria*. Executive Officer Kekichi Kato noted it in a post war interview. "When the *Chokai* approached the enemy, the main battery of the first ship that we saw, which I think was the last ship in the column, was not trained on either of our groups of ships."[17] It was clear that the American ships were not yet aware of the Japanese presence.

The *Chokai* opened the engagement with the northern force by firing a spread of four torpedoes at 1:48 A.M. at a range of almost 10,000 yards.[18] The spread was most likely aimed at the *Vincennes*. Two minutes later the Japanese ships prepared to open fire. The *Chokai* snapped on her searchlight illuminating the *Astoria* at a range of 7,800 yards. The *Aoba* and *Kako* quickly followed suit illuminating the *Quincy* and *Vincennes* respectively. All three of the American cruisers, and at least one of the escorting destroyers, could now be clearly seen by the Japanese. In only a matter of seconds, the *Chokai* let go with her first main battery salvo. Each time one of the *Chokai*'s eight-inch guns fired, a deadly 277 pound projectile was sent hurling towards the *Astoria*.[19] The first salvo missed the target, falling some five hundred yards short and two hundred yards wide to the left. A near miss so close speaks volumes to the accuracy of the initial estimates of the Japanese gunners.[20] The *Kako* immediately followed with a salvo directed at the *Vincennes*. The *Aoba* now opened fire on the *Quincy*. Before the northern force had much time to react, all three cruisers were under heavy fire.

Unlike the attack on the southern force where well placed flares silhouetted the Allied ships from behind, in this phase of the battle the Japanese were not able to benefit from the flares. The Japanese gunners instead had to rely on illumination by searchlights. When firing her initial salvos, the *Chokai* seems to have used her searchlights only intermittently to aid

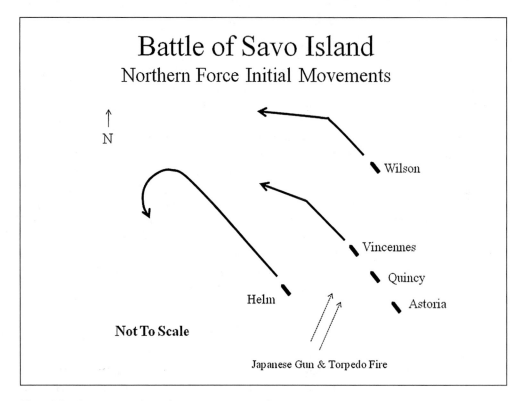

Note: Map is not to scale and represents approximate movements.

her gunners in finding their mark on the *Astoria*. The lights were quickly snapped on and off, shining for brief periods of time only when firing. To the men aboard the three American cruisers, the lights emitted a terrifying glow that seemed to last for an eternity.

Just a minute after opening fire, the *Chokai* launched her second salvo towards the *Astoria* at a range of about 7,000 yards. The shots also missed short, but were wide to the left by only about one hundred yards. Knowing that the *Astoria* was not in an immediate position to return fire, the gunners on the flagship were methodically working to find the right range. Just then a salvo fired from the *Aoba* hit the *Quincy*, landing on the main deck in the after part of the ship. It was not long before the *Vincennes* was also hit. On the third salvo directed towards the *Astoria*, the gunners on the *Chokai* found the correct deflection but were still short about five hundred yards. It was during this time that the *Chokai* was the target of two salvos from the *Astoria*, both of which missed. The *Chokai* then sighted a ship beyond the cruiser line and opened fire with her secondary battery. It was the destroyer *Wilson* patrolling off the starboard bow of the *Vincennes*. The fourth eight-inch salvo fired by the flagship landed a mere two hundred yards short of the *Astoria* and was dead on in terms of deflection. The range had fallen below 7,000 yards and it appeared that the Japanese gunners were close to finding their mark.

* * *

Just after 1:44 A.M. the *Astoria* had reached the bottom corner of the patrol box and turned right to follow the lead ship. The formation was now heading northwest. At about this juncture a series of events occurred at almost the same time. After the cruiser had settled on course, Lieutenant Commander Topper thought that he felt a distant underwater explosion, which he attributed to a destroyer dropping depth charges. Lieutenant (jg) Burkey did not feel the slight vibration. Topper wanted to make sure that everyone was alert. "I had my talker inform the officer of the watch in central station to be sure his men were on alert as depth charges were being dropped by a destroyer," he later wrote.[21] A reply came back that they were on alert, having also felt the slight tremor. Fearing that a submarine had made it through the screen and was now attacking the transports, Topper went over to the forward starboard corner of the pilot house only to find nothing amiss in the direction of Guadalcanal or Tulagi. What the *Astoria* men were hearing was most likely the end of run explosions from torpedoes fired by either the *Chokai* or *Bagley*.[22]

No sooner had Topper completed investigating the underwater sounds when reports began to reach the bridge that lookouts could hear the sound of a plane, but could not see it. Seaman First Class Lynn Hager was one of several lookouts who reported hearing planes. He had heard the noise several times from his position in sky control. Lieutenant Art McLaughlin, the officer on duty at sky control, passed the word for the men at sky forward and sky aft to keep a sharp lookout. He also made sure that the order went out over the machine gun circuit.

In an attempt to hear the planes himself, Topper went to the starboard side of the bridge and listened. The only noise that he could discern was the sound of the blowers right behind turret one. "I came back forward to the starboard window of the pilot house," he reported, "and was searching the area ahead and to the right. The destroyers and other ships in our column were in proper position." Just then the T.B.S. crackled with a message from the *Vincennes* about another delayed course change. Instead of changing at 1:50 A.M. the turn would be ten minutes later. While Burkey was on the T.B.S. acknowledging the course change, the *Patterson* was sending out her emergency warning about strange ships entering the harbor. As a result the *Astoria* did not receive the message.

Someone from the port wing of the bridge suddenly reported star shells on the port quarter. Topper directed Burkey to call the captain and stand by the general alarm as he ran to the port door of the pilot house and moved aft. He could plainly see what he identified not as star shells, but aircraft flares about 5,000 yards away. "Four flares had already fallen through the clouds and were illuminating the stern of the *Astoria*," Topper wrote. "The flares appeared to be layed [sic.] normal to our course. I hastily searched the area below the flares for any object."[23] Just then the main battery fired. "This gave me quite a surprise," Topper reported, "as I had not given any order about opening fire, nor could I make out any ships in the vicinity of the flares." As he started back towards the pilot house a second salvo was unleashed.

Looking out the port quarter Walter Putnam also saw the flares from the *Astoria*'s bridge. He initially saw only one, but almost immediately the single flare was followed by several others. He made no report as it was clear to him that others were watching the same sight. Putnam did observe some confusion on the bridge. "For the first two or three minutes after the flares were sighted," he later reported, "there seemed to be some question in the minds of the officers on watch as to what the flares were coming from."[24] Glancing at the clock, he saw it was just before 1:55 A.M. The blast of the main battery guns firing and the sound of the general alarm then occurred almost simultaneously. Before long the sound powered phones that Putnam had on went dead. He briefly ducked out onto the port wing of the bridge. As he re-entered the pilot house, the second main battery salvo fired. It was then that he noticed that Captain Greenman was on the bridge.

Up until this time Roy Radke had been occupied by his routine duties as the lead quartermaster of the watch. Hearing the report of flares, he quickly went to the port side of the bridge just in time to see a flare burning out. Four more soon appeared. "These flares were quite a distance astern of us," he noticed. "They were all about the same height and in a line about parallel to our course."[25] Re-entering the pilot house, he glanced off into the distance. "I saw a ship on our port bow at some distance open fire." It may have been the destroyer *Helm*. Radke's instincts then took over. "I rang the general alarm without orders," he wrote. "Just as I pulled the switch I heard the order, 'Stand by the general alarm.'" As the alarm was sounding the main battery opened fire. The quartermaster then ran into the chart house to record the events in the deck log.

After completing his acknowledgement of the course change to the *Vincennes* on the T.B.S., Burkey called for the captain from the door between the pilot house and emergency cabin before rushing back to the starboard side to keep on station with the *Quincy*.[26] It was then that he noticed the glare of searchlights coming from the port quarter. At the time he thought the lights were directed at the *Vincennes*. In the confusion of the moment, no one had made sure that the captain had actually been awoken. In the end it was Lieutenant (jg) John Mullen, the junior officer of the deck, who awoke Captain Greenman after realizing that he had not yet arrived on the bridge. He told Greenman that flares or star shells were off the port quarter.[27] The captain had not yet been aroused by the unfolding calamity. "Being as tired as one would be I slept more soundly and was probably more difficult to wake up," he later recounted. "Had I been more rested I would have heard some of the confusion on the bridge and wakened myself up."[28]

As the battle started Don Yeamans could see the confusion on the bridge from his position on the port pelorus. "Everyone was running around like the devil," he recalled. "I could see something on fire in the distance."[29] He later surmised that it was the burning cruiser *Canberra*.

It had not taken long for Gunnery Officer Truesdell to determine what was happening. Just after being satisfied that the fire control radar was again working properly, a lookout from sky control reported, "Star shells astern."[30] Immediately moving outside the sky control station, Truesdell noticed that the lights were evenly spaced and quickly determined that the star shells were actually aircraft flares. "Their interval of appearing was so short," he later wrote, "that it indicated that they could not have been fired by a single gun or pair of guns."[31] Truesdell knew this meant action. He rushed back into the control station, arriving in time to see the first enemy salvo fall ahead and short.

Truesdell quickly sprang into action. He alerted all stations of the sighting before training the director and main battery turrets to port. A lookout quickly reported the sighting of three Japanese cruisers thought to be of the *Nachi* type. More information on the sighting immediately became available. The range finder on the forward main battery director was able to get a range of 6,800 yards on the lead target. The speed was thought to be at least twenty-five knots. The radar operator reported seeing three distinct pips on the radar screen. Truesdell wrote, "I examined the radar screen and thought I saw four." In any case, the radar was showing a range of 7,000 yards. In response to a question from the bridge asking if what were sighted were star shells or flares, Truesdell simply told his talker to say "flares." He then asked the bridge to sound general quarters and quickly followed it with a request to open fire.

Down in the main battery plotting room, Lieutenant (jg) Marzetta received the report that three Japanese cruisers were sighted off the port quarter of the *Astoria*. The information from the lookouts and the director were being fed into his rudimentary machines to formulate a firing solution. The initial radar range for some reason did not make it to the plotting room at this time. Marzetta remembered that the general alarm sounded a short time afterwards.

Ensign Raymond McGrath was the officer in turret number two when the action started. Over the JD-2 circuit he heard the various frantic reports. "Flares on the port quarter ... the Australian is firing ... all turrets match in train to port and load." Acting as essentially a closed telephone system, the JD-2 circuit linked together the main battery gun turrets. Spot one then reported, "It's a *Nachi* type cruiser."[32] He did not have to wait much longer for his guns to fire. Truesdell could not understand why general quarters was not sounding, so he made a second request. When no reply came from the bridge on his request to open fire, he gave the order himself. The *Astoria* lurched as at least six of the nine eight-inch guns fired with a tremendous roar. A second salvo left the ship in what seemed like only a matter of seconds. Both salvos missed. The five-inch battery now also opened fire.[33]

Coming off duty at around midnight, Fire Controlman First Class Walter Johns notified his relief of the current watch situation and then decided to retire. He chose to sleep at the forward battle lookout station. "I was called by the forward battle lookouts at about 0200 who said something was wrong," Johns stated. "I dressed hurriedly and proceeded to my battle station at Batt II."[34] A large armored box, battle two was located just behind the boat deck. As he passed the forward 1.1-inch machine gun mounts, the *Astoria* opened fire with a main battery salvo. Continuing to make his way aft, Johns noticed the flares hanging about 2,000 yards away and also saw a searchlight locked onto the *Astoria* from the port side. "I heard the sound of shells passing over the ship," he reported. "Traffic was jammed on the communication platform and five-inch gun deck."

Upon arriving at battle two, Johns took immediate action. "I took my station on the seat at spot II. I manned the JC battle circuit and established communication with spot I, plot, range keepers forward and aft." The JC battle circuit connected all of the battle stations that were part of the gunnery department. The after director was quickly matched up with the forward main battery director. Among those arriving on station with Johns was Seaman First Class Jack Dean and Seaman Second Class John Bartlett. Operating in close quarters the group worked desperately to get a fix on the approaching Japanese ships. The range, relative bearing and target angle were quickly estimated and used to fire two salvos.

Chapter 17

Captain Greenman at the Helm

Aboard the *Vincennes*, Captain Riefkohl was not yet convinced that it was enemy ships that were firing on his force. He had received no information on possible enemy ships in the area from the southern force, nor did he receive the warning from the *Patterson*. His initial reaction was to send a message over T.B.S. for friendly ships to stop illuminating his force.[1] Any doubts as to the identity of the ships was quickly erased when a salvo fell just five hundred yards short of his cruiser. As the battle developed Riefkohl gave no real direction to the other cruisers of his group. The captains of the *Astoria* and *Quincy* would be on their own. It was not long into the battle that the *Vincennes* was hit by both gunfire and torpedoes.

* * *

Lieutenant Commander Topper arrived back inside the pilot house just as Captain Greenman entered the bridge. The captain entered the pilot house from the starboard door just as the *Astoria* fired her second main battery salvo to port.[2] Greenman was calm and collected as he quickly began to interpret the situation. The *Astoria* was firing at something, but exactly what he did not know, and the general alarm was sounding. Greenman noticed the flares almost immediately. "A considerable portion of them were in the sky when I got up," he later said. "At first I thought it was illumination by our vessels who had found enemy subs in the harbor."

Just then a searchlight, that appeared to be aimed at the *Vincennes*, abruptly snapped on. Greenman vividly remembers seeing two searchlights. "I could see it through the rigging over the port catapult," he later said. Glancing at the flares and searchlights, he noticed that both were inside the bay. "My first reaction was that our vessels had spotted an enemy submarine on the surface and we were firing into our own ships."[3] He immediately asked Topper, "Who sounded the general alarm? Who gave the order to commence firing?"[4] Topper replied that he had done neither. Greenman then said, "Topper, I think we are firing on our own ships, let's not get excited and act too hasty, cease firing."[5] Topper agreed with the captain's assessment of the situation. But one who surely did not was Lieutenant Commander Truesdell.

The gunnery officer stopped the firing upon receipt of the order, which came to him as, "What are you firing at? Cease firing."[6] However, he immediately called the bridge to ask permission to resume. He had just observed the *Chokai*'s third salvo fall short of the *Astoria*. Back on the bridge, the JA phone talker* announced, "Mr. Truesdell said for God's sake give the word to commence firing."[7] At almost the same time, Captain Greenman looked up to see a distant salvo straddle the *Vincennes*. He also saw the *Chokai*'s fourth salvo

---

*The JA circuit was reserved for use by the captain during combat conditions. Linking all of the main battle station areas, the communication network was used by the commanding officer to disseminate orders and receive information.

fall just short of the *Astoria* with one eight-inch shell piercing the bow well forward of turret one.[8] The projectile passed through the paint locker without starting a fire. Greenman now knew that the *Astoria* was tangling with enemy ships. "At one time I could see five indications of ships' fire," he recalled. "I could see flashes of five different ships and they were none of our ships."[9] The captain now gave the order to sound general quarters and commence firing. He then remarked to Topper, "Whether our ships or not, we would have to stop them."[10]

Word soon reached Greenman that Japanese cruisers of the *Nachi* type had been sighted and that the *Vincennes* ordered the group to increase speed to fifteen knots. He instead ordered full speed and turned the *Astoria* to the left. He wanted to bring the targets well forward and at the same time not interfere with the line of fire from the *Quincy*. Other than the order to increase speed, Greenman received no instructions from the *Vincennes* since the battle began.[11] He noticed that in addition to his ship, both the *Quincy* and *Vincennes* were now turning ten to fifteen degrees to the left of the base course. He surmised that Captain Riefkohl was intending to swing the formation to the left to better engage the approaching enemy, while allowing for all of the ships' guns to continue to train out to port while the maneuver was underway.

Truesdell wasted no time after receiving the captain's order to resume firing. The *Astoria*'s eight-inch guns fired for the third time. The salvo comprised all six guns of turrets one and two. The gunnery department used the time that elapsed as a result of the cease fire order to get a better fix on the Japanese ships. The third salvo was fired at a range of 6,200 yards and fell short of the *Chokai* by only about one hundred yards.[12] The forward turrets soon reached the limit of their ability to train out to the port side. Truesdell repeatedly reported this situation to bridge in the hopes of soon getting the ship to move more to the left. His wish was soon granted. During this time turret three temporarily lost power. As a result, the *Astoria*'s fourth salvo was fired from just two guns of turret two, the only available turret. The *Astoria* gunners had not yet found the range of the *Chokai*.

At about 1:55 A.M. the fifth salvo fired by the *Chokai* scored a direct hit on the *Astoria*. At least four eight-inch shells landed amidships. Fires immediately started on the boat deck and in the hangar, where the flames were fed by the aviation fuel in the seaplanes.[13] Each plane was loaded with 175 gallons of aviation fuel and quickly caught on fire after one of the first hits. Normal procedure was to drain the gas out of the planes each night, but this was not done due to an anticipated early morning launch.[14]

One of the shells penetrated the kerosene tank before exploding in the after mess hall. Located under the starboard ladder leading from the well deck to the top of the hangar, the tank spilled its contents across the well deck.[15] The kerosene added to the already roaring fire and created a thick black smoke. The glaring flames soon made a perfect aiming point for the Japanese gunners, who no longer needed searchlights. Shortly after the first hits were scored, a second Japanese ship began to fire on the *Astoria*. The *Kinugasa* was the last ship in the column of four heavy cruisers. With fires now burning on all three of the American ships, she decided to divide her fire. Her secondary batteries aimed at the *Vincennes*, while her eight-inch main guns opened up on the *Astoria*. Just a few minutes later she decided to direct all of her fire at the *Vincennes*.

In the meantime the *Chokai* continued to exclusively fire at the *Astoria*. The next salvo hit turret one, knocking it out of action with three direct hits. The turret had just fired and was being reloaded. The first shell hit the face plate at an almost ninety-degree angle. It left a clean cut entry hole almost eleven inches in diameter before exploding in the gun chamber. The blast killed the entire gun crew and destroyed the interior of the turret. The two additional shells, which hit almost the same time as the first, pierced the barbette. All personnel in the upper powder handling room and all but two on the shell deck were killed in the resulting explosion. The only two survivors from the latter area suffered horrible burns.[16] Powerless and dead, turret one froze in place facing the port quarter.

The *Astoria* had just unleashed her third salvo when turret one was hit. "Almost immediately afterward," Ensign McGrath noted from his position in turret two, "I felt a terrific explosion in the near vicinity, and the gun room filled with smoke."[17] He had a pretty good idea of what happened. "All communications were lost with turret one and I reported to control that turret one had been hit," McGrath later wrote. He soon had other problems to contend with as the powder hoist jammed below his turret.

Among the early hits on the *Astoria* was an eight-inch shell that penetrated the splinter shield around the number eight gun of the five-inch secondary battery. Located on the port side, the gun was even with the after stack and just forward of the aviation area. After piercing the shield the shell hit one of the nearby ready ammunition lockers and deflected upward.[18] An armored box, each ready locker stored a small amount of ammunition for immediate use by the five-inch gun crews. As a result of the hit, some of the ammunition ignited and started what would be the first of many fires on the gun deck.

* * *

The sounding of the general alarm meant a change to most of the bridge watch as officers and enlisted men alike raced to their battle stations. Captain Greenman took direct control of the ship, relieving Lieutenant Commander Topper as supervisor of the watch. As he left the bridge for his battle station at central station, Topper noticed a brief flash in the direction of the enemy ships off the port side. The ladders leading to the bridge were crowded with sailors, but he made it to central station in about a minute. When Lieutenant Commander William Guy Eaton, the ship's navigator, arrived on the bridge Lieutenant (jg) Burkey left for his battle station at secondary con. Before departing the bridge area, he saw turret one burst into flames after being hit. He heard a talker notify central station of the damage. Burkey thought the flames lasted about a minute.

Ensign Tom Ferneding became the junior officer of the deck at this time. He had boarded the *Astoria* about two months before the war started. As the signal officer he was responsible for various types of visual communications including signal flags and message blinkers.

Not leaving the bridge area as a result of the general quarters alarm was Roy Radke. He stayed on as the lead quartermaster and worked feverishly to record the developing events in the *Astoria*'s deck log. Walter Putnam also stayed on the bridge. After Captain Greenman entered the area, Putnam had a firsthand view of the confusion on the bridge in the opening minutes of the battle. "At this time shots began to fall all around us," he recorded, "and the ship was firing rapidly from both main and secondary batteries."[19]

As the battle developed, Greenman worked to zig-zag the ship with a series of ten to fifteen degree turns. Navigator Eaton and Chief Quartermaster Leo Brom were helping to keep the *Astoria* on a heading that allowed the main battery guns to maintain fire off the port side. Looking off the starboard bow, Greenman could see both the *Quincy* and *Vincennes* off in the distance. Both were burning brightly amidships but were still returning fire at the enemy cruisers.

Chapter 18

Below Deck

Neither of the two northern force destroyers was able to make much of a difference in the fight. The captains of both ships seemed to see the battle as a confusing mess.[1] Early in the battle Captain Riefkohl directed the two destroyers to attack the enemy with torpedoes, but there was no coordinated effort to do so. The *Wilson* had started the battle off the starboard bow of the *Vincennes*. The destroyer did pick up the *Patterson*'s warning message. She opened fire after seeing the enemy searchlights illuminate the cruisers. Her five-inch guns sent shells screaming over the *Vincennes* toward the *Kako*, but scored no hits. Although her torpedo battery stood ready, the *Wilson* made no attempt to fire owing to the confusion of the battle and the uncertain locations of the other American ships.[2] At one point the destroyer had to increase speed and make a hard turn to avoid the *Helm*, which had suddenly appeared out of the darkness.

The battle largely passed by the *Helm*. She was never able to get a certain fix on the Japanese ships and fired only four rounds from her five-inch guns and no torpedoes. The destroyer then turned off to chase a strange ship off her starboard bow. It turned out to be the *Bagley*. Although a few salvoes were directed toward the destroyers, the Japanese kept their focus on the bigger ships.

It did not take very long for the Japanese to gain the upper hand in the battle. The group of Japanese ships that was being led by the *Chokai* passed southeast of the northern force, effectively crossing the "T" across the sterns of the three American cruisers. The second part of the split Japanese column passed to the west. The movements allowed the Japanese to catch the American ships in a murderous cross fire.

After scoring early hits on all three cruisers, the Japanese gunners locked on and gave the ships a terrific pounding. An early hit on the *Vincennes* started a large fire amidships in the aviation area. Subsequent hits wrecked the main battery control station, severed the main steam lines, and disabled key internal communication networks. At least two torpedoes fired by the *Chokai* slammed in her port side. The lead ship of the northern force was now dying fast.

The *Quincy* was able to fire off two full salvoes before being smothered by a rain of enemy gunfire. An early hit set aflame one of the planes in the aviation area making a perfect aiming point for Japanese gunners. A parade of hits devastated the ship both above and below the waterline. One hit fatally wounded the captain and killed almost everyone in the pilot house. If the situation was not bad enough, two torpedoes fired from the light cruiser *Tenryu* struck the *Quincy* on the port side. However, in the course of the short battle she was able to return fire, hitting the *Chokai* in the flag plot just behind the bridge.[3] The shell exploded in the operations room burning up the flagship's charts and maps. Reduced to a burning derelict, the *Quincy* slowed to a stop.

***

From his position in the *Astoria*'s main battery control station, Lieutenant Commander Truesdell noted the volume and accuracy of the Japanese fire. "The accuracy of fire was excellent," he recorded. "Once the enemy started to hit they continued to hit. It seemed that we were hit [by] each salvo. In the beginning I am quite certain that we were fired upon by only one ship and later I think we were concentrated upon."[4] The gunnery officer was correct in all of his assumptions.

Being the last ship in the northern force column put the *Astoria* closest to the Japanese ships that were being led by the *Chokai*. With her view of the *Vincennes* obscured by the burning *Quincy*, the *Kako* shifted her fire to the *Astoria*. The *Kinugasa* did the same a short time later. The *Aoba* also briefly directed her fire on the *Astoria* but soon went back to focusing on the *Quincy*. For a five minute stretch of time beginning at about 2:00 A.M. the *Astoria* came under concentrated fire from multiple Japanese heavy cruisers.[5]

Guns were not the only weapons being aimed at the *Astoria* during this time. At about 2:00 A.M. the *Kako* took aim with her torpedo tubes. The *Astoria* was 8,500 yards away when four torpedoes jumped out of the Japanese cruiser's port side tubes at a speed of fifty knots. The *Kako*'s war diary recorded that one of the torpedoes found the mark. "Observed one direct hit about five minutes later and after the few minutes that target appeared to sink."[6] In actuality the *Astoria* was not sinking and all of the torpedoes missed. About five minutes after the first round, the *Kako* tried again, sending two more torpedoes at the *Astoria*. The target turned left a short time later causing both torpedoes to miss.

***

Keeping the *Astoria* moving was the responsibility of Lieutenant Commander John D. Hayes. The engineering officer oversaw the cruiser's fire rooms, engine rooms, diesel generators, and the like. He commanded a cadre of machinist's mates, water tenders, and firemen who kept the boilers lit and the steam generators turning.

Just prior to the start of the battle, the engineering department was running smoothly. Like the rest of the *Astoria*, the department was at condition two. The officer of the watch was Ensign F.M. Long. Chief Machinist's Mate Carl Weaver was the junior officer of the watch. The ship's electrical officer, Lieutenant (jg) J.T. McNulty was on duty with a repair party one deck above the engineering spaces. All of the heavy hatches below the second deck were kept closed except for the passage of personnel. Four boilers spilt between two fire rooms were online. The other four could be cut in within fifteen minutes, and all of the electric generators were in operation. Talkers from the engineering compartment were tuned in to the ship's key communication circuits.

When the battle started Hayes was asleep in his cabin. He was awoken by either the sound of the general quarters alarm or by Machinist's Mate First Class John Bengel. A member of the amidships repair party, Bengel stopped by the cabin. "The shells are sure flying up there," he told the engineering officer.[7] Like most of the amidships repair party, Bengel was destined to perish during the night. Hayes grabbed his flashlight and headed for the forward engine room. By the time he arrived, the engineering force was at battle stations. Shortly after his arrival speed was increased to fifteen knots. The order soon came in to increase speed even more. Then the engineering spaces started taking hits.

As the first hits landed on the *Astoria*, the emergency alarm from the number two fire room began ringing. The noise signified that steam for the forward engines would now have to come from the number four fire room. The engineering staff quickly opened the necessary valves. Problems were soon apparent as the starboard engine was able to make revolutions for over twenty knots of speed, but the port engine could turn for only thirteen. Before long the steam pressure began to fall. The engines seemed to be operational except for the lack of steam.

At about this time the forward engine room began to fill with smoke. "I decided to examine the mess hall above," Hayes reported of the time. Water started to come down as the dogs on the center escape hatch were being loosened and the hatch was immediately resealed. "The other hatch was opened and I proceeded to the mess hall above."[8] The air was filled with a haze of smoke. Surveying the situation, Hayes noticed a mangled bulkhead through the smoky air. The mess hall was filled with wreckage. "Serious fires were burning and the only living person I noticed was Lieutenant (jg) McNulty," Hayes later wrote. "He appeared to be in a dazed condition."[9] McNulty had made it to his battle station in the after engine room at the start of the battle, but may have gone up to the mess hall to investigate conditions. Hayes never saw McNulty again and the electrical officer did not survive the night. Hayes tried to douse some of the flames in the mess hall with a fire extinguisher sent up from the engine room below. It soon became apparent that the available firefighting equipment was ineffective. Hayes had no choice but to order the forward engine room abandoned. He did so immediately except for the talkers, who he ordered out a short time later. In the hope of possibly returning, key pieces of equipment were secured as the engineers departed.

In the company of Chief Machinist's Mate R. L. Davis and a few others, Hayes made his way to the forward mess hall. In that compartment they found Chief Machinist's Mate Harry Ray, a member of the amidships repair party, lying on the deck. As Hayes slung the wounded man over his shoulder, Davis led the group into the after mess hall. The flashlight that Hayes had grabbed as he left his cabin was still attached to a lanyard around his neck. It had been most useful up to this time. "I became very weak at this time," Hayes reported. "The last I remember is dragging myself along holding on to bunks in what must have been the fifth division compartment."[10] The engineering officer then blacked out.

The forward engine room was just one of many engineering compartments that were put out of commission during the height of the battle. However, four other key compartments would go out first. The number two fire room was the first to go off line, followed just a short time later by the after engine room. Fire rooms three and four fell out of action in advance of the forward engine room.

No men were known to have escaped from fire room number one. Off line when the battle started, it had been directed to get on line as soon as possible. All communication with the room was then lost. An eight-inch shell is believed to have penetrated the port side of the cruiser just above the waterline and exploded in the fire room.[11] The remaining three fire rooms were all abandoned largely due to smoke that filled the rooms from adjacent areas.

The after engine room was taking steam from the number four fire room when the action started. A pair of first class machinist's mates was working feverishly adjusting valves. Both William Lewis and William Stoessel had been off duty when the general alarm sent them rushing to their battle stations in the after engine room. Changing sets of valves as fire rooms went out of commission, they were trying to get steam to the engines so that the *Astoria* could pick up speed. Early in the battle smoke and flames from a hit in the compartment above came down through an exhaust trunk. The flames may have caused the generators to momentarily stall, resulting in the temporary loss of power to turret three. Lieutenant (jg) McNulty was able to get the generator up and running again in short order.

Just a short time later the room filled with thick black smoke that came in from the blower trunk. It was not long after that the after engine room lost power and superheated steam started to enter from one of the fire rooms.[12] The after engine room was ordered abandoned a short time later. Crewmen tried in vain, to open the escape hatch from the inside. Finally, someone from the damage control party opened the hatch from above. About fourteen men emptied out of the engine room into to the mess hall above, arriving just in time for the area to receive a direct hit. The flash and explosion killed and maimed many, leaving a grisly scene of dead and dying.

Among the enlisted men exiting the after engine room was Machinist's Mate Second Class Abe Santos. The instant the mess hall was hit Santos saw a flash and felt a sensation that he likened to standing next to a hot campfire. The force of the blast hurled him into the metal gedunk stand. Commonly found on larger warships, the bar-like stand was an area where sailors could purchase soda and snacks. "I was slammed right up against it," he later said, "and I indented it."[13] Recovering from the effects of the blast, he found Fireman First Class Art McCann. The two were good friends from the engineering division. McCann was seriously wounded. "He told me not to let him die," Santos said. Before much else could be done a second hit rocked the mess hall and the room became pitch black. Groping through the darkness, Santos made his way around by memory searching for a way topside. "I knew exactly were I was ... just by feel. I knew where the gedunk stand was, the tailor's shop, and so I knew then there's a trunk going up." His journey topside led him past bodies and parts of bodies that were strewn about various compartments. He saw an officer sitting up against a bulkhead wearing a gas mask, apparently dead. Santos was one of the lucky ones to make it out of the after mess hall. "Only three or four of us come out of there after the second blast." He came topside at the after part of the ship and proceeded towards the fantail. He was one of the lucky sailors to make it out from below deck.

Chapter 19

The Battle Continues

Captain Greenman's zig-zagging probably helped the *Astoria* evade the two spreads of torpedoes that were fired by the *Kako*. Given the worsening situation in the engineering compartments, the ship would not be able to keep moving for much longer. The heavy fire being directed at the *Astoria* was beginning to take a toll. A direct hit by an eight-inch shell in the chart house struck down Navigator William Eaton and Chief Quartermaster Leo Brom. Both were killed.

Don Yeamans' battle station had him just outside of the chart house when the shell hit. "It was just a steel wall between us," he recalled. "I was stunned."[1] When the blast hit he saw white but does not remember much else. The force of the explosion knocked Yeamans off his feet and pushed him about ten feet from where he had been standing. He was hit with some shrapnel and had an eardrum blown out. The next thing he knew two men were picking him up off the deck asking if he was all right.

With the death of Leo Brom, Yeamans lost both a friend and teacher. The chief quartermaster who had been on the *Astoria* at the start of the war had left. "He had just made chief," Yeamans remembered of Brom. "I was a striker and I worked under him. He was first class most of the time. He never gave anybody problems. Just do your job, that's all."

The *Astoria* was now beginning to close on the *Quincy*. "If I turned to the left," wrote Captain Greenman, "I would cross her line of fire, so I ordered right standard rudder to let her draw ahead. It was my intention to turn with left rudder as soon as *Quincy* drew ahead"[2] At about this time the *Kako* opened fire with her secondary guns. She had been tracking the *Astoria* since firing torpedoes and reported, "We fired high angle guns and twenty-five mm. machine guns at her, getting hits in her bridge area causing great damage."[3]

The turn was not yet started when the *Kako*'s fire hit home, raking the starboard side of the *Astoria*'s bridge. Among those knocked down was Ensign Ferneding. He had been standing just inside the pilot house. "I was hit in the right leg," Ferneding recounted, "either by a fragment of a six-inch shell or by some wreckage when the shell struck the bridge of the cruiser."[4] Trying to stand up by his own power, he staggered, and fell back down to the deck. Walter Putnam rushed to his aide. "I moved him against the bulkhead and gave him a cigarette," recalled the yeoman.[5]

Also felled were the helmsman, Quartermaster First Class Houston Williams, and Boatswain's Mate First Class Julian Young. For a brief period of time there was no one at the helm. Putnam stepped in to grab the wheel for a few minutes. "When I took the wheel the ship was swinging right," he noted. "I reported to the captain that I was unable to steer because the compasses were shot away." Just then Young, who had been badly wounded, struggled to his feet to take over. Following Greenman's order he began to swing the rudder to the left. The *Quincy* suddenly appeared close off the port bow, burning from stem to stern. "It looked as if we were going to hit her," recalled Young. "The captain ordered a hard left and I threw the wheel full left and we passed clear astern."[6] The *Quincy* passed out of site after the near collision.

Captain Greenman now noticed that the *Astoria* was losing speed and inquired as to the situation below. Engineering Officer Hayes reported that the after engine room was being evacuated and that there were problems in the boiler rooms. He added that the ship could not make over eight knots.[7] Greenman felt that the ship was under the heaviest fire at this time. "Shells were falling on all sides," he reported, "and the ship was being hit repeatedly from the foremast aft."[8]

Growing weak from his wounds, Julian Young was now about at the point of collapse. The captain's orderly summoned Roy Radke, who had been tending to the wounded in the chart house, to take over the helm. Taking over the wheel, he quickly learned that the steering control had been lost and immediately reported such to the captain. Greenman then ordered steering control shifted to central station. By telephone the captain ordered the ship to steer south and continue to zig-zag.

* * *

As the *Astoria* was being repeatedly hit, Gunnery Officer Truesdell continued to return fire with his two available main battery turrets. After turret two had momentarily lost power, two additional salvos were fired. The fifth salvo was comprised of all six guns of turrets two and three. The shells were fired at an estimated range of 5,500 yards, which was well short

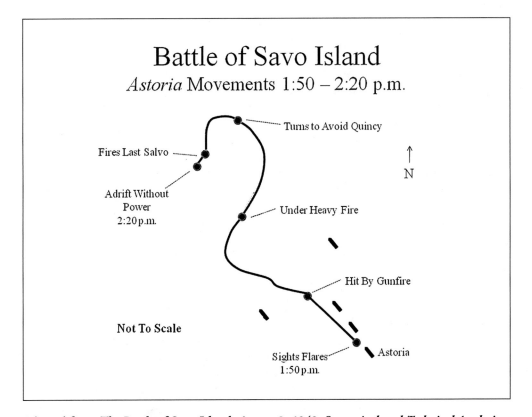

Adapted from *The Battle of Savo Island, August 9, 1942: Strategical and Technical Analysis.*

of the actual Japanese position. The Japanese ships were no longer using searchlights at this time, and no additional radar ranges were obtained after the *Astoria* was first hit.[9] With no searchlights to aim for, the *Astoria's* firecontrol men could not get a good fix on the enemy, and all of the cruiser's salvos were falling well short of their intended targets. The sixth salvo comprised only five guns fired at a range of 5,300 yards. Over the course of the next few firings, turret three was intermittently losing power.

The *Astoria's* movement to the right, coupled with the location of the Japanese cruisers was now making it difficult for the forward director to track the targets. The *Chokai* was passing across the stern of the *Astoria* at a high rate of speed moving from the port to the starboard quarter. Turret two could no longer bear on a target off the port side. "Director I kept training aft and could not see because of the fire amidships," Truesdell wrote after the battle. "I then ordered plot to shift control to control aft and director II."[10] Not long after the shift had taken place, the after main battery control station reported that they could not see anything due to their position being engulfed in smoke. No less than two salvos were fired under the control of director two. Both missed the mark. The latter salvo, the *Astoria's* eighth, was set at a range of about 5,000 yards. It fell well short of the *Chokai*, who was now about 6,500 yards off the stern of the *Astoria*.[11]

As the lead enemy cruiser passed from the port to starboard sides, the forward director now trained out to starboard and was again able to pick up the targets. On Truesdell's order, main battery control was again shifted back to director one. Turning to starboard, turret two was now again able to train on the target. At this juncture two more salvos were fired using targeting information from director one. The five guns of turrets two and three comprised the ninth salvo. Since the *Chokai* had now drifted somewhat out of the battle, the shots were most likely directed at the *Aoba* as she was now the closest Japanese cruiser at a distance of about 7,900 yards off the *Astoria's* starboard quarter.[12] The next eight-inch salvo also fell well short of the same ship.

Shortly after the tenth salvo was fired, the forward main battery control station shuddered from at least one Japanese shell landing in close proximity. Filling with smoke and hot gas, all communications to other stations were severed. "All phones were tested to no avail," Truesdell recalled. "The smoke and gas were so thick that the majority of the personnel had to leave their station."[13]

The last director-controlled salvo was fired at about 2:07 A.M. with the after director in control. The shells from turret three missed an enemy cruiser that was slightly to the port of the *Astoria's* stern. The ship was most likely the *Kinugasa*, which at the time was behind the *Aoba* and *Kako*, with the *Chokai* having drifted slightly off to the east. In eleven tries the *Astoria* gunners were unable to score a hit on any of the Japanese heavy cruisers.

While other personnel left the area, the gunnery officer stayed in the forward station trying in vain to re-establish some type of communications. He noticed that the Japanese fire seemed to have stopped and that the *Astoria* was no longer being hit.

Well below the scene of destruction that was unfolding above, Lieutenant (jg) Marzetta and his staff continued their duties in the main battery plotting room. "We were now being hit and sharp concussions were felt above us," he reported, "though no gear was loosened from the bulkheads nor was anything loose being knocked about; the blows did not appear to us to be exceptionally heavy."[14] When all attempts to contact turret one failed, it was assumed to be out of action. As smoke began to seep into the plotting room, the men worked through the process of shifting the control back and forth between the two directors.

As the smoke became worse, men began to cover their noses with handkerchiefs in an effort to breathe. "Rags were now stuffed in the ventilating ducts in order to keep smoke out," Marzetta continued, "but that didn't seem to help." The *Astoria* was no longer firing. The JA communications circuit was still intact, although contact with the bridge and main battery control were out. The floor plates of the room were now unscrewed and lifted out in order for crewmen to check for fires, but none were found. The fire control switchboard was turned off to prevent any possible short circuits. The men stood ready to turn the board back on if the ship needed to resume firing. The JA talker reported that the topside fires were getting worse. With the room full of smoke, the men broke out their gas masks. A request to abandon the plotting room was denied at this time. All Lieutenant Marzetta and his men could now do was to wait.

With all the activity Walter Johns missed an order to abandon battle two. He continued to work trying to keep the after director fixed on the Japanese ships and keeping communications open with other areas of the gunnery department. "At about this time smoke cleared sufficiently so that I caught a quick glimpse of the silhouette of a *Nachi* type cruiser through my spotting glass," he reported.[15] The director became jammed again after a hit somewhere in the general vicinity. Johns then received word that other areas were being evacuated. "I ordered my director personnel to leave their stations."

Lieutenant Jack Gibson was in command of the after main battery control station. The small armored box was located behind the boat deck on a machine gun platform that was perched just over the top of turret three. Adjacent to battle two, the area served as a secondary control center for the main battery guns. Off duty when the battle started, Gibson arrived just after the cruiser was first hit. He quickly noticed the nearby fires on the boat deck. "The smoke from these fires was very dense and swept back through batt II [battle two] and control aft," he reported.[16] Fighting smoke and nearby flames, Gibson and his crew worked through at least one director jam to provide target information for three main battery salvos.

During the height of the battle, a five-inch shell pierced the after portside bulkhead of the control station. It passed under the seat of the sight-setter, causing him to fall down to the deck, before exiting out through battle two. Miraculously the shell did not explode. If it had, then Gibson and his men would likely have been killed. The sight-setter and trainer were slightly wounded by fragments as the shell whizzed past.

Before long the heat from fires was causing the paint on the walls to peel. In a flash of light, Gibson looked down to catch a brief glimpse of some of his men lying dead on the floor. The deck below him was coated with blood. With his men choking from fumes and smoke, Gibson had no choice but to leave. "I removed my phones," he later wrote, "ordered the director crew to abandon the director, and went out to the after machine gun platform." Just then the director jammed again. "Plot was notified of this, and the director was abandoned because the smoke was now making the director untenable, and turret three had lost power."[17] Moving out onto the machine gun platform revealed a grisly scene. The thin splinter shield around the area was shattered and torn. The platform was filled with dead and dying. Among those lying dead was Lieutenant Art McLaughlin, the officer who back in January had asked young Henry Juarez to join his division.

Grabbing the first aid kit from the control station, Gibson and his men began to tend to the wounded, giving each a shot of morphine. The fires had spread to battle two just behind the control station. A fire hose was brought up to the area with the help of some men on top of turret three, but there was no water. With the ladders going down to the main deck blocked by fire, the situation for Gibson and his men seemed desperate.

* * *

Crewmen aboard the *Astoria* huddle around a five-inch gun during target practice in the spring of 1942. Only months later many gunners died at their posts during the Battle of Savo Island as direct hits and exploding ammunition extracted a heavy toll (U.S. Navy / Naval Historical Center).

At about the time the *Astoria* fired her second eight-inch salvo, the five-inch guns joined the battle. The gun deck, as the area around the five-inch gun batteries was known, would be the scene of some of the worst carnage aboard the *Astoria* that night. By the time five-inch battery officer Lieutenant (jg) Vincent Healey arrived, the port guns were already firing. "I took station at gun number six to observe the firing of the battery," he later wrote. "At the time the ship was being illuminated by three searchlights"[18] Located on the port side exactly even with the space between the two stacks, the gun was firing in automatic control. "After about the eighth salvo the boat deck was hit and burst into flames," Healey continued. "About then we lost power."

The sound powered phones were still working, and word came down for each gun to fire in local control. Each gun would now have to sight its own target instead of relying on information from the director. A short time later the number four and eight five-inch guns were hit. Gun number two had already been hit, with an explosion blowing apart the gun barrel. Sometime later the area around the number six gun was rocked by a large explosion followed almost immediately by flames shooting into the air.[19]

The movement of the *Astoria* soon put the port batteries out of the battle. As fires on the port side raged, the remaining men from the port batteries donned life jackets and ran to help those on the starboard side. A fierce fire was burning between gun mounts three and five. A hose was brought up but was not long enough to reach the fire. "When we turned on the water, a weak stream came out and still we could not reach the fire," Healey added. "I directed the men present to begin cutting down the life rafts from the loading machine platform."[20] Other men began unloading the remaining ammunition from the ready boxes throwing the shells over the side. Most of the five-inch guns now fell silent. Just after 2:00 A.M. only the number one five-inch gun on the starboard side was still firing.[21]

* * *

After arriving at central station from the bridge, Lieutenant Commander Topper felt a light jarring and heard the sound of metal flying overhead. "Within one minute after my arrival in central," Topper reported, "we received a very heavy hit followed by much rattling of metal."[22] As the ship's first lieutenant, he was responsible for damage control.[23] It was his job to keep the ship from sinking using central station as the nerve center to the direct damage control efforts. Seaman First Class Vance Largent was manning the damage control circuit and reported that all of the repair stations had checked in except for the midship repair party. All attempts to raise that group since the general alarm sounded had failed.

It did not take long for the first reports of damage started to flow into central station. First to arrive was word that turret one had been hit. Soon afterwards the after engine room was reported to be full of smoke. Someone in that room was asking for the repair party to open an escape hatch from above. It was promptly done. From about this time forward an almost constant stream of damage reports came flooding into central station at an increasingly rapid pace: fire main risers were severed in multiple locations, all communications with the after battle dressing area lost, the main radio room was out of service, large fires were burning on the gun deck, the after engine room was abandoned and several fire rooms were out of commission. The fires on the well deck and in the hangar had spread considerably since the initial hits, and planes on both catapults were ablaze. No part of the ship seemed to be untouched.

Bridge personnel inquired as to the status of the fire fighting parties. Central station soon reported back that the midship repair party had been killed and that all of the fire risers to the upper decks had been severed. No water was available to fight the fires at this critical time. Just then a series of three heavy explosions rocked central station from above. Topper called Engineering Officer Hayes, asking him to send any available spare men to help fight fires in the hangar and on the boat deck.

A report soon came in that there were many wounded men in the vicinity of the bridge. "While receiving this report," Topper noted, "large pieces of hot sparking metal, burning rubber, and debris dropped on deck in central station just below an armored wiring tube."[24] A shell had apparently exploded just above. Chief Electrician's Mate Louis Halligan quickly sprayed the debris with a fire extinguisher and then covered it with sand. "The hatch cover in the tube was completely demolished," Topper remembered. "This caused some smoke in central, which continued to fill up the space. It was impossible to plug the large opening in the armored tube."

Topper and his staff did what they could to direct the various damage control parties that were stationed around the ship. A talker from the after repair party said that Carpenter L.C. Martin had not arrived on station. "I then directed that Mr. [Seaman Second Class Herbert] Field go aft and supervise fire fighting," Topper wrote, "for at this time I realized that Carpenter Martin must have met with an accident." The carpenter was later listed as having been killed. "We were yet unable to get communication with mid repair, so I directed forward repair to send up as many men as possible topside to fight fires on the gun deck." But the forward repair party was pretty busy at this time. An eight-inch shell had just hit under the port side of turret two and exploded in the dispensary. A second had crashed into the armory just forward of the wardroom. Part of the sick bay and the dentist's office were in bad shape.

Just then Topper looked up and noticed that full speed had been rung up on the engine order telegraph, but that the ship was actually going much slower. After inquiring about the situation, a talker in the forward engine room reported that three of the four fire rooms and the after engine room were out of commission. It was about this time that Captain Greenman shifted steering control to central station. All power was lost a short time later.

*   *   *

At about 2:08 A.M. a searchlight appeared off the port beam. It was that of the *Kinugasa*. The Japanese cruiser had already ceased firing and may have been trying to ascertain the extent of the *Astoria*'s damage. Lieutenant Commander Walter Davidson, the ship's communications officer, jumped into turret two. With the turret in local control he trained it on the light. "It fired and landed in the searchlight," Captain Greenman recorded. "I myself followed the shells in flight and saw the flash when they hit. It must have been about 4,000 yards."[25]

The shells did score a hit, but not on the intended target. The volley actually sailed over the *Kinugasa* and landed on the *Chokai*, which was somewhere to the east. Turret one of the flag ship was hit and damaged. One of the barrels was split in half and considerable damage was done to the inside of the gun chamber.[26] The executive officer aboard the *Chokai* simply observed, "One shell hit the port side of the forward turret, killing ten men."[27]

Captain Greenman surely must have known that his ship was in serious trouble at this time. With the engineering spaces off line and abandoned, the *Astoria* lost all power and the burning ship slowly glided to a halt. "Almost coincidentally with the loss of power in the ship," Greenman noted, "the enemy ceased firing and apparently withdrew."[28] It was about 2:15 A.M.

Chapter 20

Escape

By 2:16 A.M. all of the Japanese cruisers had ceased firing as Admiral Mikawa and his staff pondered their next move. In less than an hour of battle, the Japanese had demolished two groups of Allied cruisers, leaving Mikawa with a critical decision. Having destroyed the two largest groups of opposition, he was now in a position to carry out his original plan of attacking the transports. While inflicting heavy damage on the enemy, the Japanese ships had suffered little in return. Other than the destroyer *Yunagi*, which had turned back to cover the line of approach, all of Mikawa's ships were now east-northeast of Savo Island. But his cruisers were scattered. In addition to being divided into two separate groups that were running somewhat parallel, in the haze of battle the *Chokai* had ended up being last in her group of heavy cruisers.

Mikawa had serious concerns about proceeding across the sound to attack the transports. He estimated it would take about three hours to reassemble the cruiser force, which meant that an attack on the transports would take place just before dawn.[1] Although the location of the American carriers was not known, the flattops were certainly thought to be close by. Mikawa had no way of knowing that Admiral Fletcher had already withdrawn. If he stayed in the waters off Guadalcanal, Mikawa felt that his force would likely be subjected to heavy air attacks by carrier planes. If he were to withdraw immediately, the ships would be well up the Slot by the time the carrier planes attacked and might lure the American carriers north into a position to be attacked by land-based planes from Rabaul.

By 2:25 A.M. Mikawa made his decision and ordered, "All forces withdraw."[2] The Japanese ships began the process of reforming into a single column before increasing speed to thirty knots and heading towards the Slot.[3] For the men of the *Astoria*, the battle with the Japanese had ended, but the struggle to save their ship had just begun.

* * *

The *Quincy* was the first cruiser of the northern force to sink. At about 2:35 A.M. she capsized to port, twisted completely around, and went down bow first.[4] She would be the first of many ships, both American and Japanese, to occupy the ocean floor in the waters around Guadalcanal. Critically damaged, the *Vincennes* lived on for only a short time before sinking just before 3:00 A.M.

* * *

It was not long after the shooting stopped that Lieutenant Commander Truesdell came to realize that his position in the forward main battery control station was tenuous at best. Much of the area above the bridge was on fire. At some point during the battle, a five-inch shell hit the battle lookout platform exploding near an ammunition storage room. By this time all of the anti-aircraft guns had stopped firing. "Many of these crews had been killed and wounded," Truesdell recalled. "I then took charge of clearing these areas of wounded and administering first aid ... I sent Ensign Middleton down for a hose as the 1.1 sprinkling system had been severed."[5] The hose arrived a short time later, but there was no water. With no hope of putting out the flames, Truesdell gave the order to clear the area. "I then saw to it that all wounded were evacuated from these upper levels and the dead noted." Each severely wounded man was tended to, given a shot of morphine and carried below.

The gunnery officer then made his way down to the bridge. "After the evacuation of topside levels," Truesdell wrote, "I reported the situation to the captain and advised him to leave the bridge and get below on account of the danger of the 1.1 clipping room fire." Captain Greenman quickly realized that he would have to leave the bridge. "The usefulness of the bridge as a control station was gone," the captain noted.[6] He then ordered all of the wounded and able-bodied be assembled on the forecastle.

When Greenman ordered the bridge evacuated, Don Yeamans was among those who left the area. With few available escape routes, he climbed down a ladder and went to the forecastle. All of the other areas of the ship seemed to be on fire.

Wounded in the right leg, Tom Ferneding was losing blood and was unable to leave the bridge under his own power. His savior appeared in the form of an unknown rescuer who tied a rope around his waist. He was lowered down to the main deck.

At the captain's direction Truesdell took control of the evacuation process of the bridge area. He saw to it that each level was cleared as he made his way down. The captain then moved to a new station on the communications deck just forward of turret two. It was just after 2:15 A.M.

* * *

Truesdell was only one of many to make it down from the forward gunnery control area. On watch as the battery officer, Gene Alair made sure that his 1.1-inch gun mounts could be made ready to fire in short order. The start of the battle brought quick action for the men in his area. The instant that flares appeared off the port quarter, Alair ordered his two guns to load and reported the sighting to sky control. Searching the distant horizon, he could not see any targets. "I left the forward machine gun platform," he recalled, "and started up the starboard ladder to the 1.1-inch director and heard our turrets open fire to port."[7] In what seemed to be only a few short minutes, the *Astoria* was illuminated by a searchlight. The general alarm sounded just as Alair observed two enemy salvos fall short of his ship. "We knew that we were going to get hit," he though after seeing the salvos; "one came in short and one was over."

From his position in the forward control station, Lieutenant Commander Ellis Wakefield ordered the forward 1.1-inch guns to open fire on the searchlights.[8] Alair immediately directed the starboard gun to commence firing. "My director crew had not arrived, so I ordered mount I to fire with power motor in local control," he said. Training out over the starboard beam, the gun rattled off a string of bullets. "It may have been futile," he felt looking back on the fire. "The 1.1 is good at about thirty-five to thirty-eight hundred yards, and I imagine the searchlight I was shooting at was probably forty-five hundred yards. The searchlight went off after I'd shot for a few minutes." The gun expended eighty-eight rounds of ammunition. The target was most likely the *Aoba*, which at the time was almost 6,000 yards away.[9]

From his vantage point high up on the superstructure, Alair could look down and see a wide view of the ship. "We had been hit on the boat deck, and the plane on the starboard catapult was on fire," he observed.[10] The entire ship seemed to be burning.

By this time the area around the 1.1-inch guns had taken multiple hits. Among the first men to fall was a loader on the starboard gun mount. He was killed as he moved to put an ammunition clip into the right gun. "At this instant we took a direct hit on the navigation bridge below us," Alair continued. "The smoke and flying debris was intense." A shell then struck the port side 1.1-inch director, knocking it out of commission. An explosion near the number two mount killed members of the gun crew and started a fire in the ammunition clipping room. The room housed not only 1.1-inch ammunition clips, but also twenty millimeter rounds. It was not long before both types of shells started exploding from the heat of the flames. Alair, who was up near the starboard 1.1-inch director was momentarily spared from the carnage at the gun mount below. "We knew we were on fire underneath us," he recalled, "but we were up above it probably ten or twelve feet."

Hearing of the clipping room fire over the phones from one of his gun captains, Alair ordered him to turn on the sprinklers in the room and then try to fight the fire with the remaining gun crew survivors. "I then left the director and climbed down to inspect the mount and clipping room as to damage," Alair continued. He quickly learned that there was no water available for the sprinklers. The crewmen used the only available fire extinguisher to attack the flames. "It did little good," Alair reported.[11]

For Alair and his men, the battle now shifted from fighting the Japanese to one of survival. As a precaution the ensign ordered the 1.1-inch magazine flooded. Located below the waterline, it was a long way from his position. Someone from the signal bridge then called up to Alair and told him to prepare to abandon ship. By this time Truesdell had in fact ordered the entire upper superstructure area abandoned. In what proved to be anything but an orderly evacuation, Alair was directed to bring his men down to the main deck and assemble near the port side of turret two. "There was lack of communication, number one," he recalled of the time, "and there was confusion and chaos."[12]

Before he was able to get very far, Alair was stopped by Lieutenant George Baker who requested his help destroying the secret documents. "He was in charge of all the radio shack communications," Alair remembered. He ordered Gunner's Mate Third Class Earl Smock to continue to lead his men down.

Baker and Alair together gathered up restricted publications, which were in what was left of the radio shack adjacent to the bridge. First to be located was all of the printed materials, which were put into canvas bags weighted down with lead. "We threw the bags over the side," Alair said. Next were the code machines. "We destroyed the ECM wheels, which are the coding machine wheels," Alair explained. "The wheels aren't very big actually, they're about the size of a patty in a hamburger, and we just threw those things away. We were suppose to put them in boxes and lead 'em and sink 'em." Baker told him not bother with the boxes and just to throw the wheels over the side. "Baker and I got rid of all of the confidential and restricted materials."

Believing that he was among the last to leave the bridge area, Alair separated from Lieutenant Baker and made his way down to the main deck. Alair's path was strewn with grievously burned sailors, all of whom he felt were dead. "I am not sure we were the last two," he remembered, "but I doubt that there was anybody left when he and I left."

* * *

Among those manning the forward 1.1-inch gun mounts during the late evening hours was Seaman Second Class William Kuphaldt. He was both tired and apprehensive when he came off watch at midnight. Like many others he had heard the rumors that Japanese ships were on the way. "I was a little apprehensive about the prospects of a battle with enemy ships firing at us," he later wrote, "since this would be an entirely new experience."¹³ Kuphaldt had seen plenty of action since reporting aboard the *Astoria* slightly more than a month after the attack on Pearl Harbor. However, all of the battles had been limited to air attacks, and he was not sure what role his light anti-aircraft gun would serve in a surface fight. Deciding not to go down to his bunk, he chose to stay in close proximity to his starboard side gun. "I decided to lay down on the deck near the gun to get some sleep before the next action," Kuphaldt recalled. "In spite of my concern, I did manage to fall asleep."

Kuphaldt was asleep for less than two hours when he suddenly awoke to the sound of the general alarm. "As I jumped to my feet I was told we were being fired upon," he wrote. He soon noticed that the ship was being brightly illuminated by flares. "It was light enough to read a newspaper," he remembered. Coinciding with the blast of the *Astoria's* main battery, he saw a distant flash followed by a splash some distance away from his ship. The first splash was quickly followed by another, and then the *Astoria* was hit by what seemed to be a continuous rain of shells. "I observed continuous balls of fire heading towards the *Astoria*, with many finding their target," he remembered of the moment. "It appeared they were all aimed directly at me."

During the rapid sequence of events, Kuphaldt's gun opened fire on one of the enemy searchlights that was trained on the *Astoria*. The rattling of the gun sent a steady stream of tracers jumping out towards the light. Kuphaldt had previously only seen the gun fire during daylight at airplanes. "The display at night was spectacular," he recalled, "as we watched the stream of fire head towards the searchlights. My main thought during this period was to keep the gun I was responsible for properly loaded, and it was only after the lights were extinguished and we stopped firing that I realized we were in serious trouble."

Looking down from his position, Kuphaldt could see the fires raging on the gun deck below. He noticed members of the five-inch gun crews lying near their guns, many presumably dead or dying. A thought crossed his mind about moving down to the main deck in case the ship had to be abandoned. Just then the battle lookout platform was rocked by an explosion. The source was most likely a five-inch shell that came from the starboard side and exploded in the clipping room.¹⁴ "It was at this point that I was hit and experienced a sensation of floating down to the deck, much like a feather would do," he recalled. "I realized I had been hit in the head and thought I had reached the end of the line." Having been hit with shrapnel in the nose and right eye, he was seriously wounded and almost immediately lost consciousness.

Although badly injured, William Kuphaldt made a daring escape from the *Astoria*'s upper superstructure on the ship's final night. Almost four years later he was awarded the Purple Heart (courtesy William Kuphaldt).

Directly opposite Kuphaldt's position, the men on the port side 1.1-inch gun did not fare much better. The hit in the clipping room devastated the gun crew. Among those manning the mount were Seaman Second Class Eugene Hardy and Seaman Second Class Forest Loomer. The gun captain was Gunner's Mate Third Class Robert Riddell. "We took a hit," Hardy re-lated. "I guess it went right through our magazine right in back of us." Sitting in the trainer's seat on the right side of the gun, Loomer was killed in-stantly. "He was cut right in half, seat and all," Hardy said.[15] Hit in the foot, Hardy staggered down to the main deck where he eventually made it off the ship. Gun captain Riddell was hit by shrapnel in both legs. His last recollection was of nudging Loomer to train the gun on another searchlight that had appeared.

When William Kuphaldt awoke the main part of the battle was over. Somewhat dazed and not able to see very well, he was happy to be alive. No one in the vicinity of his starboard gun mount seemed to be still living. Struggling to get to his feet, he placed his hand on his head to try to determine the extent of his injuries. "I knew I needed help to get down to the main deck," he recalled. "Since I knew we had been under fire from ships to the starboard side, with some difficulty, I found my way over to the port side to seek help." It was near the port side gun mount that Kuphaldt and Riddell found each other.

After being wounded in both legs, Robert Riddell's next recollection was that of sitting on the deck with his back leaning up against something, possibly the foremast. Unable to get up to walk, he saw the nearly blind Kuphaldt staggering about and called him over. The two exchanged information about their conditions and decided that their best chance of escape was to work together. Riddell told his comrade about the fire in the nearby clipping room. They decided to try to put it out before the whole room exploded. Together they struggled to make it over to the closest fire extinguisher, but in spite of a concerted effort they were unable to unfasten it from the bulkhead. "I know I was most anxious to get down and away from the clipping room," Kuphaldt later wrote. A way out was a ladder that led one level down to the navigation bridge. Movement required the use of one man's eyes and the other's legs. It would be a long and perilous journey down to the main deck, but it was their only hope for survival.

Just as the two wounded men were moving toward the ladder, help arrived in the form of Seaman First Class Earl Holler and an unknown marine. Holler was a member of the starboard 1.1-inch gun crew. The two had come up to look for survivors. The marine took Kuphaldt, while Holler grabbed onto Riddell. Both men were safely brought down to the communications deck near turret two.

* * *

Someone from the radar staff came to John Powell just before the battle started. "He was the one that woke me up because my head was against the cage and he had to open the door," he remembered. A short time later Powell was startled when the beam of a searchlight hit the *Astoria*. Assuming that general quarters would sound shortly, he started for the forward five-inch director. His lifejacket and helmet were already there. "I was climbing the ladder when the first rounds came in," he said.[16] But Powell was not able to get into his battle station. "You can't get in the director until it's lined up fore and aft, because that's where the ladder matches," Powell continued. When he arrived the director was trained out on the searchlight. "I'm down there banging on the bottom of the director saying, 'let me in' ... they were trying to get on a target." He finally made it in after the director aligned as a result of the turning motion of the *Astoria*.

Getting into position, Powell was able to visually scan the hazy horizon. Suddenly

A closeup of the upper bridge area of the *Astoria* shows a 1.1-inch machine gun mount and an array of fire control equipment. Gene Alair, John Powell and William Kuphaldt all made perilous escapes from high atop the superstructure (U.S. Navy / Naval Historical Center).

there was movement off in the distance. Something started to emerge from the haze. "I saw a cruiser come out of the haze with three turrets forward." Remembering the odd configuration from seeing a Japanese cruiser on a pre-war trip, he knew right away it was the enemy.

Also arriving at the director was Lieutenant Donald Willman. He put on the headset just in time to hear the cease fire order given by Captain Greenman. However, just moments later he received the order to fire on the searchlight. "I ordered the director on the light and began firing," Willman reported.[17]

Before the firecontrol men could get a fix on the enemy cruiser, shells started landing near the director. At least two hit the director itself. "Fortunately they never exploded," Powell said gratefully. One shell passed through the equipment, entering on one side and going out the other, while another hit knocked him down. One of the shells caused the training gear to become stuck, resulting in the equipment becoming jammed and unworkable. Off in the distance Powell could still see the *Quincy* and *Vincennes*. At one point he saw the latter cruiser rocked by a massive explosion that he assumed was a torpedo hit.

When it became time to abandon the director, Lieutenant Willman gave the order to leave. "I received the order from Sky Control to go down to the [five-inch] battery and take over in local control," he reported. "I gave the order to abandon the director and proceed to the gun deck." Getting down from the director would not be easy. "We had a hell of a time getting out," Powell recalled. With the director locked in place, it was not possible to get out the bottom ladder. There were not too many good options for escape. "You could jump off and land on top of the main battery [director], but if you slid off of that it was a long drop all the way down to the main deck," he said. There was a small platform on each side of the director that was used for scorekeeping during gunnery exercises. The angle the director was facing put one of the platforms about three feet from the foremast. Protruding high into to the air and located right behind the director, the mast had ladder rungs on the side. Powell and the others decided to climb out onto the platform, jump to the main mast, and slide down. It was a routine that had been practiced during training exercises. "If you missed the mast it was about a ninety foot drop to the deck," Powell recalled.

Each man had two choices. Keeping his feet flat on the top of the director, one could lean and fall forward to grab onto the mast ladder, or he could just jump. Powell chose the latter and jumped toward the mast. "I just grabbed the ladder and slid right down," he said. "I didn't even put my feet in the rungs. I just slid right down the side of the ladder." He ended up at the door for the main battery director that was just below his battle station. Finding some morphine shots in a first aid kit, Powell stopped to attend to couple of wounded men that had been on the 1.1 inch gun mounts. "I gave them morphine; that's all I could do."

Entering the bridge area, Powell found it abandoned and in shambles. "Out of the director, I think we were the last ones down because it took us longer to get out of there." The only light was from the various fires that were burning, both on the bridge and elsewhere. He suddenly came across a grisly scene. Pinned up against a ladder railing was a corpse that had been sliced in two, presumably by a shell. The portion of the body with the head was hanging near the ladder, while the remainder was on the deck where he had been standing.

Working with a small group of men from his director, Powell stayed in the general area of the bridge for fifteen or twenty minutes trying to get wounded men out of adjacent areas. Any man that showed the faintest sign of life was dragged over to a ladder and slid down to the signal bridge where others took over the process of getting them to the communications deck. "Anybody that was alive, that we thought was alive, we put down there," he said. "I'm sure we sent a couple of guys down the ladder that were dead." Powell and Yeoman Second Class Gaylord McCampbell found a wounded electrician's mate who had been manning one of the searchlights right in front of the forward stack. He was in bad shape but still alive. One of his legs had been partially blown off and was still attached by just a thin strand of skin. Powell and McCampbell dragged the wounded man to the communications deck, where he later succumbed to his wounds. After everyone was accounted for, Powell went down to the communications deck himself. He caught a brief glimpse of Captain Greenman who was directing the effort to save the ship. "He was standing right under the barrels of turret two giving orders," Powell remembered. "I though he did an outstanding job."

* * *

Just a short time after power was lost, the crew of the forward five-inch handling room opened the escape hatch that led directly into central station and notified Lieutenant Commander Topper that they had been ordered to abandon their compartment via his room. "This additional personnel crowded central considerably," Topper wrote, "and besides there was considerable smoke in this compartment."[18] Attempts to open the upper escape hatch out of central station met with great difficulty due to debris cluttering the area above the hatch and one dog jammed in the closed position. Electrician's Mate First Class August Jesser, with help from both above and below, was finally able to get the hatch open. By this time all communications with other parts of the ship had been lost with the exception of steering aft. Topper directed the men from the five-inch handling room and others from a repair party to go topside. The process was somewhat sluggish at the beginning as the men from the handling room were not familiar with the escape route. Topper led the group up through officer's country and out a hatch that led up to the main deck.

Returning to central station, Topper ordered the hatch leading to the main battery plotting room to be opened. Lieutenant Marzetta's men began to make their way out. Marzetta notified all of the stations that the plotting room was going off line before staying behind to ensure that everyone made it out. "Central station was found [to be] even more smoky than plot," he noted.[19] The men from the plotting room made their way topside, coming out onto the forecastle near turret one.

Making sure that the watertight doors and hatches were all sealed around central station, Topper now headed topside with his crew. On his journey he was able to get a brief glimpse of the some of the damaged compartments. "The lockers and bunks in the marine compartment had been knocked all over the place," he recalled. Compartments all around seemed to be in shambles, including the armory, gunnery spare parts storeroom, dental office, and the doctor's office. Some areas were covered with several inches of water. "At least two people were laying on deck in the vicinity of sick bay who were dead," Topper recalled.[20] He soon spotted Boatswain Raymond Ward, a member of the forward repair party, at the foot of a ladder in the area of the forward repair station. "He told me that all of their fires were out and that holes had been plugged." Ward reported that all of the fire main risers in the forward part of the ship were knocked out in the first ten minutes of the battle and the small arms magazine had been flooded. "He also told me that the trunk leading down to the gasoline room had a $Co2$ blanket on it," Topper continued, "and that the paint mixing room had been given a blanket of $Co2$ to extinguish a fire that started there at the very beginning of the battle."[21]

Finally making it topside to the forecastle, Topper soon learned that Captain Greenman was looking for him. "I reported to the captain on the starboard side of forecastle just aft of turret one," Topper wrote. "The ship appeared to be blazing all the way from the navigation bridge aft."

* * *

After the shooting stopped, Ensign McGrath and his men stayed at their station in turret two. Scanning the horizon for any sign of a target, he saw something. "I ordered the trainer to train to port to bear on what I believed to be an enemy ship." McGrath wrote.[22]

As the turn was completed, all power to the turret was lost. The ship turned out not to be an enemy at all. It was the burning *Quincy*. "I then received an order to remove my men from the turret and have them assembled on the forecastle," McGrath continued. "I then passed the word over the loudspeaker system for all stations to abandon the turret in an orderly manner." He then told the gunner's mate in the lower powder handling room to remain in his area until all others had left. Before departing he was to make sure that all of the hatches were closed and sealed and that the powder bags were immersed in water. "I did not flood the magazines," McGrath recalled, "because I did not know the condition of the ship and thought that firing might be resumed."

* * *

Of the eight pilots aboard the *Astoria,* only four would survive the night. As fate would have it, the senior aviators made it through the battle. All of the junior aviators were killed by the explosions and fires near the hangar. Each had apparently made it to his assigned battle station only to perish with the first hits.

Awakened by the sound of the first main battery salvo, Bob Schiller was in his bunk when the battle began. Putting on his pants, shirt, life vest, and helmet, he was on the way to the navigation bridge before general quarters sounded. However, he never made it to his battle station. "It had already been shot up," he remembered.[23] He did make it up to the signal bridge, where he encountered the lead pilot of the aviation group, Lieutenant Allan Edmands. Together they watched the battle unfold, seeing the incoming shells glowing through the air. "If you saw a round ball, it was going to hit the ship," Schiller remembered. A shell with a tracer line or glowing tail was a miss. As the *Astoria* was being hit continuously, Edmands took him by the hand and said, "I think this is it." Neither of the pilots seemed to think that their chances of survival were very good. The two stayed in the same area until the shooting stopped. They then separated, each going to look for friends.

Schiller eventually joined a bucket brigade near a five-inch gun mount. Pouring buckets of water down a shell hoist, he did not know that a live five-inch shell was positioned on the hoist. It went off and shot right between him and another man. Both ended up with some singed hair.

Richard Tunnell was also asleep in his bunk when the battle started. Grabbing his helmet and flight chart, he headed for the navigation bridge. Racing through the wardroom, he came to a ladder that led topside. As he stepped up the ladder several men came up right behind him. Just as he began to open the hatch an explosion in an adjacent compartment slammed it shut, hitting him on the head in the process. The aviator was knocked out cold. When he came to, all of the other men were gone and he was lying on the deck alone. He soon noticed that several of the bottom ladder rungs were blown off. Upon making it topside, he immediately saw fires and many wounded men strewn about. "I never made it to the bridge,"[24] Tunnell recalled. Coming to the radio shack, he peered in just long enough to see that everyone was dead and he decided to move on.

* * *

On the blazing gun deck the men who had manned the five-inch batteries were looking for a way to escape the heat, flames, and exploding ammunition. Under the direction of Lieutenant (jg) Vincent Healey, two life rafts were successfully unsecured and thrown over the port side. Some men leaped into the water when the line that secured the rafts to the ship gave way.

Lieutenant Donald Willman had come down to the gun deck after being ordered to abandon the forward director. He had arrived in time to be immediately injured by an explosion, which among other wounds broke his arm. Growing increasingly weak from his injuries, Willman continued to direct the evacuation of the area. He directed Healey to make his way to the forecastle. "I could not get through the smoke and fire," Healey reported. "When the ship stopped, the smoke became very bad, and Lieutenant Willman directed us to go over the side. The wounded were lowered first and then the rest of us jumped."[25] Healey's watch stopped the moment he hit the water. It was 2:37 A.M.

Chapter 21

Help at Last

Responsible for the well being of the crew, the *Astoria*'s medical staff was stretched to their limits on the night of the battle. To care for the wounded during combat conditions, two battle dressing areas were set up on the ship. Staffed by medical personnel, each served as a triage station where wounded men could be brought for immediate attention. The forward battle dressing station was located in the sick bay. The after area was in the chief petty officers' quarters near the stern of the ship. A third station was set up, but not manned, in the after mess hall. In addition to the staff in dressing areas, a small number of medical corpsmen were spread out in various locations, including one with each of the three repair parties.

The senior medical officer aboard the *Astoria* was Lieutenant Commander Charles Flower. Off duty when the battle started, he awoke to the sound of the general alarm. Quickly dressing in his cabin, he heard the ominous sounds of crashing and rattling fragments overhead. "I ran down the ladders to my battle dressing station in the sick bay," he wrote of the moment, "encountering a few people en-route ascending the ladders."[1] Arriving at sick bay he quickly noted that all of his staff was present. Assisting Flower was Lieutenant Edward O'Reilly, five corpsmen, and one striker.

As a precaution Flower ordered all of the men present to spread out and lie down flat on the floor. The sick bay began to fill with smoke shortly after a shell hit the nearby dental office, shaking the entire area. The explosion terrified O'Reilly, who was so rattled that he grabbed the hand of Hospital Apprentice First Class James Becker and tried to pull him out of the compartment. When Becker withdrew his hand, O'Reilly bolted out of the sick bay. The lieutenant did not survive the battle. He sustained serious injuries while trying to make it topside and was brought to the captain's pantry where he died a short time later.

The lights in the sick bay went out after two large shell fragments came through the outboard bulkhead at a height about even with the top of the operating table. "Explosions were occurring above us," Flower remembered, "apparently in the wardroom country and aft in the marine compartment," Checking the immediate area with a battery lantern, he found that the sick bay had not been directly hit. Checking an adjacent compartment, he saw water on deck, apparently from burst pipes. "No one in this space was alive," he recalled. Flower's brief glimpse revealed several dead men sprawled out on the deck. He recognized Chief Gunner's Mate Edward Osborn among them.

Flower now began to think about leaving the area. "With lights out, smoke filling the sick bay, and water coming in from adjoining ammunition handling area, I decided that the dressing station must be abandoned." Unable to communicate with other stations, the medical men gathered whatever supplies they could carry and headed out. They loaded a large bag full of battle dressing, gauze, morphine shots, and instruments. Other supplies were wrapped in the bed sheets. Moving with them were two wounded men who had been brought to the station during the course of the battle. Unable to enter the wardroom due to smoke and flames, the group made it up to the forecastle at about 2:25 A.M.

Coming topside, Flower and his men entered a completely different world. Gone was the *Astoria* that they had remembered, replaced with a scene of death and destruction. Flower saw fires near the bridge and heard the sounds of exploding ammunition. A member of the forward repair party arrived from below with a large first aid kit, one of three on the boat. About five small kits from various compartments were added to the mix. The group quickly set up a station and started to tend to the wounded. Assisted by many members of the crew, the men worked to render every type of aid possible, including tourniquets, burn jelly, morphine shots, etc. "It was a source of gratification to me," Flower later wrote, "to note that so many members of the crew had learned their first aid lessons well enough to be of great service at this time."[2]

Captain Greenman had ordered the seriously wounded to be moved into his cabin. About twenty-five men were moved to the smoky room, but the medical staff soon realized that they could not stay there. The deck was becoming increasingly hot from the fires below in the wardroom. Soon the position became untenable, and the wounded were transferred back to the forecastle.

The doctor then set up station at the bow of the ship near the anchor chains. Flower worked on the most seriously wounded, cutting off limbs and applying tourniquets. John Powell was among those who helped in moving the wounded. "We had to carry [the wounded] up where he was ... he had all his gear there." he said "He probably never expected any of them to live anyway. But most of them did."[3]

* * *

Roy Spurlock's wakeup call came earlier than expected. "My first consciousness that there was something wrong was when I heard muffled explosions from some distance away from the ship, closely followed by terrific bangs outside the entrance from the room I was in," he later wrote. The explosions were almost immediately followed by the general alarm. "I sat up in the cot and reached for my clothes. I remember it took forever to get dressed, or so it seemed." As he hit the deck, Spurlock could hear the terrible sounds of the *Astoria* being repeatedly hit by enemy shells. "By this time there was no doubt in my mind as to what was happening."[4]

Lying face down on the deck of his cabin, Spurlock heard the sound of a terrific explosion almost directly overhead. The blast was followed by a stinging feeling on his back and legs. Spurlock was certain that he had been hit with shrapnel. "I wondered how long it would take for me to bleed to death," he later wrote of the moment. "Finally mustering the courage to feel my back to see how bad it was, I found no blood at all. In fact, I was not wounded at all." As it turned out the blast was most likely a hit on a nearby five-inch gun. What hit Spurlock in the back was red hot paint chips that were blown off of the ceiling directly above him.

When the shelling stopped Spurlock cautiously arose and moved towards the cabin door. Before leaving the room, he noticed the damage that had been done to the steel bulkhead. "The steel walls of the captain's sitting room in which I had been sleeping were perforated," he observed, "with so many holes that it would have been quite easy to read a newspaper inside by the light from a burning five-inch ready shell locker on the deck just outside our compartment."

Spurlock remembered seeing a large first aid cabinet in a nearby compartment, most likely the wardroom. "This compartment was designed to be a major first aid station for the

A guest passenger aboard the *Astoria* during the Battle of Savo Island, marine aviator Roy Spurlock came to the aid of wounded sailors. He later became a highly decorated fighter pilot (courtesy Roy Spurlock, Jr.).

ship in the event of battle," he recalled, "and it had obviously been used for this purpose during the attack a few minutes before." However, what he found was not a functioning medical area, but a death trap. Entering the compartment he found it littered with bodies strewn about in a variety of contorted positions. No one seemed to be alive. Noticing a large shell hole, he surmised that a direct hit felled everyone in the area.

Spurlock played no role in the battle up to this point. However, that was about to change as wounded men began to wander into the area looking for help. "Here was an immediate need and opportunity to do something to help," he recalled. "There was no corpsmen to criticize or instruct, and something had to be done, so I did it." Spurlock quickly rummaged through his own belongings looking for pieces of cloth, anything that could help stop bleeding. He began to treat the wounded as best he could. "I had no antiseptics to cleanse the wounds, but I did the best I could for them all, as long as I had anything left to bandage them with. I could at least stop the bleeding." Spurlock was not prepared for what he was about to see. "As a small town man I had never seen spilled blood or appalling injuries before," he later recalled. "I found that after a certain level has been reached, the body sees and acts, but the shock no longer registers."

One of the wounded sailors who came looking for help was a muscularly built mess attendant. "As it happened, I knew him," Spurlock remembered. "He was a mess attendant in the officers' wardroom, where he dealt out ham sandwiches to the officers late at night after the mess had closed." Spurlock recalled that the wounded man had previously told him that his battle station was as a five-inch shell handler. On this night the attendant had been changed into a bloody mess. "The point of his shoulder looked like some ten-foot giant with steel clawed fingers had grasped his shoulder and ripped a great hunk of flesh right from his shoulder." The wounded man also had a deep cut on his left forearm. Spurlock did his best to stop the bleeding.

As the wounded were being assembled near the forecastle, Spurlock eventually made it topside and continued to help in any way he could. During the time he again had the opportunity to see wounded sailors up close. "The wounds were terrible," he recalled, "beyond anything I had ever seen in my life." He assisted in bringing wounded down from the bridge area. Looking back aft all he could see was fire and destruction.

At one point while on the main deck, Spurlock came across a young sailor sitting on deck with his back up propped up against the barbette of turret one. "He was a fine looking young man," he remembered. "He was the type of whom I could see as a star high school fullback." The young man appeared to be in shock and Spurlock soon saw why. A piece of jagged metal had ripped open the man's leg leaving the jagged end of a bone exposed. "At intervals he would reach down and touch the sharp jagged edge of the [bone] and would then wince as though someone had hit him in the face with a baseball bat."

In the midst of his work to help the wounded, Spurlock remembered that he had been given confidential materials relating to the air operations of the Guadalcanal invasion. The maps and codes were accompanied by a weighted bag. "I was instructed to throw these overboard if it became necessary to abandon ship," he remembered. Thinking that the end could be near, he went back down to the captain's cabin, found the documents and headed back topside. "I walked over to the edge of the deck and looked down at that dirty black water down below," he recalled of the moment. "I jettisoned the weighted bag overboard, but made an independent command decision right there that I was not going to jump into the water until the ship sank under me." Others apparently did not share the same feelings, as Spurlock saw a number of sailors go over the side.

* * *

After being evacuated down to the communications deck, William Kuphaldt lost contact with his wounded shipmate Robert Riddell. Soon after his arrival to the area near turret two, a corpsman did a check of his wounds. "I was given a shot of morphine," he recalled, "and my head was wrapped with a bandage."[5] The corpsman discovered that Kuphaldt was suffering from additional wounds. "I found out later that I had also received a one inch flesh wound in the right leg, and a small shrapnel fragment was embedded in the back of my left hand." After the initial treatment, Kuphaldt was helped down to the forecastle area.

* * *

By 3:00 A.M. almost four hundred men were gathered near the forecastle of the *Astoria*. The group included about seventy wounded and a number of dead. Captain Greenman had been hit in the back with shrapnel, most likely when he was on the bridge. The back of his life jacket was soaked with blood from the many small punctures. With information coming in from various sources, he was able to make an assessment of his ship. Lieutenant Commander Topper reported that all of the compartments forward of the engineering spaces seemed to be watertight. It seemed that men closed and sealed hatches as they left their battle stations to come topside. "I had received no indication from the engineering officer that the engine spaces were taking water when he reported that power was gone," Greenman noted.[6] A large fire in the wardroom area prevented movement aft. The situation at the rear of the ship was not known. "The ship had about a three degree list to port," Greenman explained, "which I could not account for unless some space below had been opened to the sea or the after magazine had been flooded."

Although hit badly, the *Astoria* did not seem to be in any immediate danger of sinking. Greenman decided to start salvage operations. The fires would have to be extinguished if the *Astoria* was to be saved.

As damage control officer, Topper was to play a key role in trying to save the ship. In the company of a few others, he ventured below decks. Initially going to the sail locker to look for life preservers, the group fanned out to find any type of supplies that could be useful in the salvage effort. "All buckets, mattresses, life preservers, and any material that could be used for first aid was passed to topside," Topper wrote. A couple of men were able to get into the sick bay and found two large first aid boxes that were immediately sent up to the medical staff. Returning topside, Topper soon found that a couple of life rafts had been lowered over the side. "We could only find about five serviceable life rafts,"[7] he added. Many of the rafts had been latched to the forward turrets and were destroyed in the battle. Topper then directed men to cut up any type of rope that could be found to be used as life lines in case the ship had to be abandoned.

Tending to the wounded was a high priority. "Everyone appeared to be doing all within his power to look after the wounded," Topper remembered. "All were most orderly and seemed to be most anxious to do anything to assist."[8]

A bucket brigade was established to begin attacking the fires on the starboard side of the gun deck and the forward starboard passageway. A small gas powered handybilly pump was lowered over the side and rigged to spray a small stream of water into the wardroom area. Although inadequate for the intensity of the fire, any small amount of water helped.

Lieutenant Commander Ellis Wakefield was one of the officers helping to direct the firefighting effort on the gun deck. The air defense officer had been with Gunnery Officer Truesdell in the forward control station during the height of the battle. After assisting the gunnery officer in the evacuation of the upper areas, Wakefield made it down to the communication platform behind turret two. His first order was to throw overboard all of the remaining ammunition in the ready boxes of nearby five-inch gun mounts one and two. "I could get no further than gun number three on the starboard side and couldn't get to the gun deck on the port side at all," he reported.[9] Looking at the ammunition hoists for guns one, two, and three, he noticed that shells were still on the hoists. Some of the first buckets of water available were dumped down the hoists to help lessen the possibility that the shells deeper down would explode. "At this time all of the gun deck, well deck, and boat deck was ablaze," observed Wakefield. "I then stationed myself on the communication platform and assisted in directing the water supply at the starboard rail to extinguish the gun deck fire."

Captain Greenman was initially optimistic that progress could be made on dousing the flames. "I had hoped that as the fire was driven aft on the gun deck, access might be obtained to the wardroom space from the ladder aft the captain's cabin."[10] The ladder was eventually reached only to find that the fire below was out of control. The captain's optimism now began to wane. "When the extent of this fire became evident, I ordered the forward magazines flooded," he wrote.

After departing turret two, Ensign McGrath received the order to flood the eight-inch magazine. "With my turret captain and gunner's mate from lower powder, I went below to the flooding control panel board and attempted to flood the magazines with no results," McGrath reported. "We then went to the lower powder handling room and opened the flooding valves by hand, and left closing and securing all hatches behind us."[11] McGrath and his men then returned topside to resume fire fighting and tending to the wounded. A light rain was starting to fall.

When Don Yeamans arrived on the forecastle, he knew that he was above one of the magazines and could feel that the deck was hot. "I heard someone yell abandon ship," he remembered.[12] Thinking that the official order had been given, he jumped over the side. Not having his life jacket on at the time of the jump, he grabbed onto a piece of floating material once in the water and drifted away from the *Astoria*.

Captain Greenman was satisfied that the forward eight-inch magazine had been successfully flooded. However, he had doubts about the five-inch magazine. He was just not sure that the flooding was successful. Small explosions were now being heard from the general vicinity.

John Powell remembered hearing that the heat of the fires kept people away from the five-inch magazine. The flooding valves were located on the main deck level, just forward of the wardroom. It was generally kept locked, but there was a key nearby in a glass case. "Nobody could go down to see if that place had been flooded or to flood it," he said.[13]

Greenman now faced a critical decision. He was overseeing a large group of survivors that had assembled on the forward part of the ship. Conditions near the stern were still unknown. Some progress was being made on the gun deck flames, but the intense fire in the wardroom area was still burning out of control. "The fire had also spread forward of the wardroom and to the spaces below, and it appeared that with the facilities available we were unable to effectively fight it," the captain noted. "At the same time the fire continued aft, and I became apprehensive that an explosion in a magazine might sink the ship with all survivors of the battle still on board."[14] Greenman decided it was time to leave the *Astoria*. Just then the destroyer *Bagley* was seen far off in the distance.

* * *

It was not long after he reached the main deck that Gene Alair saw the *Bagley* moving towards the *Astoria*. He then found some of his men who were congregating between turrets two and three. Like the other sailors in the forward part of the ship, Alair would soon leave the *Astoria* most likely believing that he had set foot on her for the last time.

After failing to effectively engage the Japanese cruiser force during that battle south of Savo Island, the destroyer *Bagley* moved northwest. She was the only undamaged ship of the southern force.[15] Searching the waters northwest of Savo Island, she was unable to find any trace of the enemy. Moving back into the sound, she cautiously approached a burning vessel that was about five miles northeast of Savo Island.[16] The ship was soon identified as the *Astoria*. In a twist of fate the commanding officer of the *Bagley*, Lieutenant Commander George Sinclair, had spent time as an officer aboard the cruiser.[17]

To the men on the *Astoria's* forecastle, the *Bagley* meant that help had arrived at last. By the signal of a blinker gun, Captain Greenman had initially asked the destroyer to stand by. He later asked her to move closer. At about 4:00 A.M. the *Bagley's* bow nudged up to the starboard bow of the *Astoria*. Wood planks, used for painting the side of the ship, were used to make a bow to bow crossing. The wounded were the first to transfer over to the destroyer, starting with stretcher cases. Many were carried by stretcher to the stern of the *Bagley*, dropped off and the stretcher sent back for further use. Since there were not enough stretchers, some of the wounded were laid on the planks and dragged across. The walking wounded came next followed close after by the able bodied.

Among those assisting in the transfer of the wounded were Belcher Hobson and John

Powell. A repair party survivor, Hobson had successfully escaped the flaming well deck. He was among the first to get onto the destroyer after the wounded had all been evacuated.

John Powell left the bridge area after he was directed to go down to help fight the fires. He quickly discovered what other firefighters already knew. "The hoses that were available had no water," he said, "and the pumps were all dead." He proceeded to the forecastle where he assisted in assembling wounded near the bow. "It was the only place that wasn't on fire," he recalled. Powell remembered the transfer to the destroyer as being a little uneasy. "They put two of those planks between the bow of the *Bagley* and the bow of the *Astoria* and it wasn't a very good ... it was kind of wiggly and kind of steep. But nobody fell overboard."[18] Once on the destroyer he did not re-board the *Astoria* and never saw the ship again.

When the *Bagley* came along side the stricken cruiser, all of the aviators were ordered to leave the ship. "There was a light rain falling," Bob Schiller remembered, "and the sea was very calm."[19] Schiller was fairly calm at the time he left the cruiser. "I wasn't real scared because [the *Astoria*] wasn't really sinking very fast; it was just listing a little." He walked across onto the destroyer and never saw the *Astoria* again.

Richard Tunnell eventually made his way to the forecastle where he helped the wounded as best he could. While standing with a small group of men near turret two, it suddenly fired, belching out a tremendous roar. The blast knocked the entire group down. When the *Bagley* arrived, he assisted in passing the wounded over before crossing onto the destroyer himself. As the destroyer pulled away he saw the true state of the *Astoria*, "I could see the ship almost totally on fire."[20]

When the *Bagley* came within sight of the *Astoria*, Roy Spurlock was unsure if she was friend or foe. "We did not know if we were about to be assisted or slaughtered," he recalled. Later when the transfer of wounded began, Spurlock was right there to help in the process. "Carrying wounded was something that we able bodied pilots could do, and we did as long as any wounded remained on the deck of the *Astoria*."[21]

At about 4:45 A.M. the transfer was complete. Captain Greenman was the last man to move off the bow of the *Astoria* onto the *Bagley*. The destroyer slowly backed away from the burning cruiser. "I don't think there was anybody left on the forward part of the ship when the *Bagley* pulled out," remembered Gene Alair. "I'm positive Greenman felt that everybody was off. It was raining and of course it was dark and the [*Astoria*] was burning like a torch, so there was no reason to believe that anybody was still alive on the thing."[22] Moving through the crowds of survivors on the *Bagley*, Alair found a place to rest near the torpedo tubes. "I stood for probably thirty or forty minutes just leaning up against the torpedo tubes," he remembered. A total of 450 men transferred onto the destroyer, including about 185 wounded.[23] It appeared that the end of the *Astoria* was at hand.

* * *

After jumping off the *Astoria*'s flaming gun deck during the height of the battle, Lieutenant (jg) Healey found Ensign James Boland in the water. "We swam together away from the ship until we reached a group of ten of our men," Healey later wrote. "The group of us continued to swim from the ship until we found a burning life raft." Dousing what turned out to be a small fire, the men eagerly climbed aboard. The raft was damaged from the flames and the supplies normally secured to the grating were missing. While floating in the night the raft added four additional passengers who just happened to swim by. "About dawn we heard a lot of shooting and noticed a lot of gun flashes from a direction that seemed to be near the Guadalcanal shore."[24] After spending almost six hours in the water, Healey and his men were picked up by the destroyer *Wilson*.

* * *

Among those on the stern surprised to see the approaching *Bagley* was Matthew Bouterse. Limping and suffering from a few burns, he was helped aboard the destroyer as the wounded were being evacuated off the *Astoria*. He was surprised to see Captain Greenman, who at the time was organizing the salvage party. "Had I been able to walk," Bouterse later wrote, "I think I would have jumped back aboard. I felt that strongly about my ship."[25] It was not long before the *Bagley* quickly left that area in search of a submarine contact. "I shed tears for the first time as we moved swiftly away and the lovely crippled, dying *Astoria* faded into the misty morning."

Chapter 22

Commander Shoup at the Stern

When the Battle of Savo Island started for the *Astoria*, her executive officer was not on duty. Commander Frank Shoup was asleep in his cabin when the general quarters alarm sounded. Looking at his watch, he noticed it was 1:55 A.M. as he jumped into action. "I arose and dressed very quickly, putting my clothing on over my pajamas," Shoup later wrote. "I am sure that I was out of my cabin in less than a minute."[1] He noticed a haze in the air as he ran for his battle station at the secondary conning station located at battle two. Shoup also noticed the flares in the distance and a searchlight trained on the *Astoria*. Just as he made his way onto the gun deck, a five-inch gun on the port side opened fire with a roar.

Arriving at battle two, Shoup saw that the only other person there was Quartermaster Second Class John Walker. "None of the other officers and men assigned to the station ever arrived there," Shoup recalled. "I immediately took a look on the starboard side and saw nothing. I then stepped out on the machine gun platform on the port side in order to get an unobstructed view on the port quarter."[2] Just as he leaned over the splinter shield an explosion rocked the immediate area. Sustaining burns on his hands and face, the executive officer was temporarily blinded.

Regaining his vision after only a few short minutes, Shoup saw a shell hit the base of the starboard catapult and slide across the well deck before exploding near the galley. "This started a large fire on the starboard side of the well deck," he continued, "and ignited the plane on the starboard catapult. Another hit soon ignited the boat deck. I announced this fire over the battle announcing system." The *Astoria* was now under heavy fire and being hit repeatedly by shells of all size and caliber. The entire middle part of the ship seemed to be on fire. Trying to announce each hit for the benefit of the damage control parties, Shoup soon realized that the announcing system was dead. Walker then reported that he had lost contact with the bridge and could communicate only with central station. The raging fire on the boat deck was now beginning to spread to battle two and the compartment was filling with smoke. "I looked out both sides and saw that both ladders were blocked and that there was no chance of getting down via the ordinary methods," Shoup recounted. He decided that it was time to leave and ordered the area abandoned.

* * *

Lieutenant Jack Gibson was trapped on the machine gun platform just outside of the after main battery control station. After efforts to fight the nearby fires had failed, he was looking for a way out. There was no rope long enough to reach down to the main deck. Acting on his own accord, John Bartlett went down the starboard ladder and onto the boat deck. At great risk he maneuvered past the burning twenty-millimeter clipping room and under a flaming motor launch, before making it back to the machine gun platform with a line that was long enough to reach the main deck.

With the help of Bartlett, Walter Johns, Jack Dean, and others, Gibson directed the escape. "None of these men displayed anything but coolness and bravery," Gibson later wrote of his men.³ The wounded were first lowered in slings, followed by the able-bodied who slid down the rope to the main deck near turret three. Gibson and his men joined those near the fantail under the command of the executive officer. After helping the wounded, he took a seat and noted the roaring fires amidships.⁴ The efforts of Gibson and his men caught the attention of the executive officer. "When all egress from the main mast was cut off by fire, there was no panic," Shoup reported. "When a line was obtained and rigged down to the main deck aft, the first concern was for the wounded."⁵

With the *Astoria* a mass of flames from the forward stack all the way back to battle two, trapped men were faced with the desperate situation of trying to find a way out or perishing. Gibson and his men were not the only ones to make a daring escape from the upper deck area. Four enlisted men, each from different battle stations, also found ways to make it out alive.

In the nearby after five-inch director, the battle started without warning for Theodore Torsch. He initially thought that a ship was firing at land. He asked Lieutenant Healey, "Why are they [the American ships] shooting at the beach?"⁶ After looking through his binoculars, Healey replied that it was the Japanese doing the shooting and it was directed towards them. He instructed Torsch to stay on the director and not go to his battle station at the forward five-inch magazine. Never sighting the Japanese cruisers, Torsch soon noticed that the *Astoria* was being hit in rapid succession. It seemed that shells were exploding all around him.

From his vantage point, Torsch looked down to see the seaplane on the port side catapult. Everything around it was on fire. The plane that had been on the starboard catapult just moments ago was gone. A shell then hit the base of the director, causing it to lean and destroying the ladder used to get down. Fire from explosions around and below his position burned Torsch's head, arms and back.

Lieutenant Healey then ordered the director abandoned. The men soon learned they could not escape from the director via the normal route because of a damaged ladder. They instead found a piece of rope and threw it over the side. The rope did not have any knots, meaning that the men would have to wrap their legs around it and slowly slide down. The men abandoned their station as fast as they possibly could. "When a ship is on fire," Torsch said, "you go down the fastest way to get out." The entire group went down the rope and eventually ended up on the main deck near turret three. Healey told the men that the

Seen in a postwar picture, Frank Shoup served as executive officer of the *Astoria* during 1942. Leading a group of survivors near the stern of the ship, he played a critical role in the failed effort to save the stricken ship (U.S. Navy / Naval Historical Center).

sailors on the deck near the fantail were dead. He instructed them to put the bodies into bags and sew them up in preparation for burial. The lieutenant then set out for the gun deck.

Before long Torsch thought he heard the order to abandon ship. No official order had been given, but word was spreading that the *Astoria* was on fire and that there was no way of putting out the flames. Separated from the other men from his battle station, he took off his helmet and with several others jumped into the water off the starboard side near the fantail. "We just went over the side," he recalled.

Below and forward of the after five-inch director was the area that Ed Armes called his battle station. The area was a lookout point situated on the boat deck directly forward of battle two and on top of the hangar. "This is where some of the people in the aviation division would have their lookout duties," Armes said. The station consisted of a small number of tubs that housed lookout positions and twenty-millimeter anti-aircraft guns. Positioned on the starboard side, his role was to scan the sky for enemy planes. Members of the aviation group regularly stood watch as aircraft lookouts. "We could take a quick look at a silhouette and tell the type of plane it was," Armes recalled. "We were an extra pair of eyes."[7]

Armes was on duty at his station when the battle started. Just prior to the shooting, he recalled hearing the sound of an airplane overhead. Almost simultaneously, shells began to land on the *Astoria*. The general quarters alarm sounded just moments after the first shells hit. At about the same time, Japanese searchlights suddenly trained on the *Astoria*. It did not take long for the area to become engulfed in flames. From his position Armes could see the fires forward. "A complete mass of flames," was the best description he could provide of the scene. "The well deck with the planes was all on fire." Armes could now feel the heat from the flames below him. "I was wondering how the hell we were going to get down," he said. There were two ladders that went from the top of the hangar to the well deck below and both were engulfed by fire.

Realizing that his position on top of the hangar was no longer tenable, Armes decided it was time to get down. When someone threw a rope over the side down to the main deck, some of the men near him could not decide whether to leave or stay. Having already made up his mind to leave, Armes slid down the rope and ended up on the main deck near turret three. The turret fired with a blast just as he arrived in the area, knocking him down to the deck. Briefly pausing, he looked off into the distance and saw two masses of flames, which he took to be the *Quincy* and the *Vincennes*.

Crawling across the deck, Armes headed for the stern of the ship. Once near the fantail, he lost track of many of the men from his battle station. A state of general confusion seemed to exist. "We didn't quite know what was going on," he recalled. "I saw people off in the water on the starboard side." The *Astoria* was now slowly drifting to a stop. Off to the side, a raft filled with men floated past. Just then Armes spotted a man in the water who appeared to have been burned and was yelling for someone to throw him a life vest. Thinking that the other man needed it more than himself at the moment, Armes took off his life vest. Reaching over the side, he threw it out as far as he could and the man in the water swam to it. As the *Astoria* continued to slowly drift, the man in the water began to move out of sight. Armes never saw him again. By this time the shooting had stopped and things began to quiet down a bit. Armes did not did not know what to do. He saw a life raft nearby that had three or four men in it. It was not too far from the ship. Deciding it was time to abandon ship he jumped off the starboard side and swam towards the raft.

Nestled among the small superstructure that made up battle two was the after battle lookout station. It was both the general watch and battle station for Baker Third Class George Douglas. Located above and behind the hangar, the small room served as a lookout station with four points that could be used for binoculars. No more than ten feet from his station, Douglas was off duty and asleep under a life boat when the battle started. Waking to the sound of the general alarm, he ran to his battle station as the first shells began to hit the *Astoria*. The only other man to make it to the lookout station was Seaman Second Class Fred Boatwright. The two men were soon faced with a perilous situation. "An ammunition locker outside of my battle station had taken a hit," Douglas later wrote, "and the ammo was blowing up from the heat of the fire."[8]

Deciding to leave the lookout station, Douglas and Boatwright made a run for a nearby range-finder tub. They were not in the tub for very long before a shell landed in close proximity. After ducking down, Douglas looked up and saw that the tub had a hole in the side. Boatwright was dead, having apparently absorbed the bulk of the hit. Sprayed with many small pieces of shrapnel, Douglas knew that he had also been hit but did not realize the extent of his injuries.

Douglas now seized an opportunity to escape. "Somebody from the range-finder crew above us had thrown a rope down," he recalled. It was only when he went to slide down the rope, that Douglas realized the extent of his injuries. He was only able to hold onto the rope with one hand and soon lost his grip all together. "I fell about fifteen or twenty feet to the deck." Landing on the main deck between the hangar and turret three, he was soon one of a number of wounded men who were being lowered down into the water. Not having a life jacket on at the time, he grabbed onto the side of a life ring that was floating nearby as soon as he hit the water. Eventually, someone reached down and pulled Douglas onto the ring. He recalled sitting on the lap of a wounded sailor who later died.

Also escaping from the hellish fires amidship was Belcher Hobson. He was on auxiliary watch when the sound of the general alarm sent him running toward his battle station. He was part of a twelve man repair party that met near the well deck just ahead of the uptakes at the base of the stacks. On this particular day, Hobson was assigned to wear a fireproof asbestos suit. Consisting of a pair of dungarees reinforced with sewed on sheets of asbestos, it was a homemade garment. Separating from the group, he momentarily ventured off to the port side to put on the suit. When he returned to the repair party, Hobson found that the area had been devastated by at least one shell hit in close proximity. Most of the men in the repair party, including the officer in charge, had been killed. The area was now a mass of flames. "The well deck was pretty well destroyed by fire," Hobson recalled.[9] He escaped the area by moving to the forward part of the ship.

* * *

Executive Officer Shoup and Quartermaster Walker left the smoke-filled battle two via the machine gun platform. They quickly found the rope that had been used by Lieutenant Gibson and his men for their escape. Shoup noticed that many of the men on the machine gun platform had died at their guns. Looking up he saw the *Quincy*, on fire from bow to stern, crossing in front of the *Astoria*. "All firing from the *Astoria* had ceased," Shoup noted at this time, "and also the enemy fire seemed to have ceased, although it was impossible to tell, as explosions forward were frequent."[10]

Arriving down on the main deck, Shoup found about 150 men assembled on the after portion of the ship. The number included at least twenty-five wounded men who were grouped near the fantail. Turret three had no power but was still manned and trained out to the starboard side. Men were still on duty at the after 1.1-inch machine gun mounts.

Shoup learned that an attempt had been made to fight the fire in the hangar area, but the effort had been abandoned when the water pressure was lost.

Looking forward from his position, all that Shoup could see was fire. He was not optimistic about the *Astoria*'s chances for survival. "I could not understand why the enemy fire had ceased and assumed that they were closing in to finish us with gunfire or torpedoes." Just then the *Quincy* exploded with a tremendous blast off in the distance. Shoup concluded that the *Astoria* would probably have to be abandoned and immediately began to make the appropriate preparations.

Work began to remove the wounded. All available life rafts were dropped over the side and tied by line to the ship's rail. The walking wounded began to descend down into the rafts. They were joined by an equal number of able-bodied men, some of whom were equipped with flashlights. A total of four full rafts cast away from the cruiser with orders to stay together and signal a destroyer. Those who remained on board gathered empty powder cans from turret three and lashed them together to be used as floatation devices.

While the wounded were being evacuated, Shoup conferred with Lieutenant (jg) Ira Blough about the condition of turret three and the possible need to flood the after magazines. Blough reported that his turret was manned with guns loaded, but not primed. The turret could be operated by hand power in case of further action. The magazine seemed cool, so no order to flood it was given at that time. Shoup ordered Blough to keep a close watch on the magazines and to flood them at his discretion if any sign of fire appeared. "He reported an hour or so later," Shoup recounted, "that smoke had come through the vent system into one of the magazines and that they had been flooded." The smoke likely came from the nearby third division living spaces. That compartment, along with the chief petty officer's mess hall, had been the scene of an intense fire. The flames had burned out, but lingering smoke remained.

* * *

The senior officer in charge of the after battle dressing area was Lieutenant Commander James Brown. The assistant ship's doctor, he was joined by three others from the medical division in addition to Chaplain Matthew Bouterse. When the battle started Brown arrived at the station just as the watertight door was being closed. Pushing it open to gain entry, he quickly saw that all of his staff was present. "I was closing the door when this compartment was struck by a shell and soon thereafter another," Brown reported.[11] His face was slightly burned by one of the explosions. One of the hits destroyed the medical supply locker located on the port side of the compartment. Visibility soon decreased as smoke began to flood into the area. One of the men pointed to the hole in the outboard bulkhead on the port side. Brown stumbled through the dressing station. "I was unable to reach the place on the forward bulkhead where my mask and life preserver were hanging because of the fumes, smoke, and fire."

Brown then ordered the compartment evacuated. Moving forward into the next area, the doctor found that the hatches leading up were all sealed. He then moved forward into the next compartment, crawling due to the irritating smoke. "I started forward to the midships dressing station ... but heat, flames, and smoke drove me back," Brown wrote. "I found my way up a ladder on the starboard side to the space just aft of the washroom on the main deck." As Brown momentarily paused, the previous compartment that he had just left was hit. An explosion in the nearby washroom occurred almost simultaneously. It was here that he put on the flash-proof clothing that he had been carrying since leaving his cabin at the sound of the general alarm. Making his way topside, Brown could see that the ship was on fire and burning badly. He took cover for a short time near the base of turret three until the firing stopped. He then rushed to help the wounded.

With ammunition exploding amidship, Brown ordered the wounded to be moved far aft on the main deck. The men were unable to retrieve much in the way of supplies from the after battle dressing area. "The shell fire had rendered useless or unapproachable nearly all our dispersed medical equipment," Brown remembered. "We had no splints and no morphine nor whiskey."[12] A few first aid kits were all that was available, including one that was taken out of turret three. Any available type of material was pressed into service for use as dressings: cotton from the guns, undershirts, and handkerchiefs to name just a few.

At the order of Executive Officer Shoup, Brown directed the evacuation of the wounded into the available life rafts. The first few wounded were successfully lowered down into the rafts before the process became more difficult. "No after raft remained moored to the ship long enough to permit it to be loaded," Brown later wrote. "Some of the wounded were put into life jackets and rolled over the side to be picked up by the rafts." After the last raft had pulled away, Brown quickly compared notes with Hospital Apprentice First Class Victor Molinoski. After they determined that all of the wounded who needed to be evacuated had been sent away in the rafts, the two jumped over the side. "My life jacket would not support me," Brown recalled, "but I swam some distance, found a mattress, and propelled it until I got to the rafts about three hundred yards away." He then joined the floating wounded. The group was later picked up by the destroyer *Wilson*.

* * *

Henry Juarez was almost asleep when he heard his gun captain reporting the sound of an airplane. "I got up and then I stood up," he remembered. "I didn't go back to sleep." The young sailor had no idea how long of a night lay ahead. "Then we heard that airplane again, it was kind of foggy, cloudy, overcast, low clouds. We could hear that drone of that airplane."[13] The gun captain again reported the plane to sky control, but apparently no action was being taken.

Suddenly the battle started. "Right off our port bow, three big chandelier flares dropped out of the clouds," Juarez said, "and I could see the *Vincennes* and the *Quincy* just like plain daylight." Before long the main battery of the *Astoria* opened fire with a roar. "Right after those flares dissipated ... three searchlights came on, spotlights," Juarez continued. "One came off the starboard bow, one came off the port bow, and another one came on the port quarter." Only half of the gun crew was on station at this time, so Juarez leaped into the trainers' seat and pointed the 1.1-inch machine gun at the searchlight off the port quarter. "We were ready to fire at that searchlight when we got the message from the captain to cease fire," he said. By now the *Astoria* was being hit repeatedly and fires were erupting amidship.

Looking forward Juarez saw the hangar explode into a mass of flames. Just then he spotted a wounded man crawling away from the hangar on the port side near turret three. The man was crawling across the deck using his elbows. "The fire was intense," Juarez said. "The hangar was so hot that it was just like a hot plate, the whole hangar, and we wanted to get him out of there." Almost simultaneously Juarez and his gun captain rushed to help the stricken sailor. They soon saw he was in bad shape. His legs were intact, but a large chunk of flesh around his hip had been torn off. "We drug him away from the fire," Juarez said, "and put him way on the opposite side of the turret where there was no heat. He just folded his hands and said, 'Just let me lay here.' There was nothing we could do."

While pulling the wounded man to safety, Juarez was caught dead center in the beam of a Japanese searchlight. "You talk about being scared," he remembered of the terrifying experience. "I tried to move, but I couldn't move." A shell whizzed by his position. "I ducked and I froze and to this day I don't know what made me do that. I put my hand up you know, protecting myself. Just imagine that, trying to protect myself with my elbow." Breaking free from his frozen state, Juarez began to take note of the situation around him. Ammunition was exploding from the ready boxes around the five-inch and twenty millimeter guns sending shrapnel flying in all directions. He noticed that Commander Shoup was in the area, yelling for men to take cover. Heeding the advice, Juarez ran back to his gun mount and ducked behind the shield. As the firing subsided, he joined the effort to take care of the wounded and later assisted in getting them off the ship onto the rafts. "There were about 150 of us that were back aft," he remembered. "There were guys that were really, really shocked. I was scared."

* * *

The general alarm abruptly awoke a sleeping Matthew Bouterse. The chaplain jumped out of bed and quickly put on his shoes. "I noticed that the P.A. system was still live," he remembered, "and that there were strange sounds and shouting in the background." Bouterse started his usual dash towards his battle station in the after battle dressing area. Watertight doors closed as he came running through with at least one having to be re-opened to allow for his passage. "As I ran the ship shuddered, as if either we had fired a salvo from our main batteries or we had been hit."[14]

Immediately upon arriving at the battle station, Stewart's Mate Tyrus Gullatte handed Bouterse his flash jacket. "As I put it on I asked him to get our life jackets out of the locker on the port bulkhead," Bouterse wrote. "As he did so our world came to an end!" The chaplain's next recollection was of being half conscious lying on the deck in the dark. By this time the compartment had taken one or more hits and was filled with a thick acrid smoke. The terrifying sounds of the *Astoria* being repeatedly hit filled the background.

In what appeared to be his darkest hour, Bouterse's rescuers arrived in the form of two corpsmen. The medical men may have entered the compartment looking for survivors. Bouterse followed the two men forward into adjacent compartments, moving through smoke, wreckage, and fire. The small group stopped occasionally to check on wounded sailors, some of whom were deemed to be beyond help. Just then some men came out of an adjacent compartment and warned of the decks being red hot from the raging fires amidships. Bouterse and his companions then found their escape route in the form of a ladder that led topside.

With the help of the two corpsmen, Bouterse made it up to the main deck emerging from a hatch just behind the hangar. Moving toward the stern he found a place to sit. His legs were hanging over the stern with his feet resting on the *U.S.S. Astoria* lettering that was imprinted on the ship's fantail. A light rain was falling as the dark waters below were lit up by the occasional flash of an explosion. As he gazed forward catching a glimpse of the after battle control station, he noticed a body hanging lifelessly over a rail with flames burning below and inching ever closer. Perhaps in shock, Bouterse became transfixed on that hanging body, only snapping back to reality when a sailor came to tell him that a wounded shipmate was calling for him. The chaplain found the sailor just in time to talk with him as he passed away.

* * *

After making a perilous escape from the after engine room, Abe Santos was helping the wounded near the fantail when a gravely wounded officer asked him for some water. "Don't ask me where I got the water," Santos remembered, "but I found the water."[15] Propping up the wounded man's head to his chest, Santos slowly poured the water into the officer's mouth only to have it come out of the terrible rip in his back. Although only slightly wounded with some small shrapnel hits, the experience left Santos looking like a bloody mess. The officer was still alive when he left him.

* * *

Lieutenant Commander John Hayes had blacked out during his escape from the engineering compartments below deck. When the engineering officer regained consciousness, he was lying on the main deck in the after part of the ship. He did not know exactly how he made it out from below deck. He saw fires forward and turret three trained out to the starboard side. The first person that Hayes encountered was Machinist's Mate Second Class Art Schwebel. With the help of a gas mask, Schwebel was able to find his way out of the smoky after engine room and make it topside. Schwebel told Hayes that men were being evacuated from above turret three. "At about this time I met Lieutenant Gibson, who had apparently just come down from the boat deck," Hayes recalled. "I noted about this time that most of the men from the forward engine room were not around. There were only the four talkers and two other men."[16] Hayes assumed that most of the others had been lost in the smoke on the second deck as they tried to escape. However, he later learned that many had gone over the side or left with the wounded on life rafts.

Only a short time later, Hayes met the executive officer. "He was almost unconscious from the smoke," Shoup remembered of the engineering officer, "and did not know how he had gotten out but he quickly recovered and gave me a somewhat encouraging account of the engineering spaces." Hayes reported his belief that the engine rooms and most of the fire rooms were intact. The executive officer would continue to rely on his help for the rest of the time aboard ship. "I held frequent consultations," Shoup recalled, "with him and his calm, sound advice was of great assistance to me throughout."[17]

Once the preliminary preparations needed to abandon ship were complete, Shoup then focused on trying to save the *Astoria*. A bucket brigade was quickly formed. Initially started by the executive officer, Hayes took over and was able to get the party working efficiently. Comprised of members of the after repair party, engineers, and others, the group used buckets and empty powder cans to attack the intense fire on the boat deck. The area was burning fiercely and being rocked by frequent explosions. Trying to put out the flames seemed like a daunting task. "One explosion blew a raft down," Hayes remembered. "We put the fire out on this raft and tossed it overboard, secured to a line."[18] Although it looked futile at first, the bucket brigade was able to make slow and steady progress.

At about 3:30 A.M. it started to rain. The timing could not have been better for the makeshift firefighters. "The rain considerably dampened the fire on the boat deck," Hayes recalled. The wind picked up, coming in off the starboard side to blow much of the smoke clear of the men. The bucket brigade was able to advance across the boat deck and onto the well deck extinguishing a number of small fires along the way.

Suddenly a sign of life came from the forward part of the ship. "At about 4:00 the sound of a gasoline pump was heard up forward," Shoup reported. "This was the first indication I had that there were any personnel alive in the forward part of the ship, and I began to think that she might be saved."[19] The list to port had held steady at two to three degrees. At about the same time the rain increased to a heavier downpour.

The hard work of the bucket brigade was starting to pay off. Sometime after 4:30 A.M. the firefighters had successfully fought to the forward limits of the well deck. However, their progress was blocked by a stubborn fire on the starboard side of the well deck. The fire was later determined to be cans of aviation lubricating oil that were stored in a locker at the entrance to the galley. A heavy black smoke prevented any further movement on the port side.

Just after the bucket brigade reached the forward part of the well deck, a wounded man was spotted among the flames on the starboard side. He was stuck between a whale boat davit and the break of the upper deck. The oil fire was burning above him, and a fire in the lumber stowage area was directly below. "At first I thought he was dead, but then I saw him wave his hand feebly," Shoup later wrote. Just then Shipfitter First Class Charles Watkins dashed into the flames without regard for his own safety. Reaching the corner where the man was trapped, he started to get the wounded man down and then called for help. Shipfitter Third Class Wyatt Luttrell and Water Tender Second Class Norman Touve rushed through the flames to offer their assistance. Together the three rescuers pulled the trapped man to safety. In the process the group found another trapped man in close proximity to the first and a third man hanging over the side clinging to the armor belt. Both of these men were also rescued, the latter by tossing a rope over the side. "The rescue of these three men was a heroic action," Shoup noted, "and was the finest deed I witnessed in a night when high courage was commonplace. I would not have ordered anyone in to make this rescue, as I did not think it could be done."

Small acts of selflessness and heroism were routine aboard the *Astoria* that night. Aviation Machinist's Mate First Class Harold Rogers came across a shipmate lying on deck with wounds on his ankle, thigh, hip, and forehead. Rogers evidently did not think that the man was going to be able to get off the ship. He gave the wounded man his lifejacket and then either lowered or pushed him over the side.

All efforts to squelch the oil fire were unsuccessful. Sand was used to try to smother it to no avail. Some fire extinguishers were brought in from turret three but could not put out the flames. In the meantime, a group of men tried to get to the forward part of the ship by going below the main deck. They had hoped to go under the fires and move forward, but their progress was blocked by dense smoke and a series of small fires. Although a number of rescue oxygen breathers were available, almost all were malfunctioning. "I had hoped to be able to reach the forecastle and join up with the other group," Shoup later lamented, "but it was now decided that this was impossible." With forward movement blocked, the bucket brigade turned their attention to some smaller fires and clearing wreckage from the hangar.

The executive officer now seemed positive on the possibility of saving the *Astoria*. "By daylight, the chief engineer and I had decided that there was a good chance of saving the ship," Shoup wrote, "and he thought there was a possibility of getting her underway under her own power."[20] A destroyer was then spotted off the bow of the *Astoria*.

Chapter 23

The Fight to Save the *Astoria*

After the *Bagley* pulled away from the stricken cruiser, Captain Greenman requested that the destroyer stay close by the *Astoria*. He wanted to be able to examine his ship at first daylight to determine if it was feasible to try to salvage her. At about 4:50 A.M. the *Bagley* reported the cruiser's situation to Admiral Turner via T.B.S. radio.[1] Standing clear of the *Astoria*, the destroyer used her searchlights to ply the nearby waters looking for survivors. Among those scooped out of the water was Don Yeamans, who had ended up on a raft.

It appeared to Greenman that some of the fires amidships were beginning to subside. As a result of a small flashing light spotted on the back of the *Astoria*, he learned for the first time that there were survivors near the stern of his ship. The *Bagley* signaled to the men at the stern that they had been seen before continuing to rescue men from the water. The destroyer was able to find five rafts full of *Astoria* survivors along with a few stragglers from the *Vincennes*.

At dawn Greenman directed the *Bagley* to pull along the starboard quarter of the *Astoria* so that he and Lieutenant Commander Topper could look the ship over very carefully. The true extent of the damage to the cruiser soon became apparent as parts of the ship were mangled and charred. A slight list to port was noticed almost immediately. The starboard side was riddled with a string of about eight large holes that were all positioned a couple of feet above the waterline. "The bridge had one enormous section completely blown away," Topper remembered. "The ship did not appear to be shipping any water."[2]

After the brief inspection, the *Bagley* nudged her bow up to the starboard quarter of the *Astoria*. It did not take long for the captain to find that the executive officer was not only alive and well but was leading a sizeable group of survivors. The captain conferred with Commander Shoup about the prospects of saving the ship. "He informed me that he felt there was a chance to salvage the vessel," Greenman remembered of the meeting. "The chief engineer who was also present indicated the same thing."[3] The captain immediately made preparations to re-board the *Astoria* to try to save her.

Transferring back onto the *Astoria* was a salvage crew that numbered about 325 men. The group was largely comprised of two deck divisions, repair men, engineers, and electricians, but also included all able-bodied officers.[4] The *Bagley* also passed over firefighting equipment and rescue breathing apparatus. Lieutenant (jg) Donald Smith, part of the destroyer's medical staff, was also placed aboard the *Astoria* to assist in caring for the wounded in the fantail area. All other personnel from the cruiser who were not part of the salvage crew, including many of the wounded from the after part of the ship, went aboard the *Bagley*. The transfer was completed at about 6:00 A.M.

The effort to save the *Astoria* began immediately with Greenman in direct command of the operation. If the remaining fires could be extinguished, there was a good chance that the ship could be saved. If some of the cruiser's engines could be brought back on line, then she could leave the area under her own power. Otherwise, she would have to be towed to safer waters.

In preparation for re-boarding the cruiser, Greenman gave each officer an assignment for the operation. Gene Alair remembered that the captain was calm and seemed genuinely concerned about saving his ship. "While Captain Greenman wanted volunteers to go back aboard," he said, "he also desired officers and enlisted men who he felt could evaluate conditions for him with skills necessary to save his ship."[5] Alair walked back aboard the *Astoria* on the starboard side adjacent to turret three.

Once on board the men divided into four groups under the direction of different officers. Alair was assigned to work with Lieutenant Commander Topper. "He gave us assignments to look for things," Alair said. "They knew that I knew the third division and they could not find any third division officers."

The first order of business for Topper was the organization of firefighting parties. With the fire situation in the forward part of the ship still fresh in his mind, the damage control officer quickly learned of the progress that had been made on the well deck. "The fires aft were under control except that in the aviation lubrication oil locker and lumber locker forward on the starboard side of the well deck," he wrote. "Three firefighting parties were organized."[6] Topper then made a mark on the well deck. It was a gauge that he would use to monitor the extent of the *Astoria*'s list to port.

As the firefighters attacked the flames, Topper led a group of men below decks to inspect the area aft of the number two engine room. "The smoke in these after below deck spaces had cleared up considerably," he noted. Using battle lanterns, the men slowly and carefully maneuvered through the dark spaces. The group soon came across a variety of damage. A five-inch hole on the starboard side had previously been plugged and seemed to be holding well. Another shell of the same size appeared to have passed through several compartments without exploding. The inspection of a storeroom revealed that a few rivets were loose and leaking water. A few small fires that were found to still be smoldering were quickly smothered. Topper found that most of the compartments were well sealed. "We found all hatches, drains, and ventilation valves closed," he commented. "All hatches and openings on the second deck and below were then secured." Upon leaving the area, he directed his men to make sure that all compartments were again made watertight.

Leaving the after part of the ship, Topper's group was able to find a way forward up to the forecastle. After inspecting several compartments, he was able to confirm that the forward eight-inch magazine had been successfully flooded. A fierce fire was still raging near the wardroom. "It was quite warm in this part of the ship," Topper noticed, "but the smoke had cleared up somewhat. We could not get into wardroom country due to excessive heat."

Among those venturing below decks was Gene Alair. He went down a hatch on the main deck near turret three. "I felt a degree of comfort as we went below because it had been my home for nearly one year and a half," he recalled. After starting out with Topper, they separated into two groups. The damage control officer went forward, while Alair stayed in the back area of the ship. He was in charge of a group of eight to ten men whose assignment was to examine the rear compartments to ascertain the extent of the damage and to determine the watertight integrity. "I stayed in what was called the chief's quarters," he recalled. "It was quiet, dark, and to me very eerie."

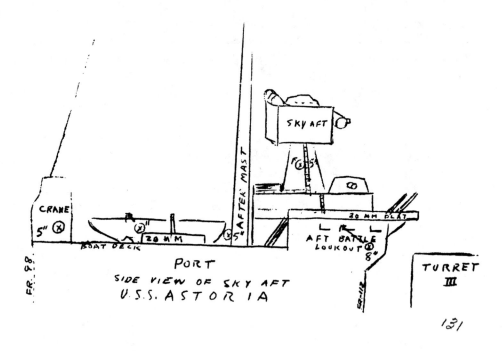

A diagram drawn by John Topper shows shell hits near the *Astoria*'s after fire control station. As damage control officer, Topper played a key role in the effort to save the ship (U.S. Navy / National Archives).

Alair entered the compartment to find about an inch of water covering the deck. A quick search revealed no apparent leaking water. A number of battery powered battle lanterns were still turned on, strewn about the area creating beams of light that crisscrossed the compartment at odd angles. "Hospital corpsmen had used the chief's quarters as a dressing station and the berths had bodies placed there, partially bandaged and severely burned," he said. No one was found to be alive.

The group next tried to gain access to the rear steering area. Alair was very familiar with the general area as he had previously been responsible for inspecting the compartment. "I tried to get down into the after steering station and couldn't get the compartment door open," he recalled. "We were trying to un-dog the thing and open the big door. It was frustrating because you knew there were guys on the other side of that compartment, but you couldn't get it open." Unknown to Alair the four men that were in the after steering compartment had escaped unharmed by going out a different hatch.

Moving forward into adjacent compartments, Alair and his men found that some of the hatches were not properly secured. A detailed search of the area revealed leaking water lines, but no apparent hull damage. Alair returned topside to report his findings.

Also going below decks was Lieutenant Commander Hayes. "After daylight, I was able to go forward and visit the forward engine room," he recounted. "At this time I did not believe that any of the engineering spaces were flooded."[7] Hayes and his men secured the battle hatches to both of the engine rooms. "All valves in the engine room were secured and the hatches dogged," he reported.

The engineering men then tried to get into the number three and four fire rooms. There appeared to be problems with both of the boilers in the number three fire room. One

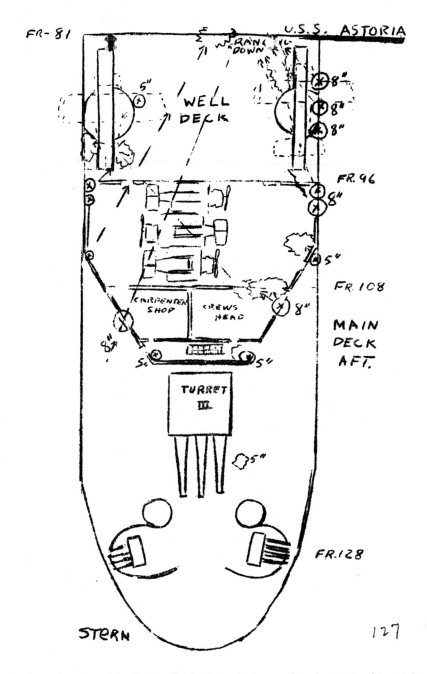

No known photographs exist of the damaged *Astoria* in the hours after the Battle of Savo Island. Sketched diagrams by John Topper, such as this one looking down on the stern of the ship, provide a record of the damage to the vessel (U.S. Navy / National Archives).

was found to be without water and burned up, while the other was too hot to be properly inspected. The number four fire room seemed to be in good condition. Smoke and flames from the fires directly above, as well as debris, blocked access to fire rooms one and two. In checking the electrical supply, Hayes found that all stored power was gone. "This was due to running down of the forward and after batteries and destruction of the batteries on the well deck," he wrote. Captain Greenman praised the efforts of Hayes and his men. "The

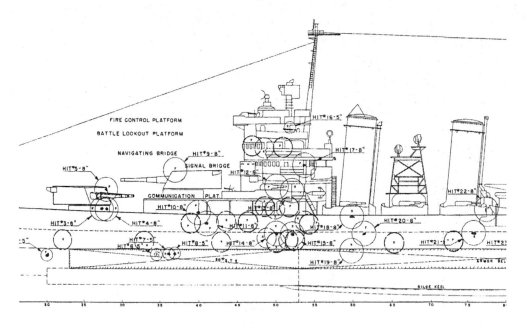

A drawing of the *Astoria*'s mid-section shows estimated positions of Japanese shell hits. The diagram was part of a damage analysis conducted by navy officials after the sinking of the ship (U.S. Navy / National Archives).

chief engineer continued in a most energetic manner to make progress in the machinery spaces," the captain wrote, "but he finally reported that the number four fire room offered the only opportunity to get up steam."[8]

While Topper and Hayes were working below deck, Shoup stayed topside. "While the fires were being fought, the captain ordered me to assemble all the accessible bodies aft for a mass burial at sea," he later wrote.[9] Teams of men fanned out to the hangar, machine gun platform, boat deck, and elsewhere with the unenviable task of collecting the dead. The sailmaker started sewing up the bodies in canvas. Each was weighted in preparation for final burial. Dog tags were also collected and put in a box.

* * *

Among the enlisted men who participated in the salvage effort were Belcher Hobson, Don Yeamans, and Henry Juarez. Once back on board the *Astoria*, Hobson spent most of his time working with others trying to find a way to restore power. Almost all of the pumps were electric and were needed to fight the fires. "We couldn't do anything without electricity," he stated, "which we never got."[10]

Don Yeamans re-boarded the ship in the company of Seaman First Class Jerry Todd. The two initially went to the hangar area, where several men were unsuccessful in trying to start a water pump. Eventually, they ended up tossing buckets of water on the raging fire near the wardroom.

Henry Juarez never left the ship. Becoming part of the salvage crew, he went to work just after daylight. Taking off his lifejacket, he joined a bucket brigade fighting fires. Juarez was paired up with Seaman Second Class Lawrence Lozano. Working with only one bucket they attacked the fire in the hangar. Lozano would start the process by filling the bucket with water from the ocean and handing it over to Juarez. He then entered the hangar from one of two back doors that were located right behind turret three, tossed the water onto the fire, and returned the empty bucket to Lozano for a refill. An inexperienced firefighter, Juarez quickly learned that he had to be careful. "I didn't know that when it gets that hot there's no oxygen," he said. "So I jumped into the hangar and it was like somebody cut my air out. I had to jump back out."[11] It did not take long for him to get the hang of it. "Finally we got the fire all simmered down. I think the fire mostly went out because it had no fuel to burn."

For his next assignment Juarez had the task of helping to collect the dead. Many sailors perished in the hangar. "I had to go and get the dog tags," he remembered. "I had to pick up the bodies." Many of the bodies were badly burned, the flesh charred black or red. Entering the hangar, he noted jagged holes in the deck and twisted metal. The area had been hit early in the battle and burned for hours. Some of the beams were still red hot. He likened it to the red hot burner of an electric stove. Paired up with another, Juarez first took the dog tags off of a body. Sliding a blanket under the body, each would grab two corners as they carried it down the main deck. The bodies were stacked between turret three and the after 1.1-inch gun mounts, while the dog tags were given to a pharmacist's mate. "We finally cleared all the bodies we could," Juarez said. "I don't know how many bodies, but there was quite a few."

After working in the hangar, Juarez made his way onto the top of the hangar by climbing up the few rungs that remained on one of the damaged ladders. From that vantage point he was able to get his first good view of the damaged ship. "From the topside of that hangar I could look forward on the ship and it looked like somebody got a can opener on both sides of the ship and just opened her up. That's just what it looked like." Returning his attention to the top of the hangar, Juarez remembers seeing many badly burned bodies strewn about. He then noticed a larger hole on top of the hangar. Peering though it he could see all the way down into the mess hall.

During the salvage operation Abe Santos retrieved Art McCann's body from below deck and brought it topside. "He weighed ... close to a hundred and eighty pounds," Santos said. "I weighed a hundred and eighteen. How I got him to topside I don't know."[12] In preparation for burial at sea, Santos rolled the body up in canvas. Finding sixty-eight dollars in his shirt pocket, he decided to leave the money with its rightful owner. "I just slipped it back in and let it go down with him," Santos said. "I even kissed him on the forehead before I covered his head."

* * *

While alongside the *Astoria*, the *Bagley* had an underwater sound contact off her port beam. As the destroyer moved away to investigate, the sailors on the back of the *Astoria* cheered, "Go get him."[13] As it turned out no definitive submarine contact could be established. After moving away from the cruiser, the *Bagley* did not return. She instead resumed her search and rescue work. She plucked additional survivors out of the water from all three northern force cruisers. The destroyer was only the first of several ships to come to the aid of the *Astoria*.

As the *Bagley* completed rescuing survivors in the water, she encountered an unknown destroyer minesweeper. It turned out to be the *Hopkins*. As the destroyer headed toward the transport area to offload survivors, the *Hopkins* was requested to stand by the *Astoria*.[14] An old World War I era destroyer modified for minesweeping duties, the venerable old *Hopkins* moved toward the cruiser.

As the *Hopkins* neared, Lieutenant Commander Benjamin Coe asked what assistance his vessel could provide. Greenman told him of his hopes to get the *Astoria* into shallow water and asked for a tow. Coe agreed to give it a try, but harbored doubts due the large size difference between the ships.[15] As the *Hopkins* slowly backed her stern up to the rear of the much larger *Astoria*, the cruiser's towing cable was passed over and fastened to the towing cleat. The first attempt to move forward failed when the cleat began to pull out from the deck. Moving back to the *Astoria*, Coe was soon ready for a second try. The cable was now wrapped around the after deckhouse of the *Hopkins*. Again the minesweeper slowly moved away, but this time the cable held. As a cheer went up from the men toiling to save her, the *Astoria* slowly began to move under tow from the *Hopkins*. After some initial problems were resolved, a speed of three knots was obtained. Pointed toward Guadalcanal, men on both ships began to believe that the cruiser could be beached.[16]

Men from the *Hopkins* passed aboard hoses and a gasoline pump to further help the firefighting effort. A power cable was also passed to the cruiser in the hopes that the power could be used to help the *Astoria* light off some of her boilers. "It was also planned to use the power to operate a submersible pump," Greenman added.[17] However, the plan to bring power failed owing to a difference in voltage of the systems aboard the two ships. Reporting through the *Hopkin's* radio, Greenman notified Admiral Turner of the condition of his ship and the hope that she could be saved if power and water were available to douse the remaining fires.

The report brought additional help in the form of another destroyer. The *Wilson* had spent a good amount of the morning rescuing survivors from the waters east of Savo Island. She had a total of 211 on board when she, along with the destroyer *Helm*, was directed to proceed toward the *Astoria*.[18] Arriving on station about two miles southeast of Savo Island, Lieutenant Commander Walter Price immediately noticed the fire in the vicinity of the *Astoria's* bridge area. At about 11:00 A.M. he brought his *Wilson* up to the starboard side of the cruiser to help in the firefighting effort.

As the *Wilson* moved close to put water on the flames, Lieutenant Healey was able to get a good look at his damaged ship. After jumping off the gun deck, Healy had been plucked out of the water by the destroyer. "I counted six five-inch holes on the starboard side below the upper deck," he later wrote. He noticed that the armor belt had been hit just below the number three five-inch gun mount and that there was plenty of damage spread around the ship. "All of the upper works of the ship was peppered with shrapnel holes."[19]

For almost an hour, the destroyer pumped water into the *Astoria* using all available hoses.[20] Additionally, the *Wilson* sent over a small work party to help in the salvage effort. With the exception of the stubborn fire in the wardroom area, some progress was being made in the salvage operation. The prospects for saving the *Astoria* now seemed pretty good. However, the optimism would be short lived.

* * *

Ed Armes missed the salvage operation entirely. After jumping off the starboard side of the *Astoria*, he made it onto the raft that he had spotted off in the distance. It turned out to be nothing more than a typical balsa wood raft that was usually found on the deck or hung on the side of a turret. It had a rope along the side and wood planks as the deck. Since the raft contained no paddles, any movement had to be done by hand. After picking up a few others, the raft soon contained six or seven men, most of whom were burned or otherwise wounded. Armes appeared to be the only able bodied man aboard.

Slowly drifting away from the *Astoria*, the burning cruiser began to fade from sight. Before long the raft was by itself, drifting along in the night. "It was pitch black," Armes recalled.[21] There was not enough room on the raft for all of the men to fit comfortably, so the men developed a rotating schedule where some would swim along side.

As the night wore on, there was disagreement among the survivors as to what to do. Some wanted to try to find a nearby island, while others wanted to take their chances by staying at sea. Someone sighted what was thought to be an island off in the distance. Armes recalled it as being nothing more than "a blur of an island." The men started to slowly paddle toward it. The movement was soon abandoned when someone realized that the land could be held by the Japanese.

Sometime after abandoning the idea of going to the island, a silhouette of a ship was sighted off in the distance. The vessel had a searchlight fanning out across the water. The men initially thought it was an American destroyer picking up survivors and started to yell in an effort to attract attention. Paddling closer, they could make out men on deck and then flashes of small arms fire. Men on the ship were shooting into the water. Armes quickly concluded that it was a Japanese ship shooting at survivors. "Let's get out of here," he told the others. They stopped yelling and slowly backpedaled away from the ship, which was still some distance away.

Armes later learned that some of the American destroyers involved in the rescue operation had men with rifles firing into the water in an effort to scare away sharks that were hovering near survivors. Dawn eventually broke revealing a foggy and misty air with limited visibility. Eventually, the destroyer *Bagley* came by and pulled the men to safety.

Chapter 24

Abandon Ship!

As the salvage crew aboard the *Astoria* fought to save the ship, medical personnel on the *Bagley* worked to save the wounded. The destroyer contained a large group of injured sailors who had been taken off the cruiser, as well as others from the *Quincy* and *Vincennes* that had been pulled from the water. After returning Captain Greenman and the salvage party to the *Astoria*, the destroyer pulled away to continue rescuing men from the water. By late morning she was en route back to the transport area.

The wounded men from the forecastle of the *Astoria* had been transferred by every possible means over to the *Bagley*. With the help of many hands, the medical staff used stretchers, cots, wood planks, and blankets to get the injured off the ship. Also transferring to the destroyer was the *Astoria*'s medical officer, Lieutenant Commander Charles Flower, and some of his staff. A large amount of medical supplies that had been assembled on the cruiser's forecastle was also taken aboard the destroyer. "Especially useful was the large number of battle dressings salvaged," Flower added.[1]

Flower and his men were joined by the *Bagley*'s small medical staff, including Lieutenant (jg) Paul Pickering, Chief Pharmacist's Mate Fredrick Barbee, and Pharmacist's Mate Second Class Leonard Benjamin. Totaling eight men, the medical party worked under extraordinary conditions to provide the best possible care with the meager resources that were available. Once on the *Bagley*, the injured were distributed to different parts of the ship based on the severity of their wounds. The most serious cases went to the wardroom.

To accommodate the emergency situation, the *Bagley*'s wardroom was turned into a makeshift operating room. A few large tables were moved together to form an operating table. Wounded men were brought in through the starboard entrance. Once an operation was completed, the patient was taken out of the port side door to await transfer elsewhere.

As burned, broken, and mangled bodies were sent into the wardroom, the medical staff worked feverishly to save lives. A number of ten gallon steel trash cans served as repositories for the bloody remnants of the emergency surgeries. Filled with amputated arms, legs, and feet, the cans were eventually tossed over the side. It was a series of horrific scenes: a pharmacist's mate cleaning out wounds and then applying sulfa before bandages; an officer being treated for a large gash across his midsection, with only the stomach lining left to hold in his intestines; and a leg being amputated with the patient only under local anesthesia. In the latter operation, Lieutenant Commander Flower used a hacksaw to cut through the bone.[2] The grisly scene was reminiscent of a butcher shop.[3]

For the less seriously wounded men aboard the destroyer, a temporary treatment station was set up in the mid-level head. With the help of some volunteers, a pharmacist's mate began to treat the walking injured. Wounds were carefully cleaned and bandaged before the men were sent on their way.

Making his way down to the *Bagley*'s wardroom, *Astoria* chaplain Matthew Bouterse did what he could to try to comfort the wounded. He seemed surrounded by horrific wounds and terrible suffering. "The officer whose breath rattled through a hole in his chest died as I watched over him," Bouterse later recalled. He saw Dr. Flowers working to sew the face back on of a sailor that he recognized as a friend. "Talking and praying with these critically wounded men," he remembered, "I began to get back some of my sanity." One of the medical men noticed the chaplain's limp and insisted that he be checked out. "In the presence of those others, I felt foolish taking up the doctor's time. I was to bury some of those men at sea a few days later."[4] After a brief checkup, a doctor concluded that his limp was not critical and gave Bouterse some ointment to soothe his burns. The chaplain could not help but think about the men who did not make it off the ship. "I thought of my shipmates still lying lifeless on our ship. At least they were beyond suffering now."

* * *

Among the wounded awaiting treatment aboard the *Bagley* was William Kuphaldt. He was initially taken to the wardroom. Since his wounds were not considered life threatening, he was placed in a waiting area. "I sat in the passageway outside the wardroom for what seemed like a very long time," he remembered. "Someone would check periodically to see if I was ok."[5]

After a long wait Kuphaldt was finally able to see a doctor. "The doctor removed the bandage, pried open my left eye, and inquired if I could see," he recalled. "To my great joy I said yes." The doctor decided to try to let the right eye heal in the hopes that his vision would be restored. "The wound through my nose was stitched and my head was again bandaged. I was then escorted to someone's bunk to try to rest." Kuphaldt vaguely remembers inquiring about the condition of the *Astoria* and being told that she was badly damaged, but still afloat.

An estimated 185 patients were treated aboard the *Bagley*, mostly from the *Astoria*. The total included fifty-seven major surgeries such as amputations and deep shrapnel wounds. Sixty men were treated who suffered from burns of various degrees of severity. The combined medical team was praised by the destroyer's executive officer for their "zeal, initiative, preparedness, and professional skill."[6] However, in spite of the best efforts put forth by the medical staff, not all of the wounded men could be saved.

Eight wounded men from the *Astoria* died aboard the *Bagley*. Among the dead were Chief Radioman Samuel Gladden and Seaman Second Class Roy Moon. Gladden died of shrapnel wounds but was able answer a few questions before he passed. He was remembered by shipmates as having drawn cartoons for the ship's newspaper, the *Astorian*.[7] Like in previous fights a shipmate had bet Moon before the battle began that the *Astoria* would make it through untouched. Moon clearly won the bet, but sadly he did not live to collect.[8] All of the bodies were buried at sea in a simple non-sectarian service that was conducted by the *Bagley*'s commanding officer. It was a mournful event attended by cruiser and destroyer men alike. "Tradition was carried out," George Sinclair simply noted in his report.[9]

The destroyer was so overloaded with survivors that John Powell was afraid she was going to capsize. "I ran up to the director, but then they started to pass the word for all of the survivors to get the hell down below." Most of the men who were use to being stationed below decks had no problem with the request. Powell was one who did not like the idea. "The engineers went down ... but I wasn't about to go down."[10] He stayed topside with Yeoman

McCampbell. The two were soon put to work helping the wounded. The doctor numbered every patient as to the order of urgency so that the volunteer helpers knew in what order to bring in the wounded. Powell and McCampbell carried men back and forth on either a plank or a stretcher through the narrow passageway that led to the wardroom. When not assisting the medical staff, the two simply tried to stay out of the way.

Once aboard the *Bagley* Roy Spurlock concluded that he was in a state of shock that was caused by the events that he had seen and participated in while aboard the *Astoria*. He searched for a warm place to rest. Eventually finding it between the stacks, he stayed there until dawn arrived. Daylight brought him a panoramic view of the damaged *Astoria*. "How anyone survived was a serious question."[11] He did not re-board the stricken ship.

* * *

Shortly before noon both the *Hopkins* and *Wilson* were called away from the *Astoria*, ordered to return to the transport area off Guadalcanal. At 11:45 A.M. the *Hopkins* dropped the tow line. About ten minutes later the *Wilson* shut off her fire hoses. The two ships, along with the *Helm*, began to leave the area. The *Astoria* was by no means being abandoned. The destroyer *Buchanan* and transport *Alchiba* had been dispatched to relive the departing ships. Operating with the cruiser *San Juan* well to the east of Savo Island, the *Buchanan* did not participate in the night battle. She was screening the transports off Tulagi when ordered to proceed toward the *Astoria*. She arrived on scene to continue the firefighting effort just after the *Wilson* had departed. Much larger and heavier than the *Hopkins*, the transport would pick up the tow line.

* * *

While the ships around her moved about, conditions on the *Astoria* began to take a turn for the worse. The stubborn fire in the wardroom began to increase with intensity. The list to port slowly increased to ten degrees as a series of small explosions were heard coming from deep below the forward part of the ship.

Early in the salvage operation, two large holes were noticed on the port side. Most likely the result of eight-inch shells, both were just above the main armor belt. One hole was about even with the forward stack, while the second was almost below the base of the catapult. Keeping these above the waterline was critical if the cruiser was to stay afloat. Lieutenant Commander Hayes and his men had been working diligently to plug the holes from the time they first ventured below deck. Mattresses and pillows had previously been forced into the openings, most likely by damage control personnel during the battle. Suitable materials to further reinforce the plugs could not be found. "Efforts were made to plug these to prevent water getting into the engineering spaces," Hayes recalled. "As the ship continued to list, these holes allowed serious flooding in the ship."[12]

At about this time Lieutenant Commander Topper heard a heavy explosion. It seemed to come from the area below and behind turret two. It was immediately followed by a small puff of yellow smoke that came out of a shell hole on the side of the ship and the sound of collapsing metal. Topper surmised it was the sound of collapsing bulkheads. He sent word of the events to the captain and executive officer, both of whom were on the after part of the ship. Checking his mark on the well deck confirmed that the list had increased.

Before moving onto the *Bagley* hours ago, Captain Greenman made known his doubts that the forward five-inch magazine had been flooded. Topper decided to try to investigate further. Moving onto the forecastle, he examined a hatch just behind turret one that was one of the last to be secured before departing on the *Bagley*. It was very hot. "I had discussed with [Chief Shipfitter Eros Vedrani] the best way to get down in the vicinity of the five-inch handling room," Topper remembered. "We decided that we would go down this hatch and fight fires aft so as to get to the flood valves of the forward five-inch handling room."[13] At about this time the forward part of the ship rumbled from another heavy internal explosion. Gas bubbles started coming to the surface off the port side about even with turret two. "A further rumbling noise was heard which possibly was the carrying away of more bulkheads below," Topper noted. He directed everyone to leave the forward part of the ship, before heading aft to personally report the situation to Greenman and Executive Officer Shoup. He noticed that the list was now increasing, a fact that was again confirmed as he passed his mark on the well deck. "The captain told me he believed that the ship would not last much more," Topper wrote, "and decided that we would make another attempt to extinguish fires in wardroom country and below with the assistance of the *Buchanan*." The destroyer was now approaching the *Astoria*'s starboard bow. Lieutenant Gibson led a small group forward to receive the ship and was soon joined by Greenman himself.

Sailors on the approaching destroyer noticed that the condition of the *Astoria* was worsening. "While maneuvering to go alongside," the *Buchanan*'s war diary recorded, "it was observed that she had taken [a] sharper list to port and was inclining rapidly."[14] With the list increasing, Topper conferred with the other senior officers at the back of the ship. "The executive officer, chief engineer, and myself, were of the opinion that the rate of list to port was so rapid that we had best make plans to abandon ship," Topper recalled. The trio went up to the forecastle and shared their concerns with the captain. Greenman agreed with the assessment and ordered all hands to return to the after part of the ship. "At that time the ship was listing so heavily," Greenman wrote, "that it was evident water was entering the holes in the second deck and she could not remain afloat much longer."

Commander Shoup also took note of the heavy explosions forward. He sensed that the ship was in trouble when the plugs gave way on the port side holes. "The salvage attempt might have succeeded," he speculated, "except for a fire raging in and below the wardroom country which defied all efforts to put it out."[15]

The *Buchanan* was directed to move to the starboard quarter to begin the evacuation of personnel. "Shortly after 12:00 [noon] the port waterway of the main deck was awash and the order was given to abandon ship," Greenman reported.[16] The *Buchanan* had not yet arrived in position and was standing about 300 hundred yards off the cruiser. Sailors aboard the *Astoria* scrambled to get off the sinking vessel in what was described by many as an orderly process. Jumping into the water, men swam toward the destroyer. A sailor summed up the feelings of many when he later stated, "We knew she was done for, but we sure hated to leave that ship."[17]

Many of the salvage crew had lifejackets. Some of those who did not clung to powder cans that had been tossed over the side. The only two remaining life rafts were also put to good use. Shoup went into the water just ahead of the captain when the ship was listing about forty-five degrees. "The port side of the main deck aft was under water almost to the barbette of turret three," he noticed as he left the ship, "and the starboard outboard propeller shaft was well out of the water."[18] The executive officer later wrote of how calm the crew seemed when it was time to leave the vessel. "When the ship was known to be doomed and was listing at an alarming angle, the men waited calmly and confidently for the order to abandon ship, and then went about it in an orderly manner."

Henry Juarez was still on top of the hangar when it came time to leave the ship. As he was surveying the area trying to figure out how he was going to get the bodies down to the main deck aft, he felt the tremor of a large blast deep below the waterline somewhere well forward. Almost immediately the ship started to list. When he heard someone yell "abandon ship," he knew it was time to leave the area. Using the same damaged ladder rungs that he had climbed up, he quickly descended back down to the main deck and headed back toward his gun mount. Still wearing his helmet, Juarez did not have his life jacket. "I left my life jacket down, because I couldn't fight fire with it," he remembered. "I put it somewhere, but somebody else got it."[19] On the main deck, Juarez had a brief encounter with Seaman Second Class Byron Hill. He knew him from boot camp back in Chicago. Hill was wearing both a life jacket and a life ring with the U.S.S. *Astoria* name on it. He had apparently survived the battle uninjured, but Juarez knew that he did not know how to swim. "He never made it," Juarez said, "I never saw him again."

By this time men were jumping off the ship. Things on deck were starting to slide as the list to port dramatically increased. Realizing that he was going to have to improvise a life jacket, Juarez rushed below deck to find a mattress. He knew how to swim, but did not want to take any chances. Below deck Juarez paused briefly when he noticed an eight-inch shell hole located right underneath his gun. "It's right underneath there and it went clear through." If the shell had been only a few feet higher, he might not have made it. With no time to speculate on what could have been, he found a mattress and returned topside. "I tied it into a ball with a quarter inch line, like a suitcase, and that was my life jacket." Juarez made his way all the way to the very back of the ship and stood there looking down. "It was going to be a long jump ... I was just making sure that there was no one down below me and somebody pushed me. I guess he thought I was scared. I was." Juarez either took his helmet off or it fell off as he hit the water.

Holding onto the mattress with all of his strength, Juarez hit the water off the stern of the *Astoria*. The water felt warm and refreshing. Thinking that he was going deep below, he paddled furiously to try to reach the surface. "I finally opened up my eyes and it's daylight." The buoyancy of the mattress had kept him from going more than a few feet underwater. "I started dog paddling, with the mattress ... and I kept looking back and that ship was rolling over." Juarez remembered that once in the water it was important to get as far away as possible from a sinking ship. "I started to swim and boy, I must've had a rooster tail because I passed everybody up," he said. "I didn't think about, you know, I was going to drown. The only thing was get away from the ship."

While paddling in the water, Juarez was able to catch a brief glimpse of a nearby ship that seemed to be heading his way. He began to think that he was moving too slow and that the sinking ship was going to pull him under. "So I let that mattress go," he said. "I just wanted to get away from the ship and I passed everybody up. I could feel the suction." The *Astoria* went down no more than two hundred feet away.

Henry Juarez was picked up by the *Buchanan* after spending about a half an hour in the water. "They threw me a life ring," he remembered.[20] The ring had a rope attached to it and the destroyer sailors pulled him aboard. "I was all wet, so I had to take all of my clothes off and air dry 'em." He does admit that he was ready to go back over the side when the destroyer later started dropping depth charges on a sub contact.

No longer on a bucket brigade, Don Yeamans became concerned about the *Astoria*'s fate while on the fantail. From his vantage point, he saw a large hole just above the waterline on the port side. When the cruiser was taken under tow from the stern, he observed water flooding into the hole. "I assumed it was an eight-inch shell hit," he recalled. "You could see the water rolling in like a river."[21] Before long the ship was getting lower in the water and some men started to get off. It looked to Yeamans that the *Astoria* was about to go down.

At the time Yeamans was in the company of Roy Radke, who did not know how to swim. As Yeamans made ready to get off the ship he quickly saw that Radke did not want to jump into the water. "I thought everyone in the navy knew how to swim," Yeamans said. He quickly found an empty five-inch shell casing. It was a silver tube with handles on each end. The two members of the quartermaster gang jumped into the water together, each holding onto one of the handles. Both were quickly picked up by the *Buchanan*.

Belcher Hobson waited until the captain gave the order to abandon ship and then jumped off the starboard side. Others near him did not wait and jumped off immediately after hearing the explosion. Hobson swam to the *Buchanan* and was soon plucked out of the water.

Gene Alair was standing near the after 1.1-inch machine gun mounts when the abandon ship order was given. He remembers that there was no panic when Captain Greenman gave the order. With the ship listing heavily to port, most men went over the starboard side. "Some of the crew who appeared hesitant to jump were locked into the arms of more confident shipmates," Alair said. "It seemed to be an orderly departure and an attitude of quiet confidence seemed common."[22] Jumping over the starboard side, Alair was not wearing a life jacket. He remembered that water surface was calm with some amount of oil near the hull and a large amount of debris floating about.

Fully clothed, Alair took off his shoes and swam to a small group of men who were huddled around a piece of a wooden crate. "I don't recall that any of them had a life jacket and we didn't have any life rafts," he remembered. Alair soon grabbed a floating life jacket and gave it to two nearby men who appeared to be wounded. "Eventually I grabbed a five-inch powder can." After being in the water for less than an hour, the group was approached by a whaleboat. It was overloaded, but was able to take aboard two injured men. "The coxswain was a pretty smart kid," Alair said. "He threw out lines and he must have had three or four lines that he had secured. We just hung onto those lines." The men eagerly grabbed on and were towed to the *Buchanan*. After letting the wounded get on board first, Alair grabbed onto a strap that was hanging over the destroyer about amidships. "I remember two guys just virtually pulling me right out of the water and right up onto the deck."

Carpenter's Mate Second Class John Fritz believes that he was the last to get off the sinking *Astoria*. He was getting ready to jump off when he noticed that one of the screws was starting to come out of the water. "I stood there to direct the men to jump forward of where I was standing so they wouldn't jump onto the screw," he later wrote.[23] Someone shouted for him to jump. "I looked around the fantail and realized that I was alone, so by then the ship was listing so badly that I just walked down the side and into the water. I had the rather dubious honor of being the last man off the ship."

The *Astoria* gently rolled over on her port side, settled slightly by the stern, and began to go under. The bow rose a few feet in the air as the gallant cruiser disappeared beneath the waves. It was exactly 12:15 P.M. The war diary of the *Buchanan* recorded that the *Astoria* sank in sixty fathoms of water, which converts to a depth of about 360 feet. The destroyer immediately put two whaleboats and three life rafts in the water to help with the rescue effort. The *Buchanan* then moved about pulling men up out of the water.

By this time the *Alchiba* had arrived on the scene and also began picking up survivors. She would rescue a total of thirty-two. While the rescue was in progress, the *Buchanan* made an underwater sound contact about 1,500 yards away. She rushed away and dropped two 600 pound depth charges, but the results were negative. Returning to the rescue area, she picked up the remaining survivors, including Captain Greenman. At 12:40 P.M. the destroyer then headed for the transport area. The entire salvage crew was saved.

Chapter 25

Survivors

As he sped away from the Guadalcanal area, Admiral Mikawa fully expected to be struck by American carrier planes. However, the attack never materialized. The admiral had no way of knowing that the American carriers were out of position. Although he did not attack the transports as planned, Mikawa had successfully executed his daring plan and won a tremendous victory.

On the approach to Bougainville Island, Mikawa directed four of his heavy cruisers to proceed to Kavieng. Further northwest, the ships would be sheltered from the air attacks that seemed to be plaguing Rabaul. The *Aoba, Kako, Kinugasa,* and *Furutaka* separated and set a course accordingly. As the four ships continued on in a single column, they came under the watchful eye of Lieutenant Commander John Moore in the old submarine *S-44*. Carefully tracking the ships, he decided to attack the last cruiser in the column and maneuvered into position as the first three ships passed by. When the last ship was only 700 yards away, Moore fired a spread of four torpedoes. His target was the *Kako*. It was close enough for the submariner to see the Japanese standing on the ship's bridge.[1] Three torpedoes slammed into the cruiser hitting her on the starboard bow, amidships, and near the stern. The *Kako* listed heavily before sinking quickly.[2] Moore took his sub deep and slipped away leaving in his wake the noises of the heavy cruiser in her death throes. A small amount of revenge had just been extracted for the Savo Island loss. Not yet knowing about the sinking of the *Kako*, Admiral Mikawa entered Rabaul to the sound of cheers.

* * *

After being hit by a torpedo and a single shell, the *Chicago*'s participation in the battle was for all practical purposes over. As the Japanese heavy cruisers moved north and east, Captain Bode kept the *Chicago* heading in a westerly direction. At no point did he seem concerned with trying to find the Japanese ships that had torpedoed him. At about 1:49 A.M. the cruiser sighted something. "A ship ahead believed to be the *Patterson*," Bode later wrote, "illuminated with searchlight two targets which appeared to be destroyers on the port bow."[3] The destroyer was in fact the *Patterson*. At the time she was firing at the light cruisers *Tenryu* and *Yubari*. However, it was the light cruisers who were using their searchlights to illuminate the destroyer.[4]

About a minute later the port five-inch battery opened fire on one of the enemy ships at an estimated range of 7,200 yards. At the same time the starboard five-inch guns fired a spread of star shells. A short time later the *Patterson* reversed course and crossed the line of fire just as the Japanese extinguished their searchlights and changed course. The director that was tracking the target then lost it. "The port battery ceased firing, having expended twenty-five rounds," Bode recorded. "Observed burst of one hit on target." The hit was most likely on the *Tenryu*, which reported being damaged at about this time.[5] At the same time the main battery director was unsuccessful in trying to get a fix on one of the dark objects previously sighted beyond the *Canberra*.

Bode then spotted a gun battle off to the northward, but made no attempt to approach it. The *Chicago* continued on a westward course at a speed of twelve knots sighting at least one friendly destroyer during the time. The forward main battery director was unable to train aft of the beam at this time most likely due to interference from the mast that was bent in by the reverberation of the torpedo blast.

Repair parties were kept busy at the forward part of the ship. "Shoring of bulkheads and hatches was in progress," Bode noted of this time. The *Chicago* did not seem in danger of sinking.

At 1:54 A.M. the *Chicago* completed decoding a message to withdraw toward the transport area. Before any action could be taken, two unidentified ships were sighted exchanging fire west of Savo Island. When the ships disappeared behind the island, Bode decided to investigate further and continued west. After about five minutes, the starboard five-inch guns opened fire with a spread of starshells. No further action was taken once the ships were determined to be out of range. What Bode actually observed was most likely the brief exchange of fire that took place between the withdrawing *Jarvis* and the *Yunagi*, the latter destroyer having turned back just as the Japanese cruiser force swung around Savo Island.

At one point the *Chicago* saw heavy gunfire near Savo Island. Captain Bode ordered the ship steered in that direction. Speed was increased to twenty knots when an unidentified destroyer was sighted off the starboard beam. "This destroyer had been tracked by radar for several minutes prior to that time," Bode recorded. No orders to open fire were given, but when the strange ship turned on a searchlight, two of the cruiser's five-inch guns fired off under the direction of the gun captains. The firing was quickly halted with a cease fire order from the bridge. When the destroyer was seen to return fire, the *Chicago* guns again opened up only to be quickly silenced by another cease fire order. The enemy was soon identified as the *Patterson*. The destroyer at this time reported seeing a strange ship approaching that resembled the *Chicago*. The brief fight ended almost as quickly as it began. Fortunately, neither ship was able to score a hit.

At about 3:00 A.M. the *Chicago* was joined by the *Patterson*, who took up a position off her starboard bow. The cruiser was now facing the Guadalcanal transport area that was about nine miles away. Bode directed the *Patterson* to stand by the *Canberra*. The stricken cruiser requested that the destroyer come along side to help fight fires, but then signaled, "You had better wait."[6] The danger posed by exploding ammunition was too great. Fierce fires were raging on the Australian cruiser with frequent violent explosions erupting. The heavy rain that was now falling did not seem to be putting a dent into the flames. An occasional clap of thunder and flash of lightning added an eerie backdrop to the scene.

Just after 4:00 A.M. the *Patterson* was able to move up to the starboard side of the *Canberra*. As the destroyer men passed over hoses and pumps, they in turn began to receive wounded from the cruiser. About an hour later the fate of the *Canberra* was sealed in the form of a radio message that the *Patterson* received from Admiral Turner reporting that the remaining ships would be leaving the Guadalcanal area during the morning hours. A second report followed almost immediately: "If *Canberra* cannot join retirement in time she should be destroyed before departure."[7]

Both the *Chicago* and *Patterson* moved toward the *Canberra*, which was now listing about twenty degrees to starboard. With the *Patterson* soon departing for the transport area loaded with survivors, Captain Bode hailed the nearby destroyer *Blue*. He directed her to take off the remaining survivors. The *San Juan* then ordered the *Chicago* to join her in the area off the yoke transports. "*Blue, Selfridge, Patterson* standing by *Canberra*," Bode reported to Crutchley. "Am proceeding to concentration area."[8] Satisfied with the performance of his crew during the events of the evening, Captain Bode noted that "all personnel performed their duties with calmness, deliberation, and efficiency."

The *Chicago* arrived off the transports at about 7:00 A.M., but had to slow down to ten knots due to the strain that high speeds were putting on the damaged bulkheads.[9] A visual message from Crutchley sent the cruiser heading in the direction of the *Australia*. "Shortly thereafter assumed designated position in screen of x-ray group," Bode reported.[10] In the meantime two destroyers set about trying to sink the abandoned *Canberra* with gunfire. A torpedo from the destroyer *Ellet* finally sent the *Canberra* to the bottom at 8:00 A.M.[11]

After patrolling near the transports for most of the day, by 3:30 P.M. the *Chicago* was under way heading southeast through the Lengo Channel on route to New Caledonia. The mangled lower portion of the bow was clearly visible just above the waterline. "We were leaving, making a wake of over a half a mile in width because of that wreckage," recalled Art King. "It was all lying over to the port side."[12] Charles Germann was able to get his first

A diver inspects the damaged bow of the *Chicago* one day after the Battle of Savo Island. The torpedo blast mangled the lower portion of the bow and sent up a towering column of water (U.S. Navy / courtesy National Archives).

look at the damaged bow the morning after the battle. He along with several others from the aviation unit decided to have a look before breakfast. "I sneaked up there and took a look," he said. "Stuff was floating out, small stores were floating by."[13]

Word had spread among the enlisted men that the ship was headed south. Leaving the battle zone gave the *Chicago* sailors time to reflect on the hectic events of the previous three days. "We had no idea what had happened that night," recalled Fred Tuccitto. "It was a slaughter."[14] Tuccitto was still hurting from being hit in the mouth with a five-inch shell during the battle. "On the morning after the battle I went to the ship's dental office," he continued. "The doctor pulled out the root of my tooth and patched my lip." Although more dental work would be needed, the visit was a first step towards recovery. "My eating habits came to a dramatic halt," he remembered. "My smile disappeared along with my front teeth."

* * *

Even as the battle subsided, Admiral Crutchley did not have a firm grasp of what had taken place. Having decided not to rejoin the southern force after his midnight meeting off Guadalcanal, he instead patrolled near the transports in anticipation of the screen being reformed at dawn. When he saw flares off in the distance shortly before 2:00 A.M., Crutchley assumed that the subsequent gunfire was from ships firing at an airplane. About five minutes later he observed that some type of action was taking place. "The gunfire was very heavy, and I thought it must have been the *Vincennes* group coming into action against an enemy being engaged by the *Australia* group," Crutchley recalled. He received no reports from any of his ships. "I was completely ignorant of the number or the nature of the enemy force and the progress of the action being fought."[15] Crutchley positioned the *Australia* on a patrol line seven miles west of the Guadalcanal landing zone so as to "intercept any enemy which got through our cruiser screen, before he could reach the transports."

When he still did not receive any reports from his cruisers, Crutchley sent out a message at 2:26 A.M. to the *Chicago*, *Vincennes*, and *San Juan* asking if they were in battle. "Were but not now," was the brief response sent by Captain Bode. No reply came from the *Vincennes*. Admiral Scott aboard the *San Juan* replied that his force was not in action, but that a battle seemed to be taking place between Savo and Florida Islands. At 2:42 A.M. Crutchley asked the *Chicago* to report on the current situation. Bode responded that his ship was heading toward Lengo Channel. Only minutes later he added, "Hit by torpedo slightly down by bow. Enemy ships firing seaward."[16] The *Chicago* captain also advised that the *Canberra* was burning and had two destroyers standing by her.

Although visibility in the direction of Savo Island was partially obscured by bad weather, Admiral Turner could see enough to determine that something was happening. From the bridge of his flagship, *McCawley,* he caught sight of an occasional gun flash and explosion.[17] It must have been no surprise when Turner received Crutchley's message just after 3:00 A.M. "Surface action near Savo. Situation as yet undetermined."[18]

As the details of the disastrous night battle began to emerge, Turner had to decide what to do with his remaining ships. During the midnight meeting of commanders, he had already decided that the transports would pull out sometime during the day. In addition to not having air cover, Turner now also had to contend with damaged ships and many wounded sailors who needed better attention than what could be provided in the Guadalcanal area. General Vandegrift hoped to delay the departure as long as possible so that more supplies could be unloaded. The transports continued to offload supplies during the morning hours.

By late afternoon Turner could wait no longer. He decided that all of the remaining ships would leave the area due to the threat of additional air attacks.[19] Led by the damaged *Chicago*, the transports, and escort ships began to move away from Lunga Point at 6:30 P.M. Almost two hours later, the Tulagi transports began to move out. The latter group, which included the flagship *McCawley*, cleared Lengo Channel at 9:45 P.M. and set a course for Noumea, New Caledonia.[20] In the meantime Admiral Fletcher's carriers spent the day moving southeast toward a refueling point near Espiritu Santo. News of the battle first reached the carrier force at about 3:00 A.M., but the admiral offered nothing in the way of assistance.[21]

The departure of Task Force 62 was the closing act in the Savo Island battle. Most of the Marines were ashore, but a considerable amount of their heavy equipment and about half of their supplies were still on board the transports.[22] With no support from the sea or air, the Marines were now truly alone.

The Battle of Savo Island was a stinging defeat that is generally considered the worst beating ever suffered by the United States Navy in battle. Back at Pearl Harbor, Chester Nimitz was grasping for answers. He could not understand how his ships could have been so soundly defeated. Nimitz was not the only one looking for answers. The Chief of Naval Operations, Admiral Ernest King, wanted to get to the bottom of the matter as well. News of the defeat was suppressed, postponed to be released at a later date.

In the aftermath of the battle, King directed Admiral Arthur Hepburn to conduct a special investigation of the matter. Completed in 1943, the report determined that surprise was the key reason for the devastating defeat and cited a host of contributory factors. The list included: an inadequate state of readiness among the various ships involved, over reliance on radar, ineffective air reconnaissance, and failures in communications. Both Crutchley and Turner escaped criticism in the report. After reviewing the document, King agreed with the recommendation of an aide to consider the matter closed.[23] After all, there was a war to fight. A more comprehensive analysis of the battle was conducted by the United States Naval War College after the war using both American and Japanese sources.

* * *

By 8:00 P.M. on August 10, the *Chicago* was located about 150 miles off the southeastern tip of San Cristobal Island. She had cleared the Solomon Islands and was in the open waters of the Pacific. The next morning various groups of Task Force 62, which had been proceeding independently since leaving the Guadalcanal area, joined to form one large armada. At the same time the *Chicago* and destroyers *Mugford* and *Patterson* assumed the designation of Task Unit 62.6.2. On orders from Turner, the unit separated from the main formation and proceeded independently toward Noumea.[24] By the end of the day, the trio was traveling roughly parallel to the west coast of Espiritu Santo. Looping around the southwest tip of New Caledonia, the ships entered the harbor at Noumea during the morning hours of August 14.

* * *

By the early afternoon of August 9, three destroyers were on route to the transport area off Guadalcanal carrying *Astoria* survivors along with a few men rescued from the *Quincy* and *Vincennes*. Although fast and nimble for rescue operations, the destroyers did not offer a good home for survivors owing to their tight spaces and cramped conditions. All of the passengers would be transferred to the larger transport ships that had carried the Marines to Guadalcanal.

The *Bagley*, carrying about 400 men including many wounded, was the first to arrive in the transport area. She pulled alongside the *President Jackson* to affect the transfer of the survivors. The *Wilson* moved almost 160 survivors to the *Hunter Liggett*. Just before 2:00

P.M. the *Buchanan* became the last destroyer to arrive with survivors. She off loaded the rescued salvage crew to the *President Jackson*. In addition to the group on the *Alchiba*, a small number of *Astoria* men ended up on the *Neville, American Legion,* and *McCawley*.[25] Among the survivors transferred off destroyers were Theodore Torsch and George Douglas. Both had been rescued after spending hours in the water.

Abe Santos remembered that the destroyer to transport transfer was accomplished with a dunk into the ocean. Able bodied survivors jumped off the destroyer that they were aboard and swam over to a nearby transport, which had a large cargo net hanging over her side. "It's like almost climbing a five story building," Santos recalled. "It was chaos, just crazy."[26]

One *Astoria* survivor who arrived at the transports ahead of the destroyers was John Powell. When the *Bagley* was off the stern of the *Astoria,* a landing craft pulled alongside to start the transfer of men to the transports. With Yeoman McCampbell in tow, Powell jumped on board. The small boat took them to the *President Jackson*. "They fed us a good meal and gave us a place to sleep," he said. "And we all went to sleep."[27]

The *President Jackson* was completed in 1940 as an ocean liner for the American President Line. Before being acquired by the navy, she completed two around the world cruises from New York City. On her voyage south from Guadalcanal, she was evacuating almost 500 survivors from the Savo Island battle and wounded Marines from the land fighting. She became the temporary home for many *Astoria* survivors, both officers and enlisted men. The transport departed for New Caledonia with the rest of Task Force 62. For the unwounded enlisted survivors there was not much to do to pass the time. The officers went to work almost immediately trying to organize the remnants of the *Astoria*'s crew.

It was on the *President Jackson* that Captain Greenman began the process of reconstructing the night action. Senior officers interviewed individuals, gathered information, and wrote notes. Others began to compile muster rolls of survivors. Ultimately, all of the information was combined into a large report that Greenman issued to his superiors. The captain also kept abreast of how his wounded men were doing through regular reports from the ship's doctor.

Roy Spurlock, John Powell, Abe Santos, Gene Alair, and Matthew Bouterse all ended up as passengers on the *President Jackson*. Spurlock, along with the other guest marine aviators from the *Astoria*, was directed to a comfortably appointed stateroom which was a throwback to the ship's days as a luxury cruise liner. As the transport steamed south, Spurlock had little to do but to talk with other survivors about what had happened the night before. For him the trip to New Caledonia marked the end of his sea duty around Guadalcanal. "Why I was spared when so many were not," he wondered, "is a mystery to me."[28]

John Powell just tried to find a comfortable place to stay out of the way. While he remembers many men being on board the ship, it did not seem overly crowded. He recalled that the survivors were given two meals a day.

Abe Santos remembered being so busy during the actual battle that the effects of the fighting did not hit him until afterwards. "You know during the battle you don't have time to think," he said. "After every battle that we were in ... after about the third day you find a little corner and that's when you go into shock because you can't visualize what's going on. You are so busy."[29]

Santos later passed the time aboard the transport by helping the corpsmen tend to the wounded. He remembers one particular burn patient who was in bad shape. Sitting on a lower bunk with his legs spread apart, the wounded man was unable to talk. "He was so bad," Santos said, "part of his ears were gone, part of his lips were gone, part of his eyelids were gone." The man was just one of many gravely wounded sailors who did not survive. Santos speculates that there were many like him. "A lot of guys we saw aboard [the transport] and we never saw after," he recalled. Another man was missing an arm and had his chest ripped open to the point where Santos saw his internal organs. A third sailor was lying motionless, apparently dead. "It's hard to talk about it," he said, "because it was so horrible."

Gene Alair remembered the confusion among the survivors aboard the transport. "We spent time trying to get organized," he recalled. "Greenman was on that same ship, and he eventually took over so that he could get us organized in to divisions."[30] Alair directed Boatswain's Mate First Class Homer Hoberock to start recording the names of everyone that he recognized from the *Astoria* on a muster sheet. "He knew all of the enlisted men in our division. We found a lot of them." Alair worked with other officers in compiling the initial survivors list. "They had a lot of casualties that were taking up all of the housing, so we didn't get quarters." Alair thinks that he probably just slept on the deck. However, he did get to eat down in the general mess area. "They were doing their best under an adverse situation," he said of the transport's crew.

Once on the *President Jackson*, Matthew Bouterse was sent down to the sick bay to rest. After a short time he opted to go topside instead. As he came out of the shock of battle he thought about one of his prized possessions that went down with the ship, a Bible given to him by the congregation of his church back in Kentucky. He slept every night on the forecastle until the ship pulled into New Caledonia. Once ashore he was able to find an army chaplain. "He very kindly sent a note to my wife stating he had seen me and that she would be hearing from me soon."[31]

Among the wounded transferred to the *President Jackson* were William Kuphaldt and Tom Ferneding. Kuphaldt remembered arriving on the transport sometime after daylight. "The transfer was accomplished by placing me in a basket stretcher," he later wrote, "which was lifted by a cargo boom to the deck of the *President Jackson*." He was placed in the sick bay where he joined other wounded men who were arranged in rows of cots. "For the first few days I needed help to do everything," he recalled, "because my entire head was bandaged."[32] When Fireman Third Class James Hughes happened by to visit, he offered to help Kuphaldt send a postcard home to inform his parents that he was all right. "We were concerned that word of the *Astoria*'s fate could have been in the news at home," Kuphaldt remembered, "and our parents would be concerned about our welfare." Neither man had any way of knowing that the news of the *Astoria*'s sinking would be kept secret for weeks. After a few days in the sick bay, Kuphaldt was transferred to a stateroom to convalesce. He was able to see pretty well out of his left eye, but his right eye still needed to be covered. A corpsman came by to check him on a regular basis.

It was not long after Tom Ferneding came aboard the transport that he was visited by an unexpected well wisher, his twin brother, John. "Thumbs up, Ferneding," was the initial greeting that the wounded man received from his sibling.[33] The two had not seen each other for months. "Each of us knew the other was in the battle, but we hadn't seen each other since we left Dayton to begin sea duty."[34] John Ferneding did more than wish his brother a speedy recovery. He directly affected it by giving him a quart of his own blood, a move that the wounded Ferneding credited with saving his life. The chance meeting did not last long, as Tom Ferneding was soon on his way back to Pearl Harbor.

As the voyage south continued, some of the injured survivors began to succumb to their wounds. There was at least one burial service a day during the trip, held at the fantail. Captain Greenman and Executive Officer Shoup attended each ceremony.[35]

William Kuphaldt was able to attend at least one of the services. He remembered it as a sad and solemn occasion. "The body was sewn in a canvas bag, weighted, placed on a stretcher, and covered with an American flag." With the sound of taps playing in the background, the stretcher was tilted just enough for the body to slide out from under the flag and into the deep. "To this day when I hear taps played I am reminded of that event," he later wrote.

* * *

After a short stay in Noumea, Matthew Bouterse boarded the transport *Wharton* for the trip back to Pearl Harbor. The ship was filled with *Astoria* survivors, some of whom were gravely wounded and dying. As the survivors' chaplain, Bouterse attended each burial at sea. "As long as I live I will never forget the sound of that canvas covered body sliding over the rail," he later wrote, "as taps was sounded by the ship's bugler." Later in the voyage, a memorial service was held for all of the sailors who perished in the Savo Island battle. When one man started to sing the whole group started to cry. "Men seldom have the privilege of publicly shedding tears together unashamedly as we did that day," Bouterse recalled. "It was a fitting memorial to a great ship and the greatest of crews." Bouterse could not help but wonder about the fate of some of his friends from the Bible study group, in particular its leader. Although the exact circumstances of his last minutes are not known, Vic McAnney did not survive the sinking of the *Astoria*. He most likely perished at his battle station, an ammunition hoist not too far from the chaplain's stateroom.

For the men of the *Astoria,* the voyage to Guadalcanal was over. Surviving the sinking was mostly likely a defining moment in their lives and one that would surely not be forgotten anytime soon. For the *Chicago* sailors surviving the battle was a second chance and a new beginning.

Part Four

The Final Voyage of the Chicago

"We just knew that we were going back to the war zone."[1]
Howard Fortney
Electrician's Mate First Class
U.S.S. *Chicago*

Chapter 26

Stateside

The short stay at New Caledonia allowed for emergency repairs to be completed on the *Chicago's* damaged bow. Work began immediately as the cruiser moored next to the repair ship *Argonne*. Divers quickly descended into the water to access the extent of the damage. "They cut as much of the wreckage away as they could with underwater equipment," remembered Art King.[1] The damaged anchor chain, which had dangled dangerously close to a minefield as the ship entered the harbor, was hoisted out of the water, and placed on deck.

Workers inside the forward compartments toiled to plug leaks and stabilize damaged bulkheads. "Upon arrival in port compartment A-402-A was pumped dry by means of an electric submersible pump," Captain Bode later wrote. "All stores and some shelving was then removed and the leak plugged. A cofferdam was then built around the leak and filled with cement."[2] Bulkheads on the second, third, and fourth decks that abutted the damaged bow were strengthened. On one deck steel plating was welded directly onto the bulkhead. Brackets were installed on other bulkheads to act as stiffeners. Bode noted that the repair work, "proceeded with the utmost dispatch, with calm purposeful determination." The captain considered the result a "commendable practical accomplishment." After a seven day stay, the cruiser put to sea and set a course for Australia.

The *Chicago* pulled into Sydney Harbor on the morning of August 28. Two days later she entered the drydock on Cockatoo Island.[3] Yard workers quickly began the task of installing a temporary bow. The true extent of the ship's damage now became visible. "The hole in the starboard side is approximately forty-four feet long by twelve feet high," noted Captain Bode. A slightly smaller hole existed on the port side.

It was not long before another discovery was made. "Upon drydocking, it was found that what is believed to have been a torpedo struck the ship, without exploding," Bode wrote. "It appears that the torpedo hit with a glancing blow from a sharp angle on the bow."[4] The weapon hit the starboard side of the ship even with the after engine room and left little more than an indentation.

Fred Tuccitto was still hurting from having his front teeth knocked loose during the night of the battle. He was hoping to get help now that the ship had made port. "I asked the dentist aboard ship if I could have something done to stabilize my teeth so I could eat," Tuccitto later wrote. "He recommended a dentist in Sydney. I was given permission to have a civilian dentist put in a bridge." The *Chicago* sailor soon found the dental resources on shore were meager, but understood the situation given that the Australians had been at war for almost three years. "The dentist had no sedatives. He told me to down six shots of whisky to soothe the pain." Tuccitto was unsuccessful in trying to get the navy to pick up the bill. "I had to pay out of my pocket," he continued. "The dentist in Sydney gave me a

The *Chicago*'s damaged bow is seen on August 14, 1942, after the cruiser pulled into Noumea, New Caledonia. It was the first stop in a long journey that ended at the Mare Island Navy Yard near San Francisco (U.S. Navy / National Archives).

break because we were fighting to save Australia from a Japanese invasion. The bill came to $24.00."[5]

Another *Chicago* sailor was hoping to get a pay raise. "My enlistment expired while we were in drydock in Sydney," Don Wallace wrote. "Remembering the item in my shipping papers about the additional pay due if I was retained beyond my normal expiration of enlistment, I went to the disbursing office to see what forms I needed to fill out or what action was necessary on my part to get that twenty-five percent additional."[6] He was soon disappointed to learn that the provision was suspended just after Pearl Harbor.

Some of the sailors wondered if the ship would be making a quick return to battle after the patchwork repairs. However, the crew soon learned that the *Chicago* was headed stateside. With her temporary bow installed, the cruiser pulled out of Sydney on September 21 for a long voyage across the Pacific. Although there were several scheduled stops along the way, her ultimate destination was the Mare Island Navy Yard near San Francisco.

* * *

The *Chicago* entered San Francisco Bay at sunrise on October 13. After discharging fuel, she moored at the ammunition dock to offload her shells. Two days later she entered the number two drydock to commence an overhaul and make permanent repairs to the bow.[7] The place where the cruiser was constructed little more than twelve years ago, Mare

Island was now a sprawling shipyard. The time spent at Mare Island was an opportunity for the crew to rest and recharge from the arduous task of war.

Ken Maysenhalder did not like the idea of staying on the ship. "There was a lot of bad feelings because we had to stay on board the ship and the ship was full of welding lines," he recalled. "They were working on the ship at the same time as we were trying to live on the ship. But the talk was that Captain Bode wouldn't allow us to go in and live in the barracks, so we had to stay on board."[8]

Maysenhalder was now a storekeeper third class. Part of a group that was responsible for controlling supplies, he worked out of a small office on the main deck just forward of the aviation area. "There was plenty to do," he noted. "We had two or three men in there with typewriters and we were making out requisitions and taking care of the stores." Maysenhalder himself spent much of his time "making out invoices for supplies that the ship would need once we were out to sea."

Charles Germann and the rest of the aviation unit left the ship for Alameda Naval Air Station near Oakland. "It was mostly a place to get us off the ship," he recalled. He passed time working on the planes. "Routine maintenance and stuff like that."[9] Germann received a ten day leave, which he used to go back home to Iowa and get married to his childhood sweetheart. The wedding bliss continued after he was able to secure a five day extension.

Don Wallace was now working as a yeoman. Not liking the harsh conditions under Captain Bode, he decided to try to leave. "I requested a transfer so that I could go to yeoman school to learn shorthand," Wallace remembered. "This was a requirement for advancement to first class." For added emphasis, he wrote a page and a half memo outlining his request and presented it to Executive Officer Adell. The request was denied with Adell responding, "Wallace, you aren't going to get off this pig boat until I do."

Howard Fortney was given a ten day leave during the time in port. He traveled back home to Clarksburg, West Virginia. It had been almost forty-seven months since he had been back to his home state.[10]

As part of the overhaul, many flammable materials were removed from the ship. Bill Grady helped with the effort. He recalled linoleum and cork being cut out and removed. It was such materials that helped fuel the belching fires aboard the doomed cruisers off Savo Island only a few months ago.

* * *

While the *Chicago* was being repaired and refurbished, a steady stream of new crewmen were assigned to the ship. There seemed to be a never ending need for additional manpower to operate the ever increasing amount of new anti-aircraft guns and radar equipment. Working under the executive officer, Don Wallace was one of men responsible for keeping track of the personnel changes. "We had almost a thousand personnel changes," he wrote of the time. "What with people being transferred, new ones coming on board, sending men to schools, etc." Keeping up with all the changes seemed to be a full time job.

* * *

Frank Dinovo joined the navy in October 1942 from Council Bluffs, Iowa. "The war broke out and I thought well, I am going to have to go one time or another, and I'd rather go into the navy," he said of his decision. "So I joined the navy."[11] Like many wartime enlistees, he went for an extremely short boot camp at Great Lakes. "I had nine days of training when ordinarily they had three months. Ours was cut exceptionally short." After going home for a ten day leave, Dinovo found himself on a train headed for San Francisco and an assignment on the *Chicago*.

The cruiser was still in drydock when Dinovo stepped aboard his new home. "The biggest thing that I ever seen was a motorboat in a lake we have in town," he recalled of the moment. "I thought, oh my god, what a huge thing." Told to stack their sea bags, Dinovo and other newly boarded recruits were free to roam around the ship until their names were called for duty assignments. He made his way to the upper decks where he found a sailor busy at work in the radio shack. "I poked my head in there because he had a chair sitting on top of a desk and he's working with all these wires. I thought that was kind of fascinating, so I stood there and watched him." The sailor soon noticed Dinovo and asked if he was a new recruit. "A new recruit wore his hat the regulation way and not like old salts," Dinovo continued. "So he knew I was a recruit without even asking me." In conversation, the two sailors learned that they were both from Iowa.

It did not take long for the radioman to ask if Dinovo wanted to work with him. The recruit jumped at the opportunity. "You stay right here, don't leave," the radioman instructed. "I'll find my commander. It might take me ten or twenty minutes, but I will be back." The radioman came back in about twenty minutes with good news. "You're in. You are going to be working for me. They won't even call your name out, but go down and get your sea bag a little later. I will get somebody to assign you a bunk."[12] Dinovo spent much of the next few weeks confined to the radio shack learning the ropes and working to ensure that each piece of newly installed radio equipment was correctly wired and working properly.

On November 27, with her new bow installed, the *Chicago* moved from the drydock to a pier to complete her overhaul.[13] The cruiser's anti-aircraft armament had been greatly supplemented. The ship now mounted sixteen of the new forty-millimeter guns and twenty of the smaller twenty-millimeter mounts.[14] Fire control radar was upgraded to the most advanced model. The CXAM surface search radar was moved from the main mast to the foremast. It would not be long before the *Chicago* would be headed back to war.

There was more than just equipment changing aboard the *Chicago*; December brought a new captain. After leading the ship for almost a full year, Captain Howard Bode was relieved of his command. Taking over leadership of the cruiser was fifty-one-year-old Captain Ralph Otis Davis. An Illinois native, he graduated from the Naval Academy

Frank Dinovo boarded the *Chicago* in late 1942 while the ship was undergoing repairs in California. He did not know what to expect when the ship headed back to war in early 1943 (courtesy Frank Dinovo).

in 1914.¹⁵ The next two decades saw Davis serving on a variety of vessels ranging from battleships to submarines. He served as the executive officer of the heavy cruiser *Indianapolis* in the late 1930s. During the first year of World War II, Davis was serving at the Naval Academy in an administrative capacity. The *Chicago* was his first wartime command, and he would soon be getting his first taste of action.

* * *

During the time at Mare Island, Art King was to feel the wrath of Captain Bode one last time. King used his leave to go home to Louisville in December. "I think it was eight days leave. Well, I was late getting back," he explained. With the help of a naval officer stationed at a local manufacturing plant, King was able to get a priority status for his return flight to San Francisco. He flew various routes before ending up stranded in Denver due to bad weather. Unable to catch a train due to the winter conditions, he sent a telegram to the ship. The priority status allowed King to catch the first flight out the next morning. "I think I reported aboard the ship at about 11:45 [P.M.]. I was due at eight o'clock that morning." The officer of the deck mentioned the possibility of putting King into the brig for the night. "I'm pretty sure he was kidding me, but I wasn't that sure of things by that time." He did not have to spend time in the brig. However, King was given a date for captain's mast, a disciplinary hearing before the captain. "I'd already forgotten about my one and only contact with Captain Bode when he came aboard," he said. "It never dawned on me that I'm going to go to captain's mast."¹⁶

Rear Admiral Ralph Davis (left) stands behind Vice Admiral Daniel Barbey in a postwar photograph. Davis was the captain of the *Chicago* at the time of her sinking in 1943. U.S. Navy/Naval Historical Center.

King made his appearance in front of Bode the very next morning. In addition to the captain, Executive Officer Adell, and King's immediate superiors were in attendance. The scuttlebutt was that Bode was tough on all officers, including petty officers, a rank that King had recently attained. During the brief proceedings, King stated his case and several officers spoke on his behalf. "I remember he wasn't saying much," he said of the captain. Bode did not seem impressed and chided King for not finding a way to get back. However, in the end the captain let him off with just a warning. Bode's tenure as the *Chicago*'s captain ended a short time later.

Chapter 27

Return to Guadalcanal

As the Marines were enduring their first month of fighting on Guadalcanal, a young man in San Bernardino, California, decided to join the corps. Tom Sheble joined the Marines in August 1942. He remembered debating with a buddy while growing up as to which branch of the military service was best. "He was always for the navy and was going to join the navy," Sheble remembered. "I was always going to join the Marines. So we used to argue and fight over which was the best service. I was always for the Marines and he was always for the navy. After the war broke out I went in to join the Marines. I enlisted and had to have my parents sign up for me."[1]

Upon graduation from boot camp, each recruit was asked to choose a specialty. Sheble wanted to go to sea school, a path that would lead to being stationed aboard a navy ship. Although there was no guarantee that an individual would get his request, he was among a small group who was selected. The school took place in San Diego and lasted almost ten weeks. The men were taught basic ship nomenclature, navy regulations, and anti-aircraft gunnery. Training took place on twenty and forty-millimeter anti-aircraft guns. About eight men were selected for actual ship duty.

Sheble was assigned to the *Chicago* and arrived at Mare Island in December 1942. He immediately noticed the large radar that was mounted high on the ship. It reminded him

of a bed spring. He was struck by the size of the ship. "I had never seen a ship that big," he recalled. "It was just amazing. I never expected anything like that, and of course it wasn't the biggest thing that we had in the navy, but it was a heavy cruiser and it was quite large." Sheble became part of a small marine detachment that served about the ship. "We had the captain's orderly, the brig, and the twenty-millimeter batteries," he said. "That's what the marine detachment took care of."

Sheble was assigned to a twenty-millimeter gun mount at the bow of the ship. It was one of the many new anti-aircraft guns added during the stay at Mare

Marine Tom Sheble opted for sea duty after joining the Marines in 1942. He soon found himself manning an anti-aircraft gun as the *Chicago* left California on her final voyage (courtesy Tom Sheble).

27. Return to Guadalcanal 175

Island. "There was about four of us," he remembered of the gun crew. "There was a gunner, the loader, and two others that would handle the magazines." During his first weeks aboard the ship, Sheble became well acquainted with the gun mount. "Everybody had to learn all of the positions," he said. "You had to learn how to do everything."

* * *

Less than a month after leaving the drydock, the *Chicago* was ready to put to sea. A short run in the waters off San Francisco was all that was needed to test out new equipment and confirm that the new bow was seaworthy. For the veteran sailors, it was nothing to get excited about. Returning to the ship along with the rest of the aviation group, Charles Germann summed up the feelings of many of the veterans. "Just a routine trip," he recalled. "Out and back."[2]

For newcomers like Tom Sheble, the short shakedown cruise was a memorable experience. "That was my first time at sea," he said. "When we passed under the Golden Gate Bridge and got out there [the ship] was riding the waves pretty good." As the *Chicago* picked up speed and began to ride rough in the open waters, Sheble struggled to stay upright at

The *Chicago* is seen entering San Francisco Harbor in December 1942. The short trip out to test the seaworthiness of the new bow was the first time at sea for many of the new recruits who had boarded the cruiser while she was stateside for repairs (U.S. Navy / National Archives).

his gun mount. "The bow was dipping down and you had to hold your damn breath and you went under water, then the thing came back up. It was just like a real big coaster ride." Before long the force of the waves bent the splinter shields on the gun mount. "It just bent those back and wrapped them around that gun." Sheble's stomach soon had all that it could take. "I started getting sick," he said. "And I tell you I was sick." The gun mount was eventually abandoned and the new marine survived the experience to become a veteran seafarer. Once the *Chicago* returned to port, Sheble was given liberty. "I was one of the first to get off," he recalled.[3]

Repaired, overhauled, and sea tested, it was time for the *Chicago* to return to war. The cruiser pulled out of San Francisco Bay during the last days of 1942 bound for the Pacific. The crew did not know the ship's ultimate destination, but many surmised that they were headed for the war zone. Many of the veteran sailors knew what to expect but still felt a level of uneasiness about returning to war. "With the action I had seen, along with all the death and destruction, I was no longer the cock-sure immature youth I had been when the war started and now realized that perhaps I wasn't so indestructible after all," wrote Don Wallace. "So it was with a certain amount of trepidation that, still on the *Chicago* I sailed once again to the South Pacific." Frank Dinovo was among the new sailors who wondered what the future held. "I remember standing at the stern of the boat looking at the Golden Gate Bridge and wondering if I'd even see it again."[4] The California coast slowly faded into the distance as the *Chicago* began her journey back to war.

Dinovo made it through his first time at sea without getting sick, but that was about to change. "When we went out on the shakedown cruise I was so damn busy, I never had time to get seasick," he said. He was not so lucky when the *Chicago* left San Francisco for the Pacific. "We headed out to sea for good; there was some idle time there and I just got sicker than a dog." As a recommended cure for seasickness, the old hands told him to "load up" on food. "That was the worst damn thing you could do," he said. "But the old salts got a kick out of that. I thought that was the end of the world, the way I was vomiting."[5] He learned not to repeat the same mistake in the future.

Heading out into the Pacific, the *Chicago* escorted some troop ships that were also going to the war zone. As he looked at the transport off in the distance, marine Tom Sheble wondered what it was like to be aboard that ship. Knowing the conditions that he enjoyed, he did not envy the troops that were crammed abroad the transport.

The long voyage gave the crew an opportunity to become acquainted with their new captain. Ken Maysenhalder recalled Captain Davis being well liked by the crew with most considering him to be a friendly officer.[6] Tom Sheble served as the new captain's orderly for a short period of time while the ship was on route to the South Pacific. One night during a stop in New Caledonia, two seaplanes were getting ready for a late night departure. Two lieutenants were transferring off the ship and needed the captain's signature on an authorization. Davis had already turned in for the night, so the two approached Sheble who was stationed outside the captain's cabin door. The marine immediately informed the visitors, "The captain is asleep and cannot be disturbed."[7] The marine eventually went into the cabin, somewhat reluctantly, and found the captain to be sound asleep. He said, "Captain," but here was no response. A second attempt in a louder voice also failed to rouse the sleeping leader. After Sheble barely touched him, Davis bolted up from a sound sleep. The captain grumbled, but signed the orders in what proved to be a somewhat awkward situation for both men.

***

In the aftermath of the defeat at Savo Island, the *Chicago* had departed from what surely was a desperate situation for the U.S. Navy. While the cruiser was stateside, the fight for Guadalcanal continued unabated. It was a seesaw struggle with control of the immediate waters around the island often in firm American hands during daylight hours, only to slip into Japanese hands during the dark of night. Five large naval battles, two of which were largely between carrier aircraft, were fought in the four months that followed the Battle of Savo Island. A critical, momentum changing naval battle took place in mid–November. It was a resounding American victory. During the three day slugfest, a large American convoy was able to successfully land fresh troops and supplies on the beleaguered island. A similar Japanese convoy met a horrible fate at the hands of American warplanes. In the two associated naval battles, both vicious night gunfights near Savo Island, the Japanese suffered serious losses including two battleships. However, it came at a terrible price as the Americans lost ships, many sailors, and two admirals.

Progress in the Guadalcanal area was by no means limited to the sea. In spite of repeated attempts, the Japanese were unable to wrestle control of Henderson Field from the Marines. A major American land offensive was started on January 10.[8] By the time the *Chicago* arrived back in the area in early 1943, the poorly supplied, starving, and outnumbered Japanese defenders were being pushed into an ever decreasing portion of the island.

After making a stop at Pearl Harbor, the *Chicago* made her way back to the South Pacific. Her voyage ended in the New Hebrides. "We went there and we anchored," remembered Art King. "In the distance we could see what turned out to be a group of ships that were put together for a specific purpose. The captain left the ship to make his call on the admiral, who was on the *Wichita*. We were in dungarees. We could see on the *Wichita* everyone was in whites."[9] King remembered Captain Davis preparing the crew to get ready to change into their white uniforms, which were not the normal fare in the forward operating area of the South Pacific.

The individual that Davis made the courtesy call to was Rear Admiral Robert C. Giffen. Using the heavy cruiser *Wichita* as his flagship, Giffen had sailed halfway around the world to join the fight in the South Pacific. He had previously served in the Atlantic, where he led a task force into battle off the North African coast in late 1942.[10] Giffen was new to the Pacific and had plenty to learn. He was given command of a newly formed task force that included the *Chicago*.

Task Force 18 comprised a variety of different types of ships that had arrived from different destinations. The building blocks of the force were a trio of heavy cruisers: the *Wichita, Chicago,* and *Louisville*. Also included were the new light cruisers *Montpelier, Cleveland,* and *Columbia*. Added to the mix were two small escort carriers, the *Chenango* and *Suwannee*, which came from the Atlantic. A total of eight destroyers rounded out the force. It would not take long for the new force to see action.

Chapter 28

The Last Battle of the *Chicago*

The last days of January 1943 had what appeared to be all of the ingredients for another big naval battle around Guadalcanal. More than two months had passed since the ferocious battles of mid–November. American naval leaders noted that "an increase of enemy shipping at Buin and Rabaul, intensification of air activity, and other indications pointed to prospective vigorous operations by the Japanese in the Southern Solomons."[1] Reports placed Japanese heavy fleet units operating near Ontong Java Atoll, almost directly north of the Solomon Islands. Since the Japanese had shown willingness in the past to throw large numbers of reinforcements into the struggle for Guadalcanal, it seemed plausible that the trend would continue. The idea of a large Japanese movement towards the embattled island was also supported by radio intelligence reports.[2] Coupled with the apparent imminent threat was the need to send another group of reinforcements to the army and marine units on the island.

If the Japanese were to make a move towards Guadalcanal, the navy was ready with "the greatest concentration of U.S. naval power yet assembled in the South Pacific."[3] A total of five American task forces were ready to ensure the safe arrival of the reinforcements. On the morning of January 27, a convoy of four transports and four destroyers pulled out of Noumea bound for Guadalcanal.

Task Force 18 was assigned to provide close cover for the reinforcement transports. The force would be in a good position to meet any surface units that the Japanese might move into the area. Additional powerful forces lurked to the south. Two carrier groups, built around the *Enterprise* and *Saratoga*, moved towards a rendezvous point. A third task force contained the new battleships *Washington*, *North Carolina*, and *Indiana*. A fourth group of cruisers and destroyers was moving to join up with the battleships.[4] The various task forces operated well behind the transports and cover group, with some ships being almost 400 miles to the south. All of the American commanders were given the general directive of "destroying any Japanese forces encountered."[5]

The *Chicago* and the rest of Task Force 18 departed Efate, New Hebrides, late in the day January 27. After shadowing the transport group north, Admiral Giffen was to meet up with a group of destroyers already on station in the Guadalcanal area. The forces were to combine southwest of the island on the morning on January 30 and make a daylight sweep up the Slot while the transports discharged off Lunga Point.[6] On January 28, the transports and cover group proceeded without incident towards Guadalcanal.

Being new to the Pacific, Giffen lacked a firm understanding of Japanese tactics and the seriousness of the threat from the air. However, his experience in the Atlantic had taught him to beware of the threat from below. Information received from various American commands on January 29 indicated that from three to ten Japanese submarines were thought

28. The Last Battle of the Chicago

The *Chicago* and *Louisville* (background) are seen from the *Wichita* during the last days of January 1943. The cruisers were providing close cover for a convoy headed to Guadalcanal when attacked by Japanese planes (U.S. Navy / National Archives).

to be lurking in the general area that the task force was to operate. The same information warned that the Japanese might try a night air attack.[7]

As an added difficulty, Giffen had to contend with having the two escort carriers as part of his force. The speed of the mini-flattops slowed the pace of the cruisers. When it became clear that the task force would not be able to make its scheduled rendezvous, he ordered the *Chenango* and *Suwannee* to break off from the main group. At 2:00 P.M. on January 29, the carriers and two destroyers cleared the main formation. The small group was to proceed to the southwest and provide air cover for the cruisers as best as possible during the remaining afternoon hours and the next morning.[8]

Giffen took no chances regarding the submarine threat. With the departure of the carriers, he organized his cruisers into two parallel columns. The heavy cruisers made up the starboard side with the *Wichita* in the lead followed by the *Chicago* and *Louisville* at 2,500 yard intervals. The three light cruisers comprised a similar line on the port side. The six remaining destroyers formed a semi-circle almost two miles ahead of the cruisers. The arrangement made for a sound disposition against submarines and offered the ability to rapidly move into action against a surface force. However, the formation was less than satisfactory for a threat from the air owing to the lack of a destroyer screen on the sides and to the rear.[9] The force zigzagged as it continued on at a speed of twenty-four knots. Giffen ordered his ships to adhere to complete radio silence. He seemed determined to make the rendezvous on time.

As the escort carriers slowly slid away from the cruisers, the air around the task force seemed to be abuzz with activity. Radar operators in the cruisers were kept busy during the afternoon hours with a variety of unidentified contacts. Groups of planes circled the task force at distances of forty to fifty miles. One or more would occasionally move to within twenty miles. It was difficult to determine whether the planes were friend or foe.[10] Giffen surely surmised that at least some of the strange contacts were Japanese planes shadowing his task force.

Just after 2:00 P.M. the *Chenango* launched two radar-equipped torpedo planes and four fighters. The planes sped off in search of Japanese scout planes thought to be in the vicinity of San Cristobal Island. The escort carriers added additional planes to form a protective cap over the cruisers. A determined search found no Japanese snoopers. However, one pilot sighted what he believed to be a twin-engine Japanese bomber. The enemy quickly escaped into the clouds and was not seen again. The last of the fighter planes landed for the night as the sun slowly slid below the horizon just before 7:00 P.M. The sea was smooth, a light wind blew from the southeast and most of the sky was overcast. It looked as though the coming night would be black and nearly moonless.

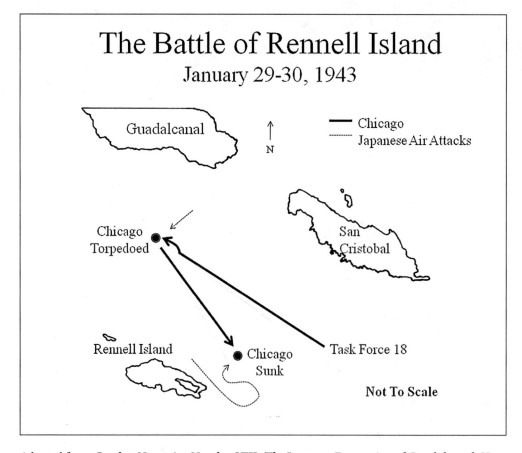

Adapted from *Combat Narrative Number VIII: The Japanese Evacuation of Guadalcanal.* Note: Map is not to scale and represents approximate movements.

***

The Japanese had in fact located Task Force 18. In what would prove to be a busy day for enemy search planes, two flying boats and thirteen land-based bombers scoured the southern Solomons. No large formations of American ships had been sighted since January 25. However, a scout bomber reported the presence of a large group of ships in the waters south of San Cristobal Island.[11] The ships certainly were Task Force 18. A succession of search planes were dispatched to keep careful watch on the American ships as the Japanese prepared an attack.

Sixteen twin-engine attack bombers took to the air from Rabaul in the early afternoon. A second group, fifteen strong, was launched just ten minutes later. Each plane was loaded with a deadly aerial torpedo. The planes headed southeast to strike the lucrative American target.

***

As the last glimpse of daylight slowly faded away, the *Chicago* plodded along in her position directly behind the *Wichita*. The ships were now almost directly south of Guadalcanal, about fifty miles off the northern coast of Rennell Island. Captain Davis had his ship in darkened condition. Most critical watertight hatches were closed except those required for immediate access or ventilation. The crew stood at condition two with all of the antiaircraft guns manned.

At about 7:10 P.M. the CXAM radar picked up a large group of unidentified planes twenty-five miles to the west. The contact was immediately reported to the flagship. "These 'bogies' were tracked and found to be drawing aft and closing slightly," Davis later wrote. "At first it was believed that they would pass clear of the formation."[12] Over the next ten minutes the planes made a wide circle ending up about fourteen miles off the stern of the *Chicago*. "Search and firecontrol radars showed that the planes had divided into two groups at ranges of approximately 10,000 yards and 17,000 yards," Davis continued. With the general alarm sounding, the *Chicago* prepared for battle.

The cruiser was no stranger to the incoming attackers; she had battled the same type of Betty bombers off Guadalcanal the previous August. For this fight the *Chicago* gunners had a new advantage. The ship was equipped with new proximity fuse anti-aircraft ammunition. Instead of actually having to hit a plane, the shells would explode nearby, but close enough to cause serious damage.[13]

The sixteen planes of the Japanese 705th Air Group were the first to attack. As the planes approached from the right side of the task force, the eastern sky made for a perfect dark background. At 7:24 P.M., the destroyer *Waller*, located almost directly off the *Chicago's* starboard beam, opened fire on the approaching planes.[14] The starboard anti-aircraft batteries of the cruiser quickly followed suit. The cruiser's five-inch and forty-millimeter batteries were operating under full radar control. All the ships of the task force were soon firing on the planes.

One plane was seen to come down almost immediately between the *Chicago* and *Waller*, perhaps a victim of the combined fire from both ships. "Two planes approached from two points abaft the starboard beam, one launching a torpedo at a range of 500 to 600 yards," Davis noted of the moment. "These two planes crossed ahead of the *Chicago* and were apparently not damaged." Lookouts combed the waters for a torpedo wake, but found nothing. "Immediately thereafter one plane crashed off the port quarter of *Chicago* as a result of hits from the *Chicago*'s automatic weapons," David added.

Although Captain Davis reported hearing the impacts of bombs on the water near the

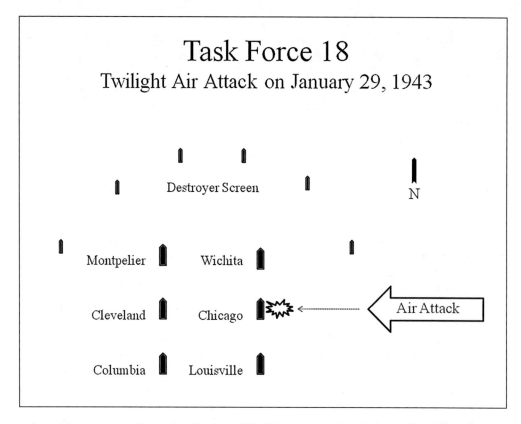

Adapted from *Combat Narrative Number VIII: The Japanese Evacuation of Guadalcanal*. Note: Map is not to scale and represents approximate movements.

light cruisers *Cleveland* and *Columbia* at this time, neither ship was damaged. However, a dud torpedo may have hit the *Louisville*.[15] The *Chicago*, and the rest of the task force, survived the attack. Admiral Giffen decided to discontinue zigzagging and increased speed in an effort to keep on course for the planned rendezvous.

The Japanese were not yet done for the evening. Scout planes now dropped a string of flares marking the cruisers' path and illuminating the ships. Additional flare clusters of red and green gave important information to the fifteen bombers of the Japanese 701st Air Group. The planes were now closing in for the attack. The formation was led by Lieutenant Commander Joji Higai, an experienced and respected naval aviator.[16] The twilight had now faded into complete darkness.

Just before 7:40 P.M. the starboard five-inch batteries on the *Chicago* opened fire on the planes at a range of 10,000 yards. "The automatic weapons took up the fire as the planes approached the extreme ranges of these weapons," Captain Davis wrote. One Betty quickly went down behind the *Waller*. Just moments later Higai's plane began to falter as it headed directly towards the *Chicago*. The bomber trailed flames as it careened into the water in a mass of flames just off the cruiser's port bow. "The flames from this plane were very brilliant and hot and undoubtedly silhouetted the *Chicago* for the following planes," Davis noted.

The death of the Japanese flight leader was not to be in vain. Unknown to the men aboard the *Chicago*, multiple torpedoes were now speeding towards their ship. At about 7:40 P.M. a torpedo slammed into the starboard side of the cruiser. "The wake of this torpedo was not seen," Davis reported. "It was completely dark by this time." The torpedo hit even with the after engine room with a thunderous explosion. Just two minutes later a torpedo wake was sighted approaching the ship from the starboard beam. It hit directly under the hangar near the number three fire room. As the *Chicago* reeled from the two explosions, the anti-aircraft gunners continued to hammer away at the enemy bombers, the last of which were now speeding away from the immediate area.

Not on duty at the time, marine Tom Sheble ran to his gun station when the general alarm sounded. He had recently moved to a twenty-millimeter gun mount above the bridge. "It was kind of dark during the attack," he said. "You were shooting at the blue flame that you could see coming out of the side of the engine, the exhaust."[17] Throughout the attack Sheble's gun rattled away. The gun crew cheered whenever a plane was seen to go down in flames. He was in the gun sling at the time the first torpedo hit and felt the ship rise up and then fall back into the water. "I never heard such an explosion; it was unbelievable," he recalled.

In the aftermath of the concussion, Sheble remembers hearing loud noises coming from below and thought that the whole ship was going to explode. After a short time the noises slowly subsided. Things quieted down somewhat after the order was given to hold

Flames trail a Japanese bomber going down on the evening of January 29, 1943, near Rennell Island. The wreckage continued to burn in the water, silhouetting the *Chicago* for other enemy pilots (U.S. Navy / National Archives).

fire. Later in the evening he could hear ammunition being thrown overboard to lighten up the ship. Sheble stayed at his gun through the night.

One of the new recruits aboard the *Chicago* was Seaman Second Class Charles Goldsmith. The Chicago native was among the many new sailors who came aboard at Mare Island. The air attack was his first taste of combat. The sound of the alarm sent him racing towards his battle station inside turret one. The main batteries did not fire during the attack. After the ship was hit and lost power, the crew was ordered out of the turret. With the attack still going on, he proceeded to a twenty-millimeter gun on the port side to help out as a loader. He remembers seeing one plane hit by gunfire; it was trailing smoke and flew near the superstructure.

George Pursley was on duty in the forward director at the time of the first attack. He remembered looking out the starboard porthole to see an enemy plane coming right for the ship. The bomber flew directly over his position, clipping the CXAM radar before crashing into the water in flames. Pursley stayed on duty all night, except for a brief trip down below to check on the power source.

Unlike the last air attacks near Guadalcanal, Ken Maysenhalder was no longer on a five-inch gun. His battle station was now on the starboard side of the bridge. He was a talker who was responsible for relaying orders from the bridge to the navigator. His position was mostly needed when entering or exiting a port. Since he had no formal duty during a battle, he simply manned his post and stayed at the position during the entire air attack.

Harry Blumhorst rode out the attack at his new battle station, which was to be the captain's messenger. The job required him to stand at the captain's side and act as a runner sending out information and reporting back. He remembered that Captain Davis never left the bridge during the air attacks. However, that would not be the case for him. "I was all over the ship the night she was hit," he recalled.[18]

As the enemy planes approached the *Chicago*, Frank Dinovo was one of almost ten men crowded into radio two. The station was also known as the transmitter room. Located just behind the hangar, it was fully enclosed with no windows or portholes. The blast of the torpedo hits did not damage any of the equipment, but gave the room a good shaking. "It jarred things around and some of the stuff we had stored fell out on deck," he remembered.[19]

The concussion knocked open one of the nearby five-inch ready lockers, sending live ammunition rolling towards nearby radio three. Many of the shells came to a stop near the hatch, blocking the men inside. Dinovo answered a call for a volunteer to move the shells. "I was going to free them guys up because, hell, I didn't know if we were going to go down that night," he said. "So I just started picking it up throwing it like it was rocks or something, just throwing them left and right because I wanted to get them out of there." Dinovo was fortunate that none of the shells exploded during the moving process. The four men that were trapped inside were grateful for his effort.

Just after he returned to radio two, the captain's orderly arrived with an emergency message to be sent out. "We had to dig out the emergency generator and transmitter and set it up, which we never even practiced," Dinovo said. "We got it all set up and my job was to run the generator. It had two long handles on it that you pulled it ... back and forth to get the speed up on the generator." As Dinovo worked the handles, another sailor held a flashlight to the meter. "I had to maintain [the cycles] as they read off the S.O.S. that we sent to the admiral of the fleet to tell him that we were dead in the water."

Now an electrician's mate first class, Howard Fortney's battle station was the after gyro-compass-auxiliary internal communication room. Located well below the main deck, the room housed one of the two gyrocompasses aboard the ship. Only two men were assigned to the compartment.

The blast of the torpedo hits ruptured the bulkhead between the engine room and evaporator room, flooding the latter. Water soon began to enter Fortney's room through a cable connection point. "It was supposed to be water tight, [but] was not because there was quite a bit of water squirting in and squirting on the switchboard," he recalled. "We retreated to the trunk after water got up around our knees. It was still coming in."[20] The trunk went all the way up to the second deck. "We still had communications with central control. They sent people down and opened up the hatches and we come out." The room eventually completely flooded. Fortney went topside and was later pressed into service for the damage control effort.

* * *

The *Louisville* turned sharply to avoid the slowing *Chicago*, before taking up position behind the *Wichita*. Giffen changed course and slowed the undamaged ships to fifteen knots to reduce the phosphorescent wakes. Additionally, he ordered all ships to hold fire. The Japanese planes remained in the area trying to entice American gunners to open fire in the hopes that the gun flashes would give away the ship's position. Just after 8:00 P.M. most of the bombers left the area, although a few enemy search planes remained near the force over the next few hours. The task force slowly patrolled the immediate area around the stricken cruiser.

The great ship *Chicago* was now in peril. Among the compartments that flooded immediately after the first hit were the after engine room, number four fire room, evaporator room, and the crew's space just behind the after engine room. Directly above the impacted area, the starboard bulkheads of the crew's mess were ripped apart and open to the sea. The second hit quickly flooded the number three fire room and forward engine room. Flooding extended almost 200 feet, about one-third of the length of the ship.

All steam pressure was lost causing a complete loss of power. Three screws stopped almost immediately after the first hit, while the remaining one went dead right after the second blast. Ship control was lost with the rudder locked ten degrees to the left.[21] The cruiser began to settle in the water towards the stern while a list to starboard rapidly developed. It was clear that a long night lay ahead. The *Chicago* sailors had kept the ship afloat at Savo Island and were determined to do the same now.

The damage control effort began immediately. Two emergency generators were quickly started to provide power for emergency lighting, electric pumps, and radios. Two small fires in the galley and radio two were extinguished. Repair parties worked to establish flooding boundaries, plug leaks, and reinforce weakened bulkheads.[22] "It was extremely problematical as to whether the ship would continue to float, but careful and continuous checks indicated that buoyancy was holding its own," reported Captain Davis.

Bill Grady had arrived at his battle station just as the attack began. He was part of the midship repair party that was stationed in the after mess hall. "I was on the headphones, sound powered phones," he said. "There was a chief who had told me a joke, and I was laughing when the first torpedo hit in the after engine room right below me. It turned me head over heels."[23] Having lost his phones, Grady soon found himself in total darkness. With the mess hall filling with smoke and water, the repair party went topside only to find that the guns were still blazing away at the enemy planes. They took shelter in the crew's head. When the danger subsided, the repair party formed a bucket brigade and worked through the night. "We kept her afloat," he said. "Holding more water than the books said we would."

Art King had spent most of the day down in the after engine room. "We had on aboard something new," he said. "We had a degaussing system." A series of coils wrapped around the ship, the system was used to help defend against underwater magnetic mines. It had been installed during the recent stay at Mare Island. "We had a separate motor generator to provide the voltage for each one of those coils," he continued. "The one for the main coil was down in the after engine room. Like anything else, the engine room is so compact that they had to invent a place to put this motor generator. They built this like scaffolding and this thing is way up in the air. It's brand new and we already have bearing problems." King and two others spent nearly the entire day working to fix the problem, finishing up at about 7:15 P.M. "I came up out of the after engine room on the second deck," he said. "I was going to get a cup of coffee. I think before I even got a sip of that cup of coffee, I heard gunfire."[24]

Concluding that it was something more than a drill, King decided to head for his battle station, to be part of the forward repair party in the vicinity of the wardroom. "I started walking forward, and then the general alarm sounded, and I picked up some speed and started running." He had no sooner arrived at his battle station when the two torpedoes hit, one in the after engine room. He soon realized that he had escaped a certain death by about fifteen minutes.

Once the attack ended the forward repair party took stock of the situation. The group ended up disbanding. "From then on its saving the ship," King said. "I finally left the forward repair party; we all did. I don't know whether we received words to secure or what." Many of the top officers in King's division never made it out of the after engine room. "I was trying to figure out what was going on and where and what we could do," he continued. "So I rounded up as many electrician's mates as I could find." King led the group to the well deck. He noticed that one of the men appeared to be in shock. "I found that we had another guy, a young fella that was a survivor from the *California* in Pearl Harbor," he said. "He still was only about nineteen years old and about to experience his second sinking. The young fella wasn't sitting there, he was just wandering around. So I detailed somebody else to keep an eye on him so that he didn't walk over the side." The sailor made it through the night without incident.

The group eventually went back to the number two mess hall after hearing that the area was flooded. "We go back there and hell, sure enough here's the midship repair party and they're all up on the main deck," King continued. "The hatch is open and the water is right up to the hatch level." It was about this time that Chief Carpenter's Mate Albert Bartholomew dove into the flooded compartment to find the source of the leaks. He went in alone with no lifeline tied to his waist. "Normally you would walk down the ladder, but that was under water too," King remembered. "So the only way he could get down there was to dive down. It's risky, but the ship is sinking." Bartholomew found that the hatch to the flooded after engine room was open. Through a series of dives, with short periods of rest in between, he was able to close and dog down the hatch.

King later heard that a chief running to his battle station after the first torpedo hit stopped to open the hatch after hearing cries for help from below. "He opened that door to let that guy out," he recalled. "And of course when he came out he came out with several tons of water. That water was flowing continuously then and they couldn't close the door." With the leak stopped, two submersible electrical pumps were lowered down the hatch to begin the slow process of pumping out the water.

Charles Germann was among the many veterans who had a new battle station. His was the forward searchlight platform. "I had two new guys with me who had never been aboard the ship before," he recalled. During daylight the group acted as lookouts. At night, it turned to searchlight duty. After the torpedoes hit, the station was ordered abandoned. Germann made his way down to join a bucket brigade in the number one mess hall. He joined a long line of people that stretched from the mess hall, up a ladder, and onto the main deck. "We bailed all night long," he said. "I was on the ladder. We shifted around, because you know a guy couldn't stay in one place, the ladder was hard to stand on."[25] During the night Germann and another sailor were told to check the hatch at the bottom of the mess hall to make sure it was still sealed. As a safety precaution, a rope was tied around the other man as he descended into the waist deep water. Germann stayed at the ladder with a firm grip on the other end. The two soon found that the hatch was closed and dogged down.

After the attack ended, Charles Goldsmith assisted with the damage control effort. He tried to help out wherever he could. "We were up most of the night doing work, clean up," he said. "Everywhere there was oil. We had to pick up stuff and help the wounded get down to sick bay. It was a mess," he recalled of the situation below deck. "Sick bay was horrible, all the screaming."[26]

While the *Chicago* sailors worked to keep their ship afloat, Admiral Giffen directed the *Louisville* to take the damaged cruiser in tow. The *Louisville* slowly moved towards her crippled sister ship. It was to be a delicate and difficult task. "The darkness of the night was a major difficulty," reported the *Louisville's* captain. "Added to this was the lack of power on the *Chicago* and the concern felt over the presence of enemy planes, a number of which were heard overhead and tracked in the close vicinity."[27] To further add to the tension, the destroyer *Chevalier* fired upon what she believed to be a surfaced enemy submarine just before midnight.[28]

Silhouetted against the morning sun, the *Louisville* tows the damaged *Chicago* near Rennell Island on January 30, 1943. Towing duties were later taken over by the fleet tug *Navajo* (U.S. Navy / National Archives).

One of the last known pictures of the *Chicago* shows the damaged cruiser riding low in the water on January 30, 1943. After being hit by two aerial torpedoes a day earlier, the crew worked through the night to keep the ship afloat (U.S. Navy / Naval Historical Center).

Several unsuccessful attempts were made to bring the two ships close together before the *Louisville* was able to come to a stop just ahead of the *Chicago's* bow. The passing of the tow seemed to go smoothly. The end of the heavy wire was pulled aboard the *Chicago* by the brute force of her crew and secured to the anchor chain. By the first hour of January 30, the *Louisville* was proceeding southeast toward Espiritu Santo at a speed of four knots. The destroyers *La Vallette, Edwards,* and *Taylor* screened the slow-moving twosome.

While the topside sailors were toiling to connect the two ships, others below had lit off the number four boiler at about midnight. The additional power allowed oil to be pumped away from the starboard side. The list, which had been checked at eleven degrees, slowly began to subside. Using equalizing valves, the rudder was straightened out and locked into a normal position.

An all out effort was made to save the damaged *Chicago*. In order to succeed she would have to be protected while being towed out of the range of Japanese land-based bombers. During the waning hours of January 29, Admiral William Halsey, commander of naval forces in the South Pacific, mustered the necessary resources. He ordered the two escort carriers to move into a position to provide air cover at dawn. The *Chenango* and *Suwannee* made best speed for a point sixty miles southeast of the *Chicago's* estimated dawn position. The *Enterprise* was ordered to move north to provide additional fighters and search planes for Task Force 18. A Black Cat night patrol plane was sent to fly night cover over the damaged cruiser. The fleet tug *Navajo* was directed to head for the *Chicago*. She had been en route from Guadalcanal to Espiritu Santo with the destroyer transport *Sands*. The first rays of sunlight brought new hope. The *Chicago* had made it through the night but was not yet out of danger.

Chapter 29

Rescue

It was just after 6:00 A.M. when the *Navajo* sighted the *Chicago* and *Louisville*. Maneuvering alongside the lead cruiser, crewmen successfully transferred the tow line over to the fleet tug. By 7:40 A.M. the *Navajo* had the *Chicago* in tow.[1] The damaged cruiser was trailing oil as she was pulled at a slow speed of four knots. The remaining ships of the task force were patrolling in the immediate vicinity.

The morning hours brought the welcome sight of American fighter planes to the *Chicago* sailors. Seven fighters from the *Chenango* arrived over the cruiser force just after dawn. Six more from the *Enterprise* appeared a short time later. A constant patrol was maintained throughout the day. A fighter director officer aboard the *Wichita* occasionally directed planes to investigate possible enemy snoopers that had been picked up by radar. None were located.

Art King was both relieved and happy when morning came. "We were all celebrating," he remembered. "We were celebrating because, hey, we were going to get out of here. We were thinking about getting into Sydney and all that good liberty down there. We were pretty happy."[2] Daylight meant the end of an exhausting night for Charles Germann. His hard work had paid off. "We kept her afloat," he said. "We sat down against the bulkhead. I think there were four or five of us." He returned to the aviation area after a rest. The *Chicago* had two planes aboard for the voyage. "They were both forward on the catapults. I think we were planning to take our planes off if we could."[3] It was soon discovered that one was damaged during the attack and was probably not flyable.

One of the torpedoes had struck directly below the hangar and blew a large hole in the floor. Earlier in the night, Germann and another sailor were asked to retrieve a hose that was on the hangar wall. They had to find their way around in the dark. As it turned out the pair was walking on a narrow strip that was all that remained of the floor. "That's all that was left of the deck," he recalled. "The next day if we had known what we'd done we wouldn't've went in there. My night vision ain't worth a hoot." Like most of the men aboard, Germann was just hoping that the *Chicago* would make it to safety.

* * *

During the morning hours Admiral Giffen directed Captain Davis to transfer off excess personnel to nearby destroyers at his discretion. Davis signaled back asking if the wounded could be dispatched via ship to a land hospital. Giffen said no. The admiral did not think that a destroyer could be spared given the submarine threat. Davis then decided to keep all of his sailors aboard the *Chicago* in light of the precarious stability of the ship and the probability of further enemy attacks.[4]

At about noon the two escort carriers joined up with the *Enterprise* task force. The combined force moved on a variety of courses designed to hold position about fifty miles

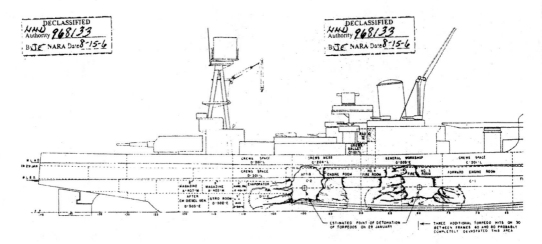

A U.S. Navy diagram shows underwater damage suffered by the Chicago when two Japanese torpedoes hit the ship on January 29, 1943 (U.S. Navy / National Archives).

southeast of the *Chicago*. Although the escort carriers later went back to operating independently, the mission of the force remained the same: to provide air cover for the retreating ships.

At 3:00 P.M. Giffen and the undamaged cruisers pulled away from the *Chicago*, having been ordered to proceed separately to Efate. He left behind a total of six destroyers, which formed a moving circle around the *Chicago* and *Navajo*. Leaving with the cruisers was the powerful assortment of anti-aircraft firepower that the ships could bring to bear and the fighter director officer aboard the *Wichita*.[5] Both would be missed as the day progressed.

* * *

The Japanese regained contact with Task Force 18 during the early morning hours of January 30. A scout plane reported the location of the force, mistaking the *Chicago* as a battleship but noting that it was under tow and trailing oil.[6] Another air attack was soon launched. Eleven bombers took off from Buka determined to sink the damaged "battleship."

At about the same time that Giffen was leaving with his cruisers, American forces on Guadalcanal issued a plain language radio message warning of eleven twin-engine Japanese bombers heading southeast. There was no doubt that the target was the *Chicago*. The commander of the escorting destroyers received the message just before 3:30 P.M. The *Enterprise* also picked up the warning and officers were able to make a reasonably accurate estimate of when the enemy planes would arrive over the *Chicago*.[7]

Just ten minutes after the *Enterprise* received the warning her fighters over the *Chicago* sighted an enemy search plane and gave chase. Four of the six fighters downed the enemy plane after an almost forty mile chase to the northeast. The plane was a scout that had been sent out in advance of the attack force to shadow the American fleet.[8] Before going down, however, the snooper provided enough information for the attack planes to find the target.

American accounts of the battle have the Japanese bombers heading first towards the *Enterprise*, before radically turning to attack the *Chicago*. However, the Japanese history of the action makes no mention of that event.[9] In either case, not all of the American fighters were positioned to clash with the enemy planes before they reached the *Chicago*. A small number of fighters were able to tangle with the enemy. At least eight bombers survived to press home the attack.[10]

At 4:20 P.M. the Japanese bombers were sighted seven miles off the starboard bow of the *Chicago*. The ship was now about thirty-five miles east of Rennell Island. "At the time our own fighter patrol was not in sight," commented Captain Davis. The *La Vallette* opened fire, quickly followed by the starboard batteries of the *Chicago*. The cruiser's guns were operating in local control, the CXAM radar having been knocked out the day before. The planes were 8,000 yards away when the barrage began. In the moments that followed, several planes were seen to fall in flames. "Another caught fire in one engine and apparently attempted to crash on the *Chicago*, but missed the stern and fell off the port quarter in flames," Davis reported.[11] More American fighters suddenly appeared on the scene and proceeded to tear into the bombers as twin-engine planes crossed the *Chicago*'s track. "Some difficulty was encountered keeping the fire of the anti-aircraft weapons off our own fighters while in local control," Davis noted.

Charles Goldsmith was on clean up duty when he took a break for some food. Cooks had set up makeshift tables on the well deck and were preparing to serve. "They were about to serve peaches," he recalled.[12] The general quarters alarm suddenly sounded. Goldsmith could soon see the enemy planes far off in the distance. He ran back to the same twenty-millimeter gun mount that he had been at the day before.

Bill Grady was resting from a night of hard work when the general alarm sounded. "I was getting a little shut eye when all hell broke loose again," he said. "I was up on the well deck because I did not have a battle station, but I was up there to do whatever they wanted me to do." He had a good look at the enemy planes as they raced toward the *Chicago*. "It was something when you are standing there and you see the fish leave the belly of that plane and there is nothing that you can do about it."[13]

Almost as soon as the attack started, the battle swept past the *Chicago*. "After the [anti-aircraft] fire had been ceased, when all enemy planes had either been shot down or were engaged by [our] own fighters, five torpedo wakes were observed to [be] approaching the ship from the starboard beam," Captain Davis later wrote. Moving at a slow speed and unable to maneuver, the *Chicago* was a sitting duck.

At 4:24 P.M. the first torpedo struck the cruiser well forward between turrets one and two. The impact sent up a tower of water and debris that came down on the bridge and forecastle. Just seconds later three additional torpedoes hit in rapid succession in a thunderous concussion. All struck dead amidships, directly under the aviation area. "The fifth torpedo missed astern," Davis added.

The hits were a devastating blow to the damaged cruiser. It was very apparent to Captain Davis that his ship would not stay afloat for very long. Four minutes after the initial hit, he gave the order to abandon ship. The word was passed over both the battle telephones and the general announcing system. Crewmen on the *Navajo* cut the tow line with an acetylene torch at 4:30 P.M. as the *Chicago* began to keel over to the starboard side. "Most life rafts and floater nets had been cut loose and placed on deck during the previous night," Davis recalled. "Considerable difficulty was encountered in launching the port life rafts and floater nets." Most of the rafts and nets did eventually make it over the side. The one remaining motor whaleboat was also launched, but it later sank.

The *Chicago* slowly rolled over and began to settle by the stern. Her colors were still flying as she slipped beneath the waves. The official end of the veteran cruiser came at 4:43 P.M. when her bow disappeared below the surface.[14]

The rescue operation was underway within an instant of the sinking. After cutting loose the tow line, the *Navajo* maneuvered to pick up survivors. The *Sands*, *Edwards,* and *Waller* joined the effort, pulling up men from rafts, floater nets or directly out of the sea.

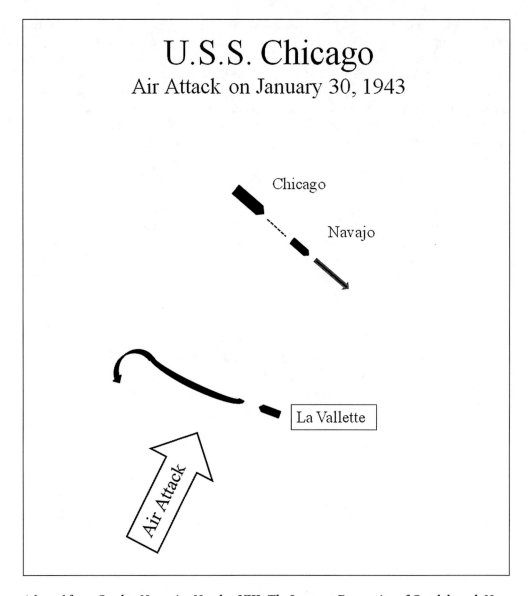

Adapted from *Combat Narrative Number VIII: The Japanese Evacuation of Guadalcanal*. Note: Map is not to scale and represents approximate movements.

* * *

When the general alarm sounded, Charles Germann did not go back to the searchlight platform. Instead, he went to a five-inch ammunition hoist. "After they told us to abandon ship, I came back up forward," he said. Moving across the flight deck, he eventually arrived near turret two. "That was my abandon ship station." He helped cut down one of the life rafts that was hanging on the side of the turret and assisted getting some wounded off the ship. "We got the guys off and I looked around and there stood Lieutenant Colonie."[15] The head of the aviation division was standing alone. With the ship going down, the two decided to jump off together.

29. Rescue

From his vantage point, Germann saw the *Chicago* sinking. "I was in the water when it went down," he said. "She went down and stuff spouted out of course. The last thing I saw was the stern go down. I hated to see it go." He was soon picked up by a motor launch and taken aboard the *Navajo*.

The day's attack again saw Tom Sheble at his anti-aircraft gun. He initially saw the planes far out on the starboard side flying in a tight formation just above the water. He noticed that the planes were "flying wing to wing and coming right at us." After the planes sped by, strafing as they passed, he looked out to see the incoming torpedoes. "You could see all of these streaks coming at you," he recalled.[16]

After the torpedoes hit, the abandon ship order quickly spread by word of mouth. Putting on his life jacket, Sheble slid down a ladder to the main deck. The ship was listing heavily with water almost coming up to the deck. Just then he saw a badly burned man emerge from below deck and immediately jump into the water. Proceeding to the forward part of the ship, he noticed that his former gun mount was still manned. He approached to find the crew busy changing the gun barrel. For some reason the men thought the barrel had become too hot. He stayed for a brief time to help, before the group decided it was time to leave. They left the gun, but could not decide where to get off the ship. "We were arguing about what side to jump off," he recalled. Deciding on the port side, Sheble stopped to think about what to do with his shoes: take them off to help him swim better in the water or leave them on. He decided to take them off and jumped off the side. He made the mistake of jumping off wearing his helmet, but soon recovered and started to swim away from the ship with a small group of others.

Sheble stopped momentarily, and looked back to see the ship rolling over. He noticed sailors still on the fantail. "For some reason they would not jump," he said. He soon saw the bow "go straight up into the air and slowly come down."

Howard Fortney had been working diligently on damage control. He assisted in getting a submersible pump lowered into a flooded compartment. "I think the water was coming in as fast as we could send it out," he said.[17] It was while operating the pump that the general alarm sounded. Fortney saw men scrambling around in all directions. Word soon spread that another air attack was coming.

Unable to go back to his flooded battle station, Fortney positioned himself in the passageway below the five-inch guns. The whole ship shook when the torpedoes hit. Never hearing the order to abandon ship, he made his way aft and joined several other men in cutting off a raft that was fastened to the port side of turret three. It was large and awkward to handle. "It took four of us to get it over the side," he remembered. Fortney then jumped off the port side. He had on a life jacket, but forgot to take off his helmet. His head jerked sharply when the helmet hit the water. Fortunately, it did not break his neck. He never did make it to the life raft that he helped to throw over the side. He instead clung to the floater net with at least six others.

"I knew that we were going to go down," Frank Dinovo said of the moment after the torpedoes hit. "Like everybody else, we got out of there as quick as we could." Racing out of radio two, he made his way to a nearby ladder that led down to the main deck. "Hell, there were so many guys around [the ladder] I couldn't even get near it." He soon saw a large crowd at his assigned abandon ship station. Men were already taking down a raft. Dinovo was wearing his life jacket; he had put it on shortly before the first attack and never took it off. "I said that's my raft; how the hell am I going to get it ... there were so many guys around it. I though they'll get it off of there and into the water." Dinovo slid down a rope into the water. As soon as the raft was tossed over the side, he pounced on it. He was quickly joined by about twenty others.

Dinovo looked up to see a buddy from the radio shack still up on deck. He shouted for him to "get the hell off of there!" His friend nonchalantly took his shoes off before sliding down a rope and swimming out to the crowded raft.

The group tried to move the raft away from the ship. "My buddy went berserk," Dinovo said of the time. "He started screaming, he felt the undertow as the ship compartments were collapsing. So I turned around and I slapped him as hard as I could along the side of the face. I didn't want to cause a panic." Everything seemed to be all right afterwards.

A short time later, Dinovo looked back to see the *Chicago* sliding over. "When it went under everyone that was in the water yelled, hollered, and clapped," he said. "It was a last salute. That was our salute to the *Chicago*."[18]

When the order was given to leave the ship, Harry Blumhorst made his way down to his abandon ship station, which was on the port side of turret two. Looking over the side he noticed that the water was up near the main deck and that many men were already overboard. "I took off my shoes and put my socks into them as if I were coming back someday, like you do when you go to bed," he said. He jumped off the port side and grabbed a cargo net raft, which he recalled as being "one of the worst things that I had ever seen." He was concerned about the suction that would be created when the ship went down. "We tried to get away from it as far as we could."[19] To increase speed he turned around and swam on his back. He estimated that the destroyer was about a quarter of a mile away.

Fred Tuccitto was busy at his five-inch gun during both of the air attacks. He knew it was time to leave after hearing the abandon ship order. "I reached under my seat to grab my life jacket, and it was gone," he later wrote of the moment. He began to make his way towards the back of the ship. "I kept looking for something to take into the water that would keep me afloat. I was a good swimmer. Being twenty-one years old and not afraid of the water was a gift. I somehow felt that I would get through all of this by myself."[20]

Arriving at the stern, Tuccitto saw a marine standing alone. He believed it was Private Jack Chuda. Tuccitto noticed his clean khaki uniform and that he was also without a life jacket. The two saw a large life raft on deck near turret three and decided to work together to get it into the water. "The water was up to the main deck by now," he recalled. "Together we were able to move it."

The sea was covered with oil and littered with debris. The marine's uniform was no longer clean. "I jumped over the life line first and he followed," Tuccitto recalled. "We paddled with our hands to get away from the ship, for it could explode or the oil might ignite." In less than ten minutes the raft was filled with other men, mostly wounded. Being uninjured, Tuccitto and Chuda took to the water and hung onto the side. "There was one thing that we were all sure of; we were in shark infested waters." After being in the water for three or four hours, the men were picked by the destroyer *Waller*.

From his battle station near the bridge, Ken Maysenhalder looked down at the low flying attacking planes. "You could see the wakes of the torpedoes coming at us," he said. Right after the hits, he heard the abandon ship order relayed over his talker headset. "It was a shock," he recalled. The headset cord was tucked under his life jacket and securely plugged into the bulkhead. After hearing the abandon ship order, he began to move and was quickly jerked back by the cord. He momentarily began to wonder if he was going to make it off the ship. Pulling the entire headset down through his life jacket, he left it on deck and ran down a series of ladders to the main deck. When he arrived at the stern, the water level was even with the deck and was starting to spill over. Looking off into the distance the water seemed to be full of men. He pulled off his shoes, but kept on his black socks thinking that sharks would be more interested in bare skin, and simply walked off the starboard side into the water. With all the nearby rafts full, he started swimming to a distant ship. Stopping to look back, he saw the *Chicago* go down. He momentarily thought about his locker and personal belongings that were left behind. Maysenhalder was picked up by the *Navajo* after spending about twenty minutes in the water.

George Pursley's director had no power during the second attack and had to be operated manually. When the abandon ship order came, he quickly escaped from the director through a side hatch and went down to the main deck. Kicking off his shoes, he jumped off the port bow. In the mist of his escape, he realized that he was not wearing a life jacket. He normally did not wear it on station due to the tight spaces of the director. Once in the water, he swam with a small group of men away from the ship.

Standing right below the catapults when the abandon ship order was given, Bill Grady went right into the water. "I had a life belt on," he said. "I never did learn to swim. Back in the depression days, it was either go to the water hole and learn how to swim or go to work and have fifty cents in my pocket. I would rather work and have fifty cents in my pocket, so I never learned to swim. Of course they didn't give it to us in boot camp, wasn't there long enough."[21] A swimmer or not, Grady made it to a floater net in quick order.

The rescue activity took place amid a warning that more Japanese planes were on the way. A message from Guadalcanal warned of nineteen Japanese planes in the Central Solomons heading southeast. However, no additional bombers ever arrived on the scene.

After narrowly escaping death in the after engine room the day before, Art King made what can be considered a perilous escape from the sinking *Chicago*. He was topside when he heard someone yell that more enemy planes were coming. "I went running forward and I went down to my battle station," King recalled. "There was nobody down there. It never occurred to me not to go down there."[22] With only emergency power available, the area was dark. He had just decided that he had better find his way out when the ship shook from a torpedo hit. King had on a small, un-inflated rubber life belt, the type used by engineering personnel so that they could get through the escape hatches. "I go this way and I can't get through there. I go another way. It's pitch black. Finally, I get over to the starboard side of the ship and the door is open. I get over to that door and I can look all the way down that passage way and see daylight down there." Looking towards the back of the ship, King was looking at the well deck. Another torpedo hit as he stepped through the hatch. "I see water out there where I was seeing daylight before. I see solid water out there, so I put another puff in my life jacket."

By this time the *Chicago* had started to go down. "I'm looking at all that water on the well deck and trying to figure out how come it's dry in this passageway and the well deck is underwater," King continues. "So pretty soon the water all drops as it does from one of those [torpedo] hits." Just then a man wearing a life jacket stepped out of a side compartment and disappeared by walking out into the water. "He walked aft and stepped through that hatch and got out on the well deck. He made a left turn and I couldn't see him anymore." King decided to do the same. "So once I got out on the well deck, I looked out there to figure where the hell did that guy go. It dawned on me that he must have been sucked right into that hole that that torpedo had made. So then I changed my idea about going overboard there." He knew that he had to find a different way to get off.

With the ship listing heavily to starboard, King went to the port side. He made his way up a ladder and started going forward. "I finally get up to the forecastle deck," he said. "I'm up there alongside number one turret. I can look out there at the ocean and man, there's nothing but sailors out there all over the ocean." He sees two men struggling to cut a life raft down from the side of a turret. Momentarily pausing, he thought that he could either try to help them or get off the boat before it sinks. He decided to do the latter. "I go over right to the life line and there's the boat boom, the forward port side boat boom." The narrow plank was extending straight out over the water. "Somebody had rigged it out and so I figured hey, I am going to walk out there. I was accustomed to doing that in taking care of the boats." He walked out onto the boom, quickly looked to see if the was anyone directly below and jumped off into the water.

King descended into the black water below the ocean's surface. His life belt had deflated, perhaps when it hit the water, so he had to kick and flap to try to get to the surface. "I finally popped the surface just before my lungs were about to break," he said. It was at this juncture that he determined that his life belt had ruptured. "I was a poor swimmer. I was shocked to find out that salt water is more buoyant that fresh water." Much to his surprise, he did not have a hard time staying afloat. "I figured that I have got to get away from the ship. It's going to sink any minute and it could have some explosions and I don't want to be near when that happens."

Spotting a nearby life raft, King climbed aboard. There were only two or three men on the raft, but that was about to change. "It wasn't long before some guy comes swimming up and never stopped until he got right in the raft. He was scared, he was really scared," King remembered. Paddling with their hands, the men tried to maneuver the raft away from a nearby patch of oil. The group eventually grew in number as more men were brought aboard. King and others then pulled aboard a badly burned sailor, whose scorched flesh was pulled off in the process. Now the men begin to worry about sharks. "We decided that maybe we'd better get back in the oil. Maybe the sharks might not like that oil."

By this time the *Chicago* was going under. King spied a glimpse of the bow sliding beneath the waves. "The bow looked like it was rising up in the air just sticking up there like a sore thumb and then just slowly settled back. When it started going down, everybody that was in the water started letting up a huge yell. And that was it, the *Chicago* was gone."

After hearing the abandon ship order, Don Wallace and a shipmate made their way forward. "The skipper ordered us to prepare to abandon ship and it was obvious that our beloved *Chicago* was doomed," he wrote.[23] Once at the bow, the two took off their shoes and put the pairs aside in a safe place. "We still had faith that some miracle might occur. It had been our home for four years and we still felt that even if [the Japanese] sunk every other ship in the navy that ours would still be around and we refused to believe that she was actually a goner." In spite of his hopes for a miracle, Wallace went into the water like everyone else. Swimming away from the ship, he saw the cruiser go down. "We all felt a tremendous sense of loss when we saw the big numbers twenty-nine on her bow disappear beneath the sea. It was a horrible and confidence shattering experience."

Charles Goldsmith remembers hearing the order to abandon ship by word of mouth. He already had on his life jacket and went back to the fantail. He saw at least fifteen men already in the water in the immediate area. Seeing many shoes on deck, he decided to take his off before jumping into the water with several buddies. Hitting the water hard, his life vest kept him from going under. Goldsmith soon joined on to the end of a line of men. Each was holding on to the shoulders of the man in front. He eventually decided to break off and swim on his own to a nearby ship. He remembered the sounds of the *Chicago* sinking and the bow going straight up into the air. He related it to "the dying of a beautiful friend."[24] He was later picked up by the *Sands*.

Once the *Chicago* disappeared, the nearby ships went about locating and picking up survivors. At least one of the ships put motor whale boats into the water to help in the rescue effort. Howard Fortney was rescued by the *Sands*. The destroyer transport came directly at the small group of men that were clinging to the floater net. "It looked like it was going to run us over," he recalled. Fortney soon found much company as the vessel pulled aboard 379 *Chicago* survivors including Harry Blumhorst, Bill Grady, George Pursley, and Charles Goldsmith.[25]

Frank Dinovo was able to see several destroyers in the immediate area of his raft, one of which appeared to be brand new. "It looked like it was right out of the shipyard," he said. Dinovo and a buddy decided to swim for it, but before they could reach the destroyer, a motor whale boat pull up. A coxswain asked, "Are you guys hurt?" When the reply was no, the coxswain continued "Well our orders are to pick up the injured first." Dinovo directed him in the general direction of his raft and swam on to the destroyer making it in good time. "The first thing they did was feed us," he recalled once aboard. With many of the survivors covered with oil, it did not take long for the destroyer to become a mess. "Everything you touched, why you left oil on it." Dinovo soon joined in the cleanup effort.

After only a short time in the water, a whale boat came by Art King's raft. The motorboat had a long line of life rafts in tow. The last raft threw King's group a line. Seeing the *Sands* off in the distance, the group decided not to take the line. Knowing the destroyer transport was used to take Marines up to Guadalcanal, King and the others feared that they would be issued a rifle and sent ashore. "We stayed there and about a half an hour later the whale boat comes back again," he continues. "It's all by its self." The coxswain yelled over, "I am going to throw you the line now and if you don't take it, you're staying here and I'm leaving." The raft sailors quickly decided to take up the coxswain's offer and were soon on their way to the *Sands*.

Don Wallace was among the survivors picked up by the *Navajo*. Once back at Espiritu Santo, he moved to a transport for the trip to New Caledonia. The first person he saw after climbing aboard was Executive Officer Cecil Adell. "I kept my word, didn't I," Adell said with a grin on his face. Wallace was somewhat perplexed until Adell added, "I told you that you wouldn't get off that ship until I did." Wallace now remembered Adell's statement when he had denied his request for a transfer off the cruiser back at Mare Island.

After seeing the *Chicago* sink, Tom Sheble remained in the water for some time before being picked up by the *Navajo*. He later transferred to a nearby destroyer. He was more than exhausted after making the swim in his waterlogged life jacket. Given a blanket, he lay down in a bunk and fell into a deep sleep.

After picking up all of the survivors, the rescue ships conducted a search of the immediate area. Sixty-two officers and men went down with the *Chicago*. A total of 1,069 sailors were rescued.[26]

There certainly must have been stories surrounding the men who went down with the *Chicago*. The details of most are lost forever. Chief Machinist's Mate Ben Williams is thought to have been one of the few to make it out of the after engine room when the first torpedoes struck. Badly burned, he was taken to the sick bay and never made it out when the ship sank. Seaman Second Class Albert Efigenio suffered burns while fighting a fire after the first attack. He was thought to have been at his gun station during the second attack and may have been blown overboard when the final torpedoes hit. Postell Hayes was seen jumping in the water after the abandon ship order was given. Although wearing a life jacket, he went under and only the jacket came to the surface. It was well known that he did not know how to swim.[27]

With the rescue operation complete, the *Chicago* survivors crowded aboard the *Conway*, *Edwards*, *Sands*, and *Waller*. Once at Espiritu Santo, most of the survivors made their way to the survivor's camp at Noumea. A temporary way station for sailors of sunken ships, the camp was somewhat of a tent city. "They gave us a little ditty bag, a little bag full of necessities, like a toothbrush and shaving cream and such," recalled Charles Goldsmith of his arrival at the camp.

Fred Tuccitto passed his time eating, playing ball and sleeping. "We had nothing to do," he remembered. "I was there two weeks. I was sleeping in a tent. I think I mentioned that I was not used to sleeping in a tent with a dirt floor. I don't think I would've of made a good army man."

George Pursley remembered a particular tree that seemed to attract plenty of attention. "There was a huge tree that was used for a bulletin board," he recalled. "On the board was posted ships going to the United States." When it was his time to go, Pursley had to choose between traveling on a fast unescorted ship or a slower vessel with an escort. "I chose the faster one," he said.[28]

Upon entering the survivors' camp, Frank Dinovo signed in at the administration building. "I didn't give them a rating or anything," he said. He did not give any thought to the fact that his cousin, with the same name and middle initial, was also serving in the navy. A few days later a couple of Marines came roaming through the camp looking for him. "Frank Dinovo third class cook," the soldiers were yelling. Answering the call, Dinovo told them that while it was his name, he was not a cook. The Marines did not believe him and seemed intent on taking him to the brig for not answering the call for duty in the mess hall. It took the intervention of his division officer to straighten everything out. It turned out that Dinovo's cousin had been a cook aboard the *Astoria* and went down with the ship off Savo Island. The navy had the two mixed up, with Dinovo's family having been notified that he did not survive the sinking of the *Chicago*.[29] Dinovo did survive the sinking, but he did not have to serve in the mess hall.

* * *

One day after the *Chicago* sank the Japanese announced a great victory in what became known as the Battle of Rennell Island. A total of four American ships, including two battleships, were reported to have been sunk in a series of air attacks. As we know, only one American ship was lost. It was, however, a valuable heavy cruiser that succumbed to a combination of bad luck, poor judgment, an inexperienced admiral, and new Japanese night tactics.[30] However, the events were not without some good news. As the Japanese air units focused on the ships off Rennell Island, the four transports arrived and departed Guadalcanal unharmed.

In the coming weeks the anticipated big Japanese naval operation around Guadalcanal did take place. However, it was not reinforcement, but rather the evacuation of the last remaining troops from the island. Almost six months since the sailors aboard the *Astoria* and *Chicago* had departed Koro Island for the perilous voyage to Guadalcanal, a small foothold had been firmly established on the edge of the Japanese Empire.

Epilogue: The Voyage Continued

The war was not over for the men who served aboard the *Astoria* and *Chicago*. Most would spend some amount of time in the survivors' camp at Noumea before being processed out for reassignment. Some would be granted a thirty day leave, routine navy policy for a survivor of a sunken ship. For many it was a long overdue trip home and a chance to temporarily forget about the war, visit with family, and perhaps spend time with a sweetheart.

New assignments often meant parting company with old shipmates and friends. Some would never see each other again. Others would be reunited at ship reunions decades later. For each sailor a new voyage was about to begin.

* * *

Like the other *Astoria* survivors, Lieutenant (jg) Gene Alair initially went to New Caledonia. "Most of the guys got new construction back in the states," he remembered.[1] Alair would stay in the Pacific and was soon assigned to an amphibious transport division. After initially serving as a navigator, he moved up to flag secretary. He later served in a similar capacity to the commander of a transport division. In February 1945, Alair was assigned to the Joint Army–Navy Communications School. Located at Harvard University, he taught amphibious warfare to commissioned officers. He was serving in this capacity when the war ended.

* * *

After being rescued by a destroyer, *Astoria* survivor Ed Armes was transferred to a transport that took him to the survivors' camp. He eventually made it to San Francisco via Pearl Harbor. Returning to New York on thirty day survivor's leave, he was interviewed by a reporter for *Look* Magazine. His story appeared in the December 29, 1942, issue. In the years that followed, Armes stayed in the naval aviation area. He was stationed at naval air stations in Oakland, Seattle, and Fallon, Nevada, before making his way back to Pearl Harbor. When the war ended he was getting ready to transfer to an aircraft carrier as a parachute rigger.

* * *

After spending time in New Caledonia, *Chicago* survivor Harry Blumhorst made his way back to the states. After reaching the West Coast he was granted a ten day leave. "I spent two days at home and eight days on the road," he recalled.[2] Upon returning from leave he was assigned to the cargo ship *Arrid*.

Later in the war Blumhorst moved to the amphibious force and was a crewman aboard a landing craft. He participated in the invasion of Okinawa and was on the island when the war ended.

* * *

Any aspirations that Captain Howard Bode of the *Chicago* may have had of making flag rank ended off Savo Island. On January 30, 1943, the same day that his former ship sank, he assumed command of the Balboa Naval Station near the Panama Canal. Bode shot himself in the head on April 20, 1943.[3] He died the next day at the Balboa Naval Hospital.[4] Bode's suicide occurred shortly after he was interviewed by Admiral Arthur J. Hepburn, who was conducting an inquiry into the Savo Island debacle. Hepburn's report, completed in May 1943, was critical of the actions that Bode took the night of the battle.[5]

* * *

After a short stay at Pearl Harbor, *Astoria* chaplain Matthew Bouterse was aboard the transport *Henderson* on his way back to San Francisco. "We enjoyed every safe and sane moment aboard," he remembered of the voyage, "and were finally rewarded by the sight of every South Pacific sailor's dream, the Golden Gate Bridge!"[6] He arrived back home on leave just in time to witness the birth of his daughter. After spending some quality time with family, it was time for him to go back to navy life.

Returning to sea duty, Bouterse was next assigned to the transport ship *Pinkney*. He soon found himself back in the Solomons. For almost two years the ship operated in the South Pacific carrying supplies and troops to forward bases and evacuating casualties on the return trips. In March 1944 Bouterse received orders sending him to Officers Training School in Hollywood, Florida. When the war ended he was serving aboard the transport *General J.R. Brooke*.

* * *

Captain Ralph Davis received a bronze star for his efforts in attempting to save the sinking *Chicago*. In May 1943 he assumed command of the *New Orleans*. At the time the heavy cruiser was at the Puget Sound Naval Shipyard being repaired for battle damage suffered near Guadalcanal. Before the repairs were completed, he was reassigned to the Amphibious Training Command. In June 1944 he took leadership of the command. Headquartered in San Diego, he was responsible for training amphibious personnel and maintaining equipment on the West Coast.[7] When the war ended, Davis was in command of Amphibious Group Thirteen. Now a rear admiral, he was aboard his flagship *Estes* in Pearl Harbor when word came of the Japanese surrender.[8]

* * *

Seaman Second Class Frank Dinovo went straight from the survivor's camp to an assignment aboard the battleship *North Carolina*. The now veteran radioman from the *Chicago* served aboard the ship for the remainder of the war. When the hostilities ended Dinovo and the battleship were near Tokyo Bay having participated in some of the final raids on Japan prior to her surrender.

* * *

Electrician's Mate First Class Howard Fortney left New Caledonia aboard the transport *Matsonia* bound for San Diego and reassignment. Having spent the first part of the war aboard the *Chicago*, he would spend the latter part on small ships. After a thirty day survivor's leave he was sent to sub chaser school in Miami.

Fortney was next assigned to the destroyer escort *Pope*. He put the ship into commission and while aboard made chief electrician's mate. He later transferred to the *Raymond* and was aboard the destroyer escort on October 25, 1944, when she bravely defended a group of escort carriers against Japanese fleet units in the Battle of Leyte Gulf. He remained aboard the ship for the rest of the war.

* * *

After the sinking of the *Chicago*, Aviation Machinist's Mate Second Class Charles Germann never served aboard a ship again. Staying in the aviation area, he became part of a carrier aircraft service unit. Often positioned near a naval air station, the group repaired carrier based planes. Germann spent time in California before returning to the Pacific where he was based on Espiritu Santo and in the Philippines. When the war ended Germann was at home in Grinnell, Iowa. He was on leave while in transit from the Pacific to a new assignment in Florida.

* * *

Unlike many of the other *Chicago* survivors, Charles Goldsmith did not get a leave. He was assigned to a work detail on New Caledonia when the last group of sailors shipped out. "I was one of a few that got left behind," he recalled of the disappointment.[9] While still at the survivors' camp, he was assigned to the *Edgar Allan Poe*. A damaged ship without engines, she was towed to various Pacific islands where she served as a supply ship for destroyers.

After a stay aboard the cargo ship *Flying Mist*, Goldsmith returned to the states. His final wartime assignment was as a storekeeper at Bay Meadows in Albany, California. A former horse racing track near Oakland, the base served as a storage area for landing craft.

* * *

Seaman Second Class Bill Grady ended up staying on New Caledonia for almost two years working as a storekeeper in the naval disbursement office. He hoped to be aboard the new *Chicago* that was under construction. Instead, he was sent back to California in late 1944 for duty aboard the *Kittson*.

Putting the transport into commission, he served aboard her during the final stages of the Philippines campaign and during the invasion of Okinawa. When the war ended Grady was in Norfolk. He was on route to Bath, Maine, for assignment aboard the new destroyer *Noa*.

* * *

After the sinking of the *Astoria*, Captain William Greenman served the remainder of the war in a variety of staff positions. In January 1943 he began a short stay in Washington at the Bureau of Personnel. Less than two months later he was on his way back to the Pacific for duty with the Service Force Pacific Fleet. Based at Pearl Harbor, the force was responsible for the strict implementation of all logistic plans that emanated from Admiral Nimitz's staff. Greenman headed the planning section of the command.[10]

In early 1944 Greenman was on his way back to Washington where he would serve for the remainder of the war. He was assigned to the Office of the Secretary of the Navy. On May 13, 1944, Greenman was appointed director of Naval Petroleum Reserves.[11] He ended the war serving in this capacity.

* * *

Seaman Second Class Henry Juarez did not go to the survivors' camp on New Caledonia. Instead the *Astoria* survivor went directly to Pearl Harbor. "From the *Buchanan* we went to the *Wharton*," he said. "We went to New Caledonia and picked up some more survivors ... and then we went to Pearl Harbor."[12] Instead of getting a leave the young sailor was immediately assigned to work in a boat pool. He spent the next three months learning the fundamentals of boat handling.

Juarez soon found himself headed back to the war zone as an operator of a landing craft aboard the transport *Fuller*. "Back to Guadalcanal we went," he said. "We supported Guadalcanal ... I don't know how many times we went there." In November 1943 he participated in the invasion of Bougainville and spent the next nine months working there in a boat pool with the Third Marine Division. It was during that time that Juarez received a letter of commendation for his participation in the rescue of a marine battalion from behind enemy lines.

Returning stateside in 1944 after thirty-two months overseas, Juarez was found to be suffering from combat and operational fatigue. "So I ended up in the hospital," he remembered, "and that's where I got discharged." Departing from the San Diego Naval Hospital in May 1945, he was home in Los Angeles when the war ended.

* * *

Art King did not stay on New Caledonia for very long. The chief electrician's mate from the *Chicago* was at the survivor's camp for just one night when he heard his name being called out. Electrical men were urgently needed stateside for new construction. Before long he was aboard a transport on a two week voyage to San Diego.

After attending submarine chaser school in Miami, King was assigned to the new destroyer escort *Tomich*. He put the ship in commission in July 1943 and cruised aboard her in Caribbean and Atlantic waters. After about a year aboard the *Tomich*, King was commissioned an ensign. His next assignment took him to the Bremerton Navy Shipyard in Washington state where the escort carrier the *Kwajalein* was being completed. He commissioned the new ship as her electrical officer and served aboard the vessel for the rest of the war.

* * *

Seaman Second Class William Kuphaldt's stay in New Caledonia was a short one. The wounded *Astoria* survivor was transferred to the *Wharton* for transport back to Pearl Harbor. After a short stay at a naval hospital, Kuphaldt was on the move to California. "I entered the new naval hospital in Oakland in mid–September," he later wrote.

After several months of treatment, the doctors concluded that nothing further could be done to improve the vision in his damaged right eye. "I wanted to return to active sea duty, but was told this would not be possible because of the lack of vision in my right eye," he remembered.[13] Kuphaldt was given the option of limited shore duty or discharge. He chose the latter and was honorably discharged from the navy on March, 8, 1943. On September 5, 1946, Kuphaldt was awarded a Purple Heart for the wounds received while aboard the *Astoria* almost four years earlier.

* * *

Storekeeper Third Class Ken Maysenhalder was sent from the survivor's camp to San Francisco. He was to become part of the crew for the new light cruiser *Reno*. However, before the ship was commissioned he was asked if he was willing to take shore duty at the base on Treasure Island. A storekeeper on the base wanted sea duty, so the two of them ended up switching assignments. Maysenhalder was serving in this capacity when the war ended.

* * *

It was September 1942 when Fire Controlman First Class John Powell made it back to the United States. The *Astoria*'s sinking had not yet been made public. Powell spent the rest of the war on small ships. "I never went back on a heavy cruiser," he remembered.[14] His next assignment was to the destroyer tender *Cascade*. He put the ship into commission at San Francisco as part of her initial crew.

After about seven months aboard the ship, Powell was commissioned an ensign. He was expecting to only be made a warrant officer, but at the time the navy needed gunnery officers for new construction destroyers. With his credentials apparently fitting the bill, Powell soon found himself assigned to be the gunnery officer of the *Wren*. The new destroyer was being built near Seattle. Putting the ship in commission, Powell served aboard her the rest of the war spending time in the Aleutians, near Okinawa, and bombarding Japan.

* * *

The *Chicago* was the first of four ships that Fire Controlman Second Class George Pursley served aboard during the war. After a short stay on New Caledonia, and a thirty day leave to go home, he reported to Norfolk for duty on the new light cruiser *Mobile*. He stayed on the cruiser for less than a year, but saw plenty of action near Bougainville and the Gilbert Islands.

In late 1943, Pursley went east to Washington, DC, where he attended advanced fire control school. His next assignment was to the new destroyer *Putnam*. He put the ship into commission and headed back out to the Pacific, participating in operations around the Philippines, Iwo Jima, and Okinawa. It was aboard the *Putnam* that Pursley made chief petty officer. When the war ended, he had just transferred to the new destroyer *Strong*.

* * *

After leaving the burning *Astoria* on the destroyer *Bagley*, Ensign Bob Schiller rode a transport down to New Caledonia for what proved to be a very short stay. "I doubt that it was even overnight," he remembered. "I got out of there and went to Pearl Harbor."[15] He remained in naval aviation for the rest of the war. "After we got to Pearl Harbor ... they didn't have anything for us there. All the ships that were there were fully manned. So they sent us back to San Francisco"

Taking a thirty day leave he was able to go back home to Idaho. Schiller's next assignment sent him to a scouting squadron in Oregon. He later served aboard the *Halford*, an experimental destroyer rigged with a catapult for a seaplane, and the escort carrier *Saginaw Bay*. "There was nothing very much exciting," he remembered about his time aboard the carrier. "We were out on a couple of the invasions, but all we did was fly cover over the beaches." When the war ended he was an instructor at the Sanford, Florida, Naval Air Station.

* * *

Marine private Tom Sheble had his fill of sea duty aboard the *Chicago*. In the aftermath of her sinking, he declined an opportunity to go aboard the aircraft carrier *Saratoga*. The carrier had twice been torpedoed by Japanese submarines and he felt that she had a bad reputation as a result. "Every time you heard about the *Saratoga* she had a torpedo in her," he recalled.[16]

After leave and guard duty at Mare Island, Sheble went to Camp Elliott near San Diego for infantry training. He eventually ended up with the Third Marine Division. While traveling back to the war zone, he remembered his time aboard the *Chicago* wondering what it was like to be an infantryman on a troop ship. Now he knew.

Sheble was seriously injured in a mortar attack during the invasion of Guam in July 1944. Evacuated from the beachhead, he left the area aboard the hospital ship *Solace*. He eventually ended up at the Oak Knoll Naval Hospital near Oakland where he stayed for the rest of the war. It was during his stay at the hospital that he met a young nurse who later became his wife.

* * *

For his gallant effort in attempting to save the *Astoria*, Commander Frank Shoup received a letter of commendation (with ribbon) from the Commander in Chief, South Pacific Forces. His next assignment was to serve as the chief of staff to the commander of a transportation division in the amphibious force. After only two months, he was sent to Washington for duty in the Bureau of Naval Personnel and in the Office of the Chief of Naval Operations.

In December 1944 Shoup reported to San Pedro where he assumed command of the newly completed attack transport *Clermont*.[17] He commissioned the ship as her captain on January 28, 1945, and served aboard the vessel for the rest of the war. After completing a period of training, the *Clermont* transported troops to Okinawa. In September of the same year the transport put ashore troops for the occupation of Sasebo Naval Base, Japan.

* * *

For assisting the wounded in the final desperate hours of the *Astoria*, Marine lieutenant Roy Spurlock received a citation for meritorious conduct. "His coolness and courage were in keeping with the highest traditions of the United States Naval Service," the award read.[18] Spurlock went on to have a distinguished career in marine aviation. After the sinking he returned to duty as a pilot and flew combat missions in the Solomon Islands during the latter part of 1942. He returned to the United Sates in the middle of 1943 for duty in Santa Barbara, California. About a year later he returned to the South Pacific as a member of the First Marine Air Wing. Attaining the rank of major he would see combat in a variety of areas of the South Pacific. He participated in forty-nine missions during 1944 alone.

* * *

Like a number of former *Chicago* men, Seaman Second Class Fred Tuccitto was assigned to the new light cruiser *Mobile*. Upon returning to the states, he took a thirty day leave and went back home to Nebraska. "I came to Omaha and it was in the wintertime and I froze my butt off after being in the tropics … I couldn't get out of Omaha quick enough," he remembered.[19] He then traveled to Norfolk to commission his new ship.

Now an aviation ordinance man, Tuccitto became part of the ship's aviation division. He was only the one in the group who had seen combat. Although now part of a new vessel, he fondly remembered and missed the people from the *Chicago*. When the war ended, Tuccitto was on shore duty at Alameda Naval Air Station.

* * *

Lieutenant Richard Tunnell was among the many *Astoria* survivors who went stateside for new construction. After going home on a thirty day leave, he shipped out to New York City to become part of the aviation unit of the new light cruiser *Santa Fe*. "I commissioned the aviation unit," he said. "We were stationed at what is now JFK. In those days it was Floyd Bennett Field and it was a naval air station."[20] The ship completed her shakedown cruise and then went to the war.

Arriving in Pearl Harbor in late March 1943, Tunnell and the *Santa Fe* headed north to the cold waters of the Aleutian Islands. There he participated in the recapture of Attu and Kiska islands. He later flew spotting missions as the cruiser bombarded Tarawa and Wake Island. Before the year was over, the aviator was on his way back to the states. "I had applied earlier for postgraduate school and it takes months and months before those things get sorted out," he said. "I was still aboard ship, but I got orders go to postgraduate school at Annapolis for a course in aeronautical engineering."

Before going on to Annapolis, Tunnell first spent time at Barren Field near Pensacola. "I reported to Annapolis in March 1944 for postgraduate school." After completing the initial courses at the academy, he went on to a civilian college to finish his degree. As to his whereabouts when the war ended, the pilot recalled, "I was in Pasadena at Cal Tech. Kind of a tame finish."[21]

***

Having worked under the executive officer while aboard the *Chicago*, Yeoman Second Class Don Wallace was pressed into service shortly after arriving at the survivor's camp. He and others worked furiously drawing up lists of *Chicago* survivors as well as those who had been killed, wounded or were missing. He was soon aboard the transport *Matsonia* on his way back to the states.

After going home on leave, he reported to Miami for submarine chaser school. He declined an opportunity to become an instructor at the school after graduation. Wallace instead went on to his next assignment aboard the new destroyer escort *England*. Putting the ship into commission, he would serve aboard her for the remainder of the war. The ship gained notoriety for participating in the sinking of six Japanese submarines in May 1944. The vessel was later hit by a kamikaze off Okinawa and returned to the United States. "When the war ended I was in the Philadelphia Naval Hospital," Wallace recalled. He was undergoing minor non-combat related surgery. "I got out of the hospital the day the war ended."[22]

***

Seaman Second Class Don Yeamans eventually made it back to Pearl Harbor. He then went on to San Francisco and was granted a thirty day leave, which he used to go back home to Portland. The blast aboard the *Astoria* that destroyed the navigation plotting room left him with permanent ear problems, resulting in many future trips to hospitals.

Yeamans was later assigned to the *Leader*. Formerly a private yacht, she had been converted to a sonar ship and was based out of New York City. He was later put on limited duty, which meant no sea time. He was stationed at several bases in the Pacific Northwest. When the war ended he was at a naval hospital near Seattle. "I had a re-occurrence of my ear from the battle," he remembered.[23]

Chapter Notes

Part I Page
1. Art King, telephone interviews with author. Hereafter, King.

Chapter 1
1. "Conference on the Limitation of Armament, Washington, November 12, 1921–February 6, 1922." http://ibiblio.org/pha/pre-war/1922/nav_lim.html (accessed April 30, 2007), 4.
2. Norman Friedman, *U.S. Cruisers: An Illustrated Design History* (Annapolis, MD: Naval Institute Press, 1984), 110.
3. Keith Summerville and Harriotte W. B. Smith, *Ships of the United States Navy and Their Sponsors, 1924–1950* (Annapolis, MD: Naval Institute Press, 1952), 89.
4. Al Adcock, *U.S. Heavy Cruisers in Action*. Part 1 (Carrollton, TX: Squadron Signal Publications, 2001), 16 and Friedman, *Cruisers*, 472.
5. Puget Sound Navy Yard, *Christening of U.S.S. Astoria, Heavy Cruiser No. CA 34* (Bremerton, WA: Puget Sound Navy Yard, 1933), 3.
6. Friedman, 473.
7. Walter J. Eddington, *Glossary of Shipbuilding and Outfitting Terms* (New York: Cornell Maritime Press, 1944), 48.
8. Raymond G. O'Connor, "The American Navy, 1939–1941: The Enlisted Perspective." *Military Affairs*, October 1986, 173.
9. John Campbell, *Naval Weapons of World War II* (Annapolis, MD: Naval Institute Press, 1985), 110.
10. Stefan Terzibaschitsch. *Cruisers of the U.S. Navy, 1922–1962* (Annapolis, MD: Naval Institute Press, 1988), 306.

Chapter 2
1. Thomas C. Hone and Trent Hone, *Battle Line: The United States Navy 1919–1939* (Annapolis, MD: Naval Institute Press, 2006), 66.
2. "Chicago (CA-29)." http://www.history.navy (accessed November 22, 2006), 1. Hereafter, "Chicago."
3. Terzibaschitsch, 26.
4. "U.S. Navy Shipboard Radars — CXAM." http://www.history.navy (accessed July 3, 2008).
5. King.
6. Don Wallace, unpublished narrative sent to author, correspondence and telephone interview. Hereafter, Wallace.
7. Ibid.
8. Howard Fortney, telephone interviews and correspondence with author. Hereafter, Fortney.
9. Charles Germann, interview with author. Hereafter, Germann.
10. United States Navy, *The Bluejackets Manual* (Annapolis, MD: Naval Institute Press, 1946), 92.
11. Ken Maysenhalder, telephone interviews with author and unpublished narratives sent to author. Hereafter, Maysenhalder.
12. George Pursley, unpublished narrative sent to author & telephone interviews with author. Hereafter, Pursley.
13. Fred Tuccito, telephone interviews and correspondence with author.
14. "Astoria (CA-34)." http://www.history.navy (accessed November 22, 2006), 1–2. Hereafter, "Astoria."
15. Don Yeamans, telephone interviews and correspondence with author.
16. Richard Tunnell, telephone interview with author. Hereafter, Tunnell.
17. Ibid.
18. Secretary of the Navy, *Register of the Commissioned and Warrant Officers of the Navy of the United States, Including Officers of the Marine Corps* (Washington, DC: Government Printing Office, 1942 & 1943). Hereafter, *Register of Commissioned and Warrant Officers*.
19. United States Naval Academy, *The Lucky Bag* (Annapolis, MD, 1939), 106.
20. John Powell, telephone interviews with author. Hereafter, Powell.
21. Bob Schiller, telephone interviews with author. Hereafter, Schiller.
22. Karl LaVo, "The Destroyer Aviator." *Naval History*, December 2006, 53.
23. "Gene Lyle Alair." http://www.lonesailor.org (accessed June 12, 2007).
24. Gene Alair, telephone interviews and letters to the author. Hereafter, Alair.
25. "New Training Program for Candidates, Ensigns, U.S. Naval Reserve," *Information for Naval Personnel, Bulletin Number 292*, May 31, 1941, 37–38.

26. "Military Training Program Records, 1941–1949." www.library.northwestern.edu/archives/findingaids/military_training_programs.pdf (accessed June 22, 2007).

Chapter 3

1. United States Congress Joint Committee on the Investigation of the Pearl Harbor Attack. *Pearl Harbor Attack. Hearings before the Joint Committee on the Investigation of the Pearl Harbor Attack.* Vol. 26 (Washington, DC: U.S. Government Printing Office, 1946), 343.
2. Samuel Eliot Morison. *History of United States Naval Operations in World War II.* Vol. 3. *The Rising Sun in the Pacific* (Edison, NJ: Castle Books, 2001), 210. Hereafter, Morison, Vol. 3.
3. Yeamans.
4. Edward Armes, telephone interviews with author. Hereafter, Armes.
5. Ibid.
6. "40,000 Join Navy in Month, Four Times Usual Rate," *New York Times.* January 8, 1942.
7. Carol Roberts. "When Boys Became Men of War," *San Louis Obispo Tribune*, September 26, 1999, B1.
8. Bill Grady, telephone interview with author. Hereafter, Grady.
9. Roberts, B1.
10. Harry Blumhorst, telephone interview with author. Hereafter, Blumhorst.
11. Grady.
12. Ibid.
13. Blumhorst.
14. Henry Juarez, telephone interviews with author. Hereafter, Juarez.
15. John M. Bouterse. "Confessions of a Navy Chaplain." Manuscript. Courtesy of Lee Davis. Hereafter, Bouterse.

Chapter 4

1. War Diary. *USS Chicago*, December 1941. Hereafter, *Chicago* War Diary.
2. *Biographical Sketch of Captain Howard Douglas Bode.* Operational Archives Branch, Naval Historical Center, Washington, D, 1.
3. Maysenhalder.
4. Grady.
5. King.
6. *Chicago* War Diary, May 1942.
7. Morison, Vol. 3, 38–39.
8. *Chicago* War Diary, May 15, 1942.
9. *Astoria* Deck Log, December 15, 1941.
10. "Astoria," 3.
11. Bouterse.

Part II Page

1. Alair.

Chapter 5

1. Daniel Hawthorne, *Islands of the Pacific* (New York: G.P. Putnam's Sons, 1943), 134.
2. Frank O. Hough, Verle E. Ludwig, and Henry I. Shaw, *History of U.S. Marine Corps Operations in World War II, Volume I: Pearl Harbor to Guadalcanal* (Washington, DC: Historical Branch, G-3 Division, Headquarters, U.S. Marine Corps, 1958), 238.
3. Ronald H. Spector, *Eagle Against the Sun* (New York: Vintage Books, 1985), 185.
4. Wallace.
5. Grady.
6. George Dyer, *The Amphibians Came To Conquer: The Story of Admiral Richmond Kelly Turner.* Vol. I (Washington, DC: United States Navy, 1972), 295.
7. Ibid.
8. "U.S. Navy Record of Officers: William Greenman." St. Louis, MO: National Personnel Records Center. Hereafter, "Greenman Naval Records."
9. *Register of Commissioned and Warrant Officers.*
10. Samuel Eliot Morison. *History of United States Naval Operations in World War II.* Vol. 1. *The Battle of the Atlantic* (Boston, MA: Little, Brown & Company, 1959), 14–15. Hereafter, Morison, Vol. 1.
11. "Greenman Naval Records."
12. Joe James Custer. *Through the Perilous Night* (New York: Macmillan, 1944), 92.
13. *Biographical Sketch of Captain Frank Elliot Shoup, Jr.*, Operational Archives Branch, Naval Historical Center, Washington, DC, 1.
14. Alair.
15. Juarez.
16. Powell.
17. Admiral Arthur J. Hepburn, Report of Informal Inquiry into the Circumstances Attending the loss of U.S.S. *Vincennes*, U.S.S. *Quincy*, U.S.S. *Astoria*, and H.M.A.S. *Australia*, on August 9, 1942, in the Vicinity of Savo Island (Solomon Islands) (Washington, DC: Navy Department, Headquarters of the Commander in Chief, 1943,) Annex, "Interrogation of Captain W.G. Greenman, U.S.N.," 1. Hereafter, "Greenman Interrogation."
18. Custer, 79–80.
19. Clark G. Reynolds, *The Saga of Smokey Stover* (Charleston, SC: Tradd Street Press, 1978), 33.
20. Earl Schenck, "Action in the Pacific," *Liberty*, July 31, 1943, 56.
21. Juarez.
22. Bouterse.
23. Hawthorne, 139.
24. John Miller Jr., *Guadalcanal: The First Offensive* (Washington, DC: Historical Division, United States Army, 1949), 36.
25. CO Task Group 62.6, "Special Instructions to Screening Group and Vessels Temporarily Assigned." Undated. 1. Hereafter, "Special Instructions to Screening Group."
26. CO Task Force 62. "Transmittal of Commander Task Force Sixty-Two Operation Plan A3-42." July 30, 1942. Annex A, 2. Hereafter, "Operational Plan A3-42."

Chapter 6
1. Germann.
2. Campbell, 137.
3. Tuccitto.
4. Wallace.
5. King.
6. Fortney.
7. Grady.
8. Schiller.
9. Al Adcock, *U.S. Navy Floatplanes of World War II in Action* (Carrollton, TX: Squadron Signal Publications, 2006), 7.
10. Schiller.
11. Campbell, 151.
12. Ibid.
13. Juarez.
14. Powell.

Chapter 7
1. Dyer, *Amphibians*, 295; and Leonard Ware, *The Landing in the Solomons* (Washington, DC: Office of Naval Intelligence, United States Navy, 1943), 13–14.
2. War Diary Task Force 62, July 27, 1942. Hereafter, TF 62 War Diary.
3. Juarez.
4. Bouterse.
5. William Bartsch, "Operation Dovetail: Bungled Guadalcanal Rehearsal, July 1942." *The Journal of American Military History*, April 2002, 452.
6. Ibid., 452–454.
7. King.
8. Tunnell.
9. John B. Lundstrom, *The First Team and the Guadalcanal Campaign* (Annapolis, MD: Naval Institute Press, 1994), 30.
10. Roy Spurlock, *First Savo: The Lost Battle*, unpublished narrative. Courtesy of the Columbia River Maritime Museum. Hereafter, Spurlock.
11. Ibid.
12. Alair.
13. Juarez.
14. Tuccitto.
15. Grady.

Chapter 8
1. TF 62 War Diary, July 31, 1942.
2. Ibid., August 1, 1942.
3. Mochitsura Hashimotok, *Sunk: The Story of the Japanese Submarine Fleet, 1941–1945* (New York: Holt, 1954), 258.
4. Dyer, 316.
5. Ibid., 322.
6. Ware, 29.
7. Spurlock.
8. Miller, 59.
9. Custer, 90.
10. Bouterse.
11. Ibid.
12. TF 62 War Diary, August 2, 1942.
13. Lundstrom, 33.

Chapter 9
1. "Special Instructions to Screening Group," 2.
2. Blumhorst.
3. "Attack Force Approach Disposition AR-3," in "Operational Plan A3–42," 1.
4. TF 62 War Diary, August 6, 1942.
5. Deck Log. *USS Chicago* (CA-29), August 7, 1942. Hereafter, *Chicago* Deck Log.
6. *Register of Commissioned and Warrant Officers*.
7. Ware, 29.
8. *Chicago* Deck Log, August 7, 1942; and Custer, 105.
9. "Greenman Interrogation."
10. Kerry L. Lane. *Guadalcanal Marine* (Jackson, MS: University of Mississippi Press, 2004), 69.
11. Richard Tregaskis, *Guadalcanal Diary* (New York: Random House, 1943), 34.
12. Lane, 69.
13. Clark Lee, *They Call It Pacific* (New York: Viking Press, 1943), 329.
14. Lundstrom, 34.
15. Tuccitto.
16. Maysenhalder.
17. Germann.
18. Alair.
19. Juarez.
20. Tunnell.
21. "Ships' Gunfire Plan," in "Operational Plan A3–42," 2.
22. Dyer, 329.
23. Bouterse.
24. Richard B. Frank, *Guadalcanal* (New York: Random House, 1990), 60.
25. Maysenhalder.
26. Bartsch, 449.
27. "Ships' Gunfire Plan," in "Operational Plan A3–42," 1–3.
28. Miller, 69.
29. Ware, 52.
30. Ibid., 31.
31. Ibid., 52.
32. Powell.
33. Tregaskis, 41.
34. Schiller.
35. "Special Instructions to Screening Group," 3.
36. *Chicago* Deck Log, August 7, 1942.

Chapter 10
1. Japanese Self Defense Force: War History Office, *Senshi Sosho (War History Series)*. Vol. 49. *Southeast Area Naval Operations, Part I* (Tokyo: Asagumo Shibunsha, 1971), 446. Hereafter, *Senshi Sosho*, Vol. 49.
2. "Translations from Daily War Reports of the 25th Air Flotilla, August and September, 1942." Records of Japanese Navy & Related Documents, Translations, 1941–1946. Naval Historical Center.

Washington, DC. Hereafter, "War Reports of the 25th Air Flotilla."
   3. Ibid.
   4. Samuel Eliot Morison. *History of United States Naval Operations in World War II*. Vol. 4. *Coral Sea, Midway and Submarine Actions* (Edison, NJ: Castle Books, 2001), 289.
   5. Dr. Rene J. Francillon. *Japanese Navy Bombers of World War II* (New York: Doubleday, 1969), 43.
   6. Grady.
   7. Eric Feldt, *The Coast Watchers* (New York: Ballantine Books, 1959), 86.
   8. Ware, 54.
   9. CO USS *Chicago* to CinCPac. "Action against Enemy Aircraft, August 7–8 1942." August 19, 1942, 1. Hereafter, *Chicago*, "Action against Enemy Aircraft."
   10. Masatake Okumiya, and Jiro Horikoshi, with Martin Caidin. *Zero!* (New York: Dutton, 1956), 184.
   11. Saburo Sakai, Martin Caidin, and Fred Saito. *Samurai* (New York: Dutton, 1957), 211.
   12. Lundstrom, 52.
   13. Powell.
   14. Spurlock.
   15. King.
   16. Lt. Joseph R. Daley. "Shot Down in Flames," *Cosmopolitan*, April 1943, 51, 88.
   17. TF 62 War Diary, August 7, 1942.
   18. Joseph R. Daly, *Luck is My Lady* (New York: Vantage Press, 1989), 2.
   19. Daly, "Shot Down in Flames," 88.
   20. Lundstrom, 68.
   21. Medical Officer to CO USS *Chicago*. "Report of Killed and Wounded." August 10, 1942, 4. Hereafter, *Chicago*, "Medical Report."
   22. Paul Dull, *Battle History of the Imperial Japanese Navy, 1941–1945* (Annapolis, MD: Naval Institute Press, 1978), 184.
   23. *Chicago* Deck Log, August 7, 1942.
   24. Custer, 118.

Chapter 11

   1. Walter Lord. *Lonely Vigil* (New York: Viking Press, 1977), 41.
   2. TF 62 War Diary, August 8, 1942.
   3. Ware, 76.
   4. *Chicago*, "Action against Enemy Aircraft," 2.
   5. King.
   6. Maysenhalder.
   7. Tuccitto.
   8. Ware, 77.
   9. Ibid.
   10. Powell.
   11. Tunnell.
   12. Spurlock.
   13. Lundstrom, 78.
   14. Custer, 120–121.
   15. Yeamans.
   16. Bouterse.
   17. Schiller.
   18. "George F. Elliot (AP-13)." in *Dictionary of American Fighting Ships*. http://www.history.navy.mil/danfs/index.html (accessed on various dates 2006–2007).
   19. TF 62 War Diary, August 8, 1942.
   20. George W. Kittredge. "Savo Island: The Worst Defeat." http://www.navalinstitute.org/NavalHistory/Articles02 (accessed October 22, 2006), 3.
   21. Frank, 79.
   22. Bruce Loxton and Chris Coulthard-Clark, *The Shame of Savo* (Annapolis, MD: Bluejacket Books, 1997), 106.
   23. Richard Newcomb, *Savo: The Incredible Naval Debacle off Guadalcanal* (New York: Holt, Rinehart and Winston, 1961), 77.
   24. Armes.

Part III Page

   1. Santos, Abe, telephone interview with author. Hereafter, Santos.

Chapter 12

   1. Captain Toshikazu Ohmae, "The Battle of Savo Island," *United States Naval Institute Proceedings*, December, 1957, 1264. Hereafter, Ohmae.
   2. Newcomb, 24.
   3. Richard W. Bates and Walter D. Innis, *The Battle of Savo Island, August 9, 1942: Strategical and Technical Analysis* (Newport, RI: U.S. Naval War College, 1950), 44. Hereafter Bates and Innis.
   4. Ibid., 48.
   5. Ohmae, 1269–1270.
   6. David C. Evans and Mark R. Peattie, *Kaigun: Strategy, Tactics and Technology in the Imperial Japanese Navy, 1887–1941* (Annapolis, MD: Naval Institute Press, 1997), 275.
   7. Rear Admiral (JMSDF) Yoichi Hirama, "Japanese Naval Preparations for World War II," *Naval War College Review*, Spring 1991, 71.
   8. Loxton and Coulthard-Clark, 124.
   9. Samuel Eliot Morison. *History of United States Naval Operations in World War II*. Vol. 5. *The Struggle for Guadalcanal* (Edison, NJ: Castle Book, 2001), 19. Hereafter, Morison, Vol. 5.
   10. Bates and Innis, 74.
   11. Ibid., 76.
   12. Evans and Peattie, 275.
   13. Bates and Innis, 78.
   14. "CA *Chokai* Action Record." Records of Japanese Navy & Related Documents, Translations, 1941–1946. Naval Historical Center. Washington, DC. Hereafter, "CA *Chokai* Action Record."
   15. Loxton and Coulthard-Clark, 133.
   16. "Greenman Interrogation."
   17. Frank, 95.
   18. Dyer, 368.
   19. Newcomb, 92.

Chapter 13

   1. "Special Instructions to Screening Group," 1.
   2. Denis Warner, Peggy Warner, and Sadao Seno,

Disaster in the Pacific: New Light on the Battle of Savo Island (Annapolis, MD: Naval Institute Press, 1992), 75.
  3. "Special Instructions to Screening Group," 5–6.
  4. Newcomb, 91.
  5. Winston Lewis, *The Battle of Savo Island* (Washington, DC: Office of Naval Intelligence, United States Navy, 1943), 3.
  6. TF 62 War Diary, August 8, 1942.
  7. Bates and Innis, 86.
  8. "Greenman Interrogation."
  9. Bates and Innis, 87.
  10. CO USS *Patterson* to CinCPac. "Engagement with Enemy (Japanese) Surface Ships Night 8–9 August in Savo-Guadalcanal-Tulagi Island Group Solomon Islands," August 13, 1942, 1. Hereafter, *Patterson*, "Engagement with Enemy."
  11. Loxton and Coulthard-Clark, 112.
  12. Spurlock.
  13. *Chicago* Deck Log, August 8, 1942.
  14. Grady.
  15. Ibid.
  16. King.
  17. Germann.
  18. "Greenman Interrogation."
  19. Custer, 123.
  20. Yeamans.
  21. Juarez.
  22. Theodore Torsch, telephone interviews with author. Hereafter, Torsch.
  23. Tunnell.
  24. Schiller.
  25. Armes.
  26. Powell.
  27. Alair.
  28. Bouterse.
  29. Warner and Warner, 109.

Chapter 14

  1. Eric Lacroix and Linton Wells, *Japanese Cruisers of the Pacific War* (Annapolis, MD: Naval Institute Press, 1997), 121–122.
  2. "War Diary Kako from 7–10 August 1942, Solomons Sea Battle." Records of Japanese Navy & Related Documents, Translations, 1941–1946. Naval Historical center. Washington, DC. Hereafter, "*Kako* War Diary."
  3. Bates and Innis, 106.
  4. "CA *Chokai* Action Record."
  5. Bates and Innis, Analysis, 58.
  6. Lewis, 5.
  7. Rear Admiral Edwin T. Layton, Roger Pineau, and John Costello, *And I Was There: Pearl Harbor and Midway- Breaking the Secrets* (New York: Morrow, 1985), 459.
  8. Ohmae, 1273.
  9. Jack Coombe, *Derailing the Tokyo Express* (Harrisburg, PA: Stackpole Books, 1991), 23.
  10. Bates and Innis, 108.
  11. Warner and Warner, 103.
  12. Morison, Vol. 5, 34.
  13. Frank, 97.
  14. Bates and Innis, 115.
  15. Senior Surviving Officer USS *Quincy* to CinCPac. "Report of the Engagement the Morning of August 9, 1942, off Guadalcanal Island in which the U.S.S. *Quincy* Participated." August 16, 1942, 1.
  16. Warner and Warner, 117.
  17. Loxton and Coulthard-Clark, 180.
  18. Frank, 105.
  19. Morison, Vol. 5, 38.
  20. Newcomb, 106.
  21. CO USS *Bagley* to CinCPac. "Night Engagement August 9, 1942 — Tulagi Guadalcanal Area." August 13, 1942, 1. Hereafter, *Bagley*, "Night Engagement."
  22. *Bagley*, "Night Engagement," 1.

Chapter 15

  1. CO USS *Chicago* to CinCPac. "Action against Enemy Forces August 9, 1942, Guadalcanal — Tulagi Area — Report of." August 13, 1942, 2. Hereafter, *Chicago*, "Action against Enemy Forces."
  2. Bates and Innis, 129.
  3. *Chicago*, "Action against Enemy Forces," 2.
  4. Bates and Innis, 132 and Newcomb, 110.
  5. *Chicago*, "Action against Enemy Forces," 2.
  6. Loxton and Coulthard-Clark, 211.
  7. Bates and Innis, 131–132 and Warner and Warner, 133.
  8. Fortney.
  9. Grady.
  10. Germann.
  11. Daly, "Shot Down in Flames," 88.
  12. Newcomb, 111.
  13. Ibid.
  14. King.
  15. *Chicago*, "Action against Enemy Forces," 3.
  16. Bates and Innis, 130.
  17. Loxton and Coulthard-Clark, 212.
  18. King.
  19. Wallace.
  20. Pursley.
  21. Maysenhalder.
  22. *Chicago*, "Medical Report," 3; and Maysenhalder.
  23. Tuccitto.

Chapter 16

  1. Bates and Innis, 138.
  2. CO USS *Astoria* to CinCPac. "Battle Savo Island — Action of Cruisers Task Force 62.3, Early Morning August 9, 1942 — Loss of U.S.S *Astoria*." August 20, 1942, 1. Hereafter, *Astoria*, "Battle Savo Island," 2.
  3. "Greenman Interrogation."
  4. Lieutenant Commander J. R. Topper to CO USS *Astoria*, "Statement Concerning Morning Action of August 9, 1942." August 17, 1942, in *Astoria*, "Battle Savo Island."
  5. Powell.

6. Alair.
7. William H. Truesdell to CO USS *Astoria*, "Report of Cruiser Night Action, August 9, 1942, Between U.S.S. *Astoria*, Quincy, Vincennes and Japanese Vessels." August 13, 1942, 1, in *Astoria*, "Battle Savo Island."
8. Truesdell, 1.
9. King.
10. John Datko, "Statement of Datko, CRM, USN." n.d., 1, in *Astoria*, "Battle Savo Island."
11. William Cramer, "Statement of Ens. W. F. Cramer, USNR." n.d., 1, in *Astoria*, "Battle Savo Island."
12. Walter Johns. "Statement of W.W. Johns, FC1c, USN." n.d., 1, in *Astoria*, "Battle Savo Island," and Lewis, 4.
13. "Greenman Interrogation."
14. Topper, 2.
15. Newcomb, 121.
16. Frank, 107.
17. United States Strategic Bombing Survey (Pacific), Naval Analysis Division. *The Interrogations of Japanese Officials*. Vols. 1 and 2 (Washington, DC: Government Printing Office, 1946), 361. Hereafter, *Interrogations of Japanese Officials*.
18. Morison, Vol. 5, 41.
19. "Japanese Naval Ordnance." http://combinedfleet.com (accessed January 25, 2008).
20. Bates and Innis, 154.
21. Topper, 2.
22. Warner and Warner, 173.
23. Topper, 2.
24. Walter Putnam, "Statement of W.F. Putnam, Yeoman Second Class, USN." n.d., 1, in *Astoria*, "Battle Savo Island."
25. Royal Radke, "Statement of Radke, R.A., QM2c, U.S. Navy in Connection with the Action of the Astoria Aug. 9, 1942." n.d., 1, in *Astoria*, "Battle Savo Island."
26. Noel Burkey, "Statement Concerning Action against August 9, 1942." August 17, 1942, 1, in *Astoria*, "Battle Savo Island."
27. *Astoria*, "Battle Savo Island," 4 & 14.
28. "Greenman Interrogation."
29. Yeamans.
30. Truesdell, 1.
31. Ibid., 6.
32. Raymond McGrath, "Statement of Ensign R.C. McGrath, USN." n.d., 1, in *Astoria*, "Battle Savo Island."
33. Truesdell, 4.
34. Johns, 1.

Chapter 17

1. Loxton and Coulthard-Clark, 225.
2. Burkey, 2.
3. *Astoria*, "Battle Savo Island," 4.
4. Topper, 2.
5. Ibid., 3.
6. Truesdell, 2.
7. Topper, 3.
8. Bates and Innis, 194.
9. "Greenman Interrogation."
10. Topper, 3.
11. Warner and Warner, 178.
12. Bates and Innis, 195.
13. *Astoria*, "Battle Savo Island," 16.
14. Schiller.
15. Bureau of Ships, United States Navy,. "War Damage Report #29: Loss of the USS *Astoria* (CA-34)." 1942, 6. Hereafter, "War Damage Report #29."
16. Truesdell, 9.
17. McGrath, 1.
18. "War Damage Report #29," 6.
19. Putnam, 1.

Chapter 18

1. Morison, Vol. 5, 49.
2. Warner and Warner, 188–189.
3. Loxton and Coulthard-Clark, 228.
4. Truesdell, 10.
5. Bates and Innis, 218.
6. "*Kako* War Diary."
7. Lieutenant Commander John D. Hayes, "Report of the Engineering Department, U.S.S. Astoria, during and subsequent to action with the enemy, about 0200, August 9th, 1942." August 20, 1942, 6–7, in *Astoria*, "Battle Savo Island."
8. Hayes, 7.
9. Ibid., 7, 10 & 17.
10. Ibid., 18.
11. "War Damage Report #29," Plate II.
12. Abe Santos, "The USS Astoria (CA-34) and the Battle of Savo Island," *Voices from the Past: Blue Jackets Remember*, ed. Bruce M. Petty (Annapolis, MD: Naval Institute Press, 2004), 76.
13. Santos.

Chapter 19

1. Yeamans.
2. *Astoria*, "Battle Savo Island," 5.
3. "*Kako* War Diary."
4. "Navy Officer Credits Twin's Transfusion with Saving His Life." Undated newspaper article courtesy of Tom Ferneding. Hereafter, "Twin's Transfusion."
5. Putnam, 1.
6. Julian Young, "Statement of Young, J., BM1c, U.S. Navy, In Connection with the Action of the Astoria August 9, 1942." n.d., 1, in *Astoria*, "Battle Savo Island."
7. *Astoria,* "Battle Savo Island," 6.
8. Ibid.
9. Bates and Innis, 244.
10. Truesdell, 2.
11. Bates and Innis, 243.
12. Ibid.
13. Truesdell, 2.
14. D.R. Marzetta, "Statement of Lieut. (jg) D. R. Marzetta, U.S.N. Battle Station — Plotting Control Officer." August 13, 1942, in *Astoria*, "Battle Savo Island."

15. Johns, 2.
16. Jack Gibson, "Statement of J.E. Gibson, Lieutenant, U.S.N. Battle Station — Control Officer Main Battery — Control Aft." August 14, 1942, 1, *Astoria*, "Battle Savo Island."
17. Gibson, 1.
18. Vincent Healey, "Statement of Lieut. (jg) V.P. Healey, U.S.N. Battle Station — Battery Officer 5" Battery." August 13, 1942, 1, in *Astoria*, "Battle Savo Island."
19. Ellis Wakefield, "Statement of Lt. Comdr E.K. Wakefield, USN." n.d., 1, in *Astoria*, "Battle Savo Island."
20. Healey, 1.
21. *Astoria*, "Battle Savo Island," 17.
22. Topper, 3.
23. *The Bluejackets Manual*, 340.
24. Ibid., 4.
25. *Astoria*, "Battle Savo Island," 17; and "Greenman Interrogation."
26. Warner and Warner, 183.
27. *Interrogations of Japanese Officials*, 362.
28. *Astoria*, "Battle Savo Island," 7.

Chapter 20

1. Ohmae, 1276.
2. "*Kako* War Diary."
3. Morison, Vol. 5, 53.
4. Ibid., 46.
5. Truesdell, 3.
6. *Astoria*, "Battle Savo Island," 7.
7. Gene Alair, "Statement of Lt/ (jg) G.L. Alair, U.S.N.R. Battle Station —1.1 Director I." August 15, 1942, 1, in *Astoria*, "Battle Savo Island." Hereafter Alair, "Statement."
8. Wakefield, 1.
9. Bates and Innis, 246–247.
10. Alair; and Alair, "Statement," 1.
11. Alair, "Statement," 1.
12. Alair.
13. William Kuphaldt, narrative from 1993 sent to author. Hereafter, Kuphaldt.
14. "War Damage Report #29," Plate III.
15. Eugene Hardy Collection (AFC/2001/001/20428), Veterans History Project, American Folklife Center, Library of Congress.
16. Powell.
17. Donald Willman, "Statement of Lieutenant D.E. Willman, U.S.N. Battle Station — Sky Forward." August 14, 1942, 1, in *Astoria*, "Battle Savo Island."
18. Topper, 5.
19. Marzetta, 3.
20. Topper, 5.
21. Ibid., 6.
22. McGrath, 1.
23. Schiller.
24. Tunnell.
25. Healey, 1,

Chapter 21

1. Charles Flower, "Report of Medical Department in Battle of Savo Island," n.d., 1, in *Astoria*, "Battle Savo Island."
2. Flower, 2.
3. Powell.
4. Spurlock.
5. Kuphaldt.
6. *Astoria*, "Battle Savo Island," 8.
7. Topper, 6.
8. Ibid.
9. Wakefield, 2.
10. *Astoria*, "Battle Savo Island," 8.
11. McGrath, 2.
12. Yeamans.
13. Powell.
14. *Astoria*, "Battle Savo Island," 9.
15. Morison, Vol. 5, 57.
16. *Bagley*, "Night Engagement," 2.
17. Schenck, 57.
18. Powell.
19. Schiller.
20. Tunnell.
21. Spurlock.
22. Alair.
23. *Bagley*, "Night Engagement," 2.
24. Healey, 2.
25. Bouterse.

Chapter 22

1. Frank Shoup, "Night Cruiser Action off Savo Island, Early Morning of 9 August 1942." August 19, 1942, 1, in *Astoria*, "Battle Savo Island."
2. Ibid.
3. Gibson, 2.
4. Scheck, 57.
5. Shoup, 6.
6. Torsch.
7. Armes.
8. George Douglas, telephone interview with author and correspondence.
9. Belcher Hobson, telephone interviews with author. Hereafter, Hobson.
10. Shoup, 2.
11. Flower, 3.
12. Ibid., 3.
13. Juarez.
14. Bouterse.
15. Santos.
16. Hayes, 18.
17. Shoup, 3.
18. Hayes, 19.
19. Shoup, 4.
20. Ibid., 5.

Chapter 23

1. Bates and Innis, *Analysis*, 292.
2. Topper, 7.
3. *Astoria*, "Battle Savo Island," 9.

4. Ibid., 9–10.
5. Alair.
6. Topper, 7.
7. Hayes, 20.
8. *Astoria*, "Battle Savo Island," 10–11.
9. Shoup, 5.
10. Hobson.
11. Juarez.
12. Santos.
13. Hayes, 20.
14. *Bagley*, "Night Engagement," 3.
15. Newcomb, 188.
16. Warner and Warner, 208.
17. *Astoria*, "Battle Savo Island," 11.
18. CO USS *Wilson* to CinCPac. "Report of Action against Enemy Surface Ships off Savo Island, Night of August 8–9, 1942. August 20, 1942, 3. Hereafter, *Wilson*, "Action Against Enemy Surface Ships."
19. Healey, 2.
20. *Wilson*, "Action Against Enemy Surface Ships," 3.
21. Armes.

Chapter 24

1. Flower, 2.
2. Pat Jones, ed. *The USS Astoria and the Men Who Sailed Her* (Hillsboro, OR: Premier Press, 1992), 136–137, and Flower, 2.
3. Custer, *Perilous Night*, 140.
4. Bouterse.
5. Kuphaldt.
6. *Bagley*, "Night Engagement," Enclosure C and Enclosure D.
7. Jones, 135.
8. Ibid., 138.
9. *Bagley*, "Night Engagement," Enclosure B.
10. Powell.
11. Spurlock.
12. Hayes, 21.
13. Topper, 8.
14. War Diary. USS *Buchanan* (DD-484). August 9, 1942. Hereafter, "*Buchanan* War Diary."
15. Shoup, 5.
16. *Astoria*, "Battle Savo Island," 12.
17. "Astoria Survivor Tells of Jap Attack in Savo Island Battle." Undated newspaper article. Box 5, in Record Group 24. Records on the Bureau of Naval Personnel: Ships Stations, Units and Incidents, Causality Information, 1941–45. National Archives II, College Park, MD.
18. Shoup, 6.
19. Juarez.
20. Ibid.
21. Yeamans.
22. Alair.
23. John Fritz. Narrative sent to author.

Chapter 25

1. Theodore Roscoe, *United States Submarine Operations in World War II* (Annapolis, MD: Naval Institute Press, 1949), 153.

2. "*Kako* War Diary."
3. *Chicago*, "Action Against Enemy Forces," 3.
4. Bates and Innis, 133.
5. Ibid., 204.
6. *Patterson*, "Engagement with Enemy," 2.
7. Ibid.
8. Task Group 62.6, "Night Action off Savo Island," 3.
9. *Chicago* Deck Log, August 9, 1942.
10. *Chicago*, "Action Against Enemy Forces," 6.
11. Loxton and Coulthard-Clark, 246.
12. King.
13. Germann.
14. Tuccitto.
15. CO Task Group 62.6, "Night Action off Savo Island (9 August, 1942- Remarks by C.T.G. 62.6)." August 11, 1942, 1. Hereafter, Task Group 62.6, "Night Action off Savo Island."
16. Task Group 62.6, "Night Action off Savo Island," 2.
17. Morison, Vol. 5, 52.
18. Task Group 62.6, "Night Action off Savo Island," 2.
19. John Costello, *The Pacific War* (New York: Rawson, Wade, 1981), 326.
20. TF 62 War Diary, August 9, 1942.
21. Edwin P. Hoyt, *How They Won the War in the Pacific: Nimitz and His Admirals* (New York: Lyons Press, 2000), 139.
22. Miller, 80–81.
23. Frank, 123.
24. *Chicago* War Diary, August 11, 1942.
25. Flower, 5.
26. Santos.
27. Powell.
28. Spurlock.
29. Santos.
30. Alair.
31. Bouterse.
32. Kuphaldt.
33. "Lt. Ferneding, Injured in Action, Home on Leave." Undated newspaper article courtesy of Tom Ferneding.
34. "Twin's Transfusion."
35. Custer, 168.

Part IV Page

1. Fortney.

Chapter 26

1. King.
2. CO USS *Chicago* to Chief of the Bureau of Ships, "War Damage Report." August 25, 1942, 10.
3. *Chicago* War Diary, August 27–29, 1942.
4. CO USS *Chicago* to Chief of the Bureau of Ships, "War Damage Report (Supplementary)." September 18, 1942, 1.
5. Tuccitto.
6. Wallace.
7. *Chicago* War Diary, October 13–15, 1942.

8. Maysenhalder.
9. Germann.
10. Fortney.
11. Frank Dinovo, telephone interview with author. Hereafter, Dinovo.
12. Ibid.
13. *Chicago* War Diary, November 27, 1942.
14. Terzibaschitsch, 77.
15. *Biographical Sketch of Vice Admiral Ralph O. Davis*, Operational Archives Branch, Naval Historical Center, Washington, DC.
16. King.

Chapter 27

1. Thomas Sheble, telephone interviews with author. Hereafter, Sheble.
2. Germann.
3. Sheble.
4. Tim Johnson. "Veteran's Ship comes in." *The Daily Nonpareil*, Council Bluffs, IA, December 3, 2000.
5. Dinovo.
6. Maysenhalder.
7. Sheble.
8. Dan Van Der Vat, *The Pacific Campaign* (New York: Simon & Schuster, 1991), 245.
9. King.
10. "Vice Admiral Robert C. Giffen, USN (1886–1962)." http://www.history.navy (accessed November 2, 2006).

Chapter 28

1. CinCPac to Commander in Chief U.S. Fleet, "Solomon Islands Campaign- Fall of Guadalcanal, Period 25 January to 10 February, 1943. April 7, 1943, 3. Hereafter, "Solomon Islands Campaign."
2. John Wukovits, "Battle of Rennell Island: Setback in the Solomons." http://www.historynet.com (accessed May 4, 2005), 1.
3. *Combat Narrative Number VIII: The Japanese Evacuation of Guadalcanal* (Washington, DC: Office of Naval Intelligence, United States Navy, 1944), 26. Hereafter, *The Japanese Evacuation of Guadalcanal*.
4. "Solomon Islands Campaign," 3.
5. *The Japanese Evacuation of Guadalcanal*, 27.
6. Frank, 578; and Morison, Vol. 5, 352.
7. CO Task Force 18 to CinCPac, "Action Report- Task Force 18, January 29–30, 1943." February 19, 1943, 2. Hereafter, "Action Report — Task Force 18."
8. CO Task Group 18.2 to CO Task Force 18, "Operations — report of— USS Chenango and USS Suwannee from 1140L, 29 January to, 31 January 1943." February 14, 1943, 1.
9. Morison, Vol. 5, 355.
10. "Solomon Islands Campaign," 4.
11. Japanese Self Defense Force: War History Office, *Senshi Sosho (War History Series)*. Vol. 83. *Southeast Area Naval Operations, Part II (*Tokyo: Asagumo Shibunsha, 1975), 542. Hereafter *Senshi Sosho*, Volume 83.

12. CO USS *Chicago* to CinCPac, "Preliminary Report of Action with Japanese Aircraft Beginning at Dusk 29 January 1943." February 3, 1943, 1. Hereafter, "Preliminary Report of Action with Japanese Aircraft."
13. Morison, Vol. 5, 356.
14. "Preliminary Report of Action with Japanese Aircraft," 2.
15. Edwin P. Hoyt, *Guadalcanal* (New York: Stein and Day, 1982), 279.
16. *Senshi Sosho*, Vol. 83, 543.
17. Sheble.
18. Blumhorst.
19. Dinovo.
20. Fortney.
21. Bureau of Ships, United States Navy, "War Damage Report #37: USS Chicago (CA-29) Loss in Action." 1944, 1. Hereafter, "USS Chicago Loss in Action."
22. Ibid.
23. Grady.
24. King.
25. Germann.
26. Charles Goldsmith, telephone interviews with author. Hereafter, Goldsmith.
27. *The Japanese Evacuation of Guadalcanal*, 51.
28. "Solomon Islands Campaign," 6.

Chapter 29

1. *Navajo* Deck Log, January 30, 1943.
2. King.
3. Germann.
4. Preliminary Report of Action with Japanese Aircraft," 4.
5. "Action Report — Task Force 18," 7; and Morison, Vol. 5, 359.
6. *Senshi Sosho*, Vol. 83, 544.
7. "Solomon Islands Campaign," 7.
8. *Senshi Sosho*, Vol. 83, 544.
9. Ibid., 544–545.
10. Steve Ewing. *Reaper Leader: The Life of Jimmy Flatley* (Annapolis, MD: Naval Institute Press, 2002, 165.
11. "Preliminary Report of Action with Japanese Aircraft," 4.
12. Goldsmith.
13. Grady.
14. "Preliminary Report of Action with Japanese Aircraft," 5.
15. Germann.
16. Sheble.
17. Fortney.
18. Dinovo.
19. Blumhorst.
20. Tuccitto.
21. Grady.
22. King.
23. Wallace.
24. Goldsmith.
25. *Sands* Deck Log, January 30, 1943.
26. Frank, 581.
27. "Preliminary Report of Action with Japanese Aircraft," Enclosure C, 2.

28. Pursley.
29. Johnson, 6A.
30. Morison, Vol. 5, 363.

Epilogue

1. Alair.
2. Blumhorst.
3. *Bode Biographical Sketch*, 2.
4. Sandy Shanks. *The Bode Testament* (Lincoln, NE: Writers Club Press, 2001), 503.
5. Loxton and Coulthard-Clark, 263–266.
6. Bouterse.
7. *Davis Biographical Sketch*, 2–3.
8. *USS Estes, a History.* http//www.ussestes.org (Accessed June 28, 2008), 6.
9. Goldsmith.
10. Samuel Eliot Morison. *History of United States Naval Operations in World War II*. Vol. 7. *Aleutians, Gilberts and Marshalls* (Edison, NJ: Castle Book, 2001), 103–104.
11. "*Greenman Naval Records*," 10.
12. Juarez.
13. Kuphaldt.
14. Powell.
15. Schiller.
16. Sheble.
17. *Shoup Biographical Sketch*, 1–2.
18. "Service Record of Roy Taylor Spurlock." St. Louis, MO: National Personnel Records Center.
19. Tuccitto.
20. Tunnell.
21. Tunnell.
22. Wallace.
23. Yeamans.

Bibliography

Books

Adcock, Al. *U.S. Navy Floatplanes of World War II in Action.* Carrollton, TX: Squadron Signal Publications, 2006.

_____. *U.S. Heavy Cruisers in Action: Part I.* Carrollton, TX: Squadron Signal Publications, 2001.

Astoria Reunion Association. *USS Astoria CA-34 1934–1942.* Privately published, 1970.

Campbell, John. *Naval Weapons of World War II.* Annapolis, MD: Naval Institute Press, 1985.

Coombe, Jack. *Derailing the Tokyo Express.* Harrisburg, PA: Stackpole Books, 1991.

Costello, John. *The Pacific War.* New York: Rawson, Wade, 1981.

Custer, Joe James. *Through the Perilous Night.* New York: Macmillan, 1944.

Daly, Joseph R. *Luck is My Lady.* New York: Vantage Press, 1989.

Dull, Paul. *Battle History of the Imperial Japanese Navy, 1941–1945.* Annapolis, MD: Naval Institute Press, 1978.

Eddington, Walter J. *Glossary of Shipbuilding and Outfitting Terms.* New York: Cornell Maritime Press, 1944.

Evans, David C., and Mark R. Peattie. *Kaigun: Strategy, Tactics and Technology in the Imperial Japanese Navy, 1887–1941.* Annapolis, MD: Naval Institute Press, 1997.

Ewing, Steve. *Reaper Leader: The Life of Jimmy Flatley.* Annapolis, MD: Naval Institute Press, 2002.

Feldt, Eric. *The Coast Watchers.* New York: Ballantine Books, 1959.

Francillon, Dr. Rene J. *Japanese Navy Bombers of World War II.* New York: Doubleday, 1969.

Frank, Richard B. *Guadalcanal.* New York: Random House, 1990.

Friedman, Norman. *U.S. Cruisers: An Illustrated Design History.* Annapolis, MD: Naval Institute Press, 1984.

Hashimoto, Mochitsura. *Sunk: The Story of the Japanese Submarine Fleet, 1941–1945.* New York: Holt, 1954.

Hawthorne, Daniel. *Islands of the Pacific.* New York: G.P. Putnam's Sons, 1943.

Hone, Thomas C., and Trent Hone. *Battle Line: The United States Navy 1919–1939.* Annapolis, MD: Naval Institute Press, 2006.

Hoyt, Edwin P. *Guadalcanal.* New York: Stein and Day, 1982.

_____. *How They Won the War in the Pacific: Nimitz and His Admirals.* New York: Lyons Press, 2000.

Japanese Self Defense Force: War History Office. *Senshi Sosho (War History Series). Volume 49: Southeast Area Naval Operations, Part I.* Tokyo: Asagumo Shibunsha, 1971.

_____. *Senshi Sosho (War History Series). Volume 83: Southeast Area Naval Operations, Part II.* Tokyo: Asagumo Shibunsha, 1975.

Jones, Pat, ed. *The USS Astoria and the Men Who Sailed Her.* Hillsboro, OR: Premier Press, 1992.

Lacroix, Eric, and Linton Wells. *Japanese Cruisers of the Pacific War.* Annapolis, MD: Naval Institute Press, 1997.

Lane, Kerry L. *Guadalcanal Marine.* Jackson, MS: University of Mississippi Press, 2004.

Layton, Rear Admiral Edwin T., Roger Pineau, and John Costello. *And I Was There: Pearl Harbor and Midway: Breaking the Secrets.* New York: Morrow, 1985.

Lee, Clark. *They Call It Pacific.* New York: Viking Press, 1943.

Lord, Walter. *Lonely Vigil.* New York: Viking Press, 1977.

Loxton, Bruce, and Chris Coulthard-Clark. *The Shame of Savo.* Annapolis, MD: Bluejacket Books, 1997.

Lundstrom, John B. *The First Team and the Guadalcanal Campaign.* Annapolis, MD: Naval Institute Press, 1994.

Morison, Samuel Eliot. *History of United States Naval Operations in World War II.* Vol. 1, *The Battle of the Atlantic.* Boston: Little, Brown, 1959.

_____. *History of United States Naval Operations in World War II.* Vol. 3, *The Rising Sun in the Pacific.* Edison, NJ: Castle Books, 2001.

_____. *History of United States Naval Operations in World War II.* Vol. 4, *Coral Sea, Midway and Submarine Actions.* Edison, NJ: Castle Books, 2001.

_____. *History of United States Naval Operations in World War II.* Vol. 5, *The Struggle for Guadalcanal.* Edison, NJ: Castle Books, 2001.

_____. *History of United States Naval Operations in World War II.* Vol. 7, *Aleutians, Gilberts and Marshalls.* Edison, NJ: Castle Books, 2001.

Newcomb, Richard. *Savo: The Incredible Naval Deba-*

cle off Guadalcanal. New York: Holt, Rinehart and Winston, 1961.
Okumiya, Masatake, and Jiro Horikoshi, with Martin Caidin. *Zero!* New York: Dutton, 1956.
Puget Sound Navy Yard. *Christening of U.S.S. Astoria, Heavy Cruiser No. CA 34.* Bremerton, WA: Puget Sound Navy Yard, 1933.
Reynolds, Clark G. *The Saga of Smokey Stover.* Charleston, SC: Tradd Street Press, 1978.
Roscoe, Theodore. *United States Submarine Operations in World War II.* Annapolis, MD: Naval Institute Press, 1949.
Sakai, Saburo, Martin Caidin, and Fred Saito. *Samurai.* New York: Dutton, 1957.
Santos, Abe. "The USS Astoria (CA-34) and the Battle of Savo Island." In *Voices from the Past: Blue Jackets Remember*, ed. Bruce M. Petty, 74–81. Annapolis, MD: Naval Institute Press, 2004.
Shanks, Sandy. *The Bode Testament.* Lincoln, NE: Writers Club Press, 2001.
Spector, Ronald H. *Eagle Against the Sun.* New York: Vintage Books, 1985.
Summerville, Keith, and Harriotte W. B. Smith. *Ships of the United States Navy and Their Sponsors, 1924–1950.* Annapolis, MD: Naval Institute Press, 1952.
Terzibaschitsch, Stefan. *Cruisers of the U.S. Navy, 1922–1962.* Annapolis, MD: Naval Institute Press, 1988.
Tregaskis, Richard. *Guadalcanal Diary.* New York: Random House, 1943.
United States Naval Academy. *The Lucky Bag.* Annapolis, MD, 1939.
United States Navy. *The Bluejackets Manual.* Annapolis, MD: Naval Institute Press, 1946.
Van Der Vat, Dan. *The Pacific Campaign.* New York: Simon & Schuster, 1991.
Warner, Denis, Peggy Warner, and Sadao Seno. *Disaster in the Pacific: New Light on the Battle of Savo Island.* Annapolis, MD: Naval Institute Press, 1992.

Action Reports, Deck Logs and War Diaries

"CA *Chokai* Action Record." Records of Japanese Navy & Related Documents, Translations, 1941–1946. Naval Historical Center. Washington, DC.
CinCPac to Commander in Chief U.S. Fleet. "Solomon Islands Campaign — Fall of Guadalcanal, Period 25 January to 10 February, 1943. April 7, 1943.
CO Task Force 18 to CinCPac. "Action Report — Task Force 18, January 29–30, 1943." February 19, 1943.
CO Task Group 18.2 to CO Task Force 18. "Operations — Report of — USS Chenango and USS Suwannee from 1140L, 29 January to, 31 January 1943." February 14, 1943.
CO Task Force 62. "Transmittal of Commander Task Force Sixty-Two Operation Plan A3–42." July 30, 1942.
CO Task Group 62.6. "Night Action Off Savo Island (9th August, 1942 — Remarks by C.T.G. 62.6)" August 11, 1942.
CO Task Group 62.6. "Special Instructions to Screening Group and Vessels Temporarily Assigned." n.d.
CO *USS Astoria* to CinCPac. "Battle Savo Island — Action of Cruisers Task Force 62.3, Early Morning August 9, 1942 — Loss of U.S.S Astoria." August 20, 1942. (Includes officer reports and crew statements.)
CO *USS Astoria* to Secretary of the Navy. "Survivor and Casualty Lists — U.S.S. Astoria." September 3, 1942.
CO *USS Bagley* to CinCPac. "Night Engagement August 9, 1942 — Tulagi Guadalcanal Area." August 13, 1942.
CO USS *Chicago* to CinCPac. "Action Against Enemy Forces August 9, 1942, Guadalcanal–Tulagi Area — Report of." August 13, 1942.
_____. "Action Against Enemy Aircraft, August 7–8, 1942." August 19, 1942.
_____. "Preliminary Report of Action with Japanese Aircraft Beginning at Dusk 29 January 1943." February 3, 1943.
CO USS *Chicago* to Chief of the Bureau of Ships. "War Damage Report." August 25, 1942.
_____. "War Damage Report (Supplementary)." September 18, 1942.
CO *USS Patterson* to CinCPac. "Engagement with Enemy (Japanese) Surface Ships Night 8–9 August in Savo-Guadalcanal-Tulagi Island Group Solomon Islands." August 13, 1942.
CO *USS Wilson* to CinCPac. "Report of Action Against Enemy Surface Ships Off Savo Island, Night of August 8–9, 1942. August 20, 1942.
Deck Logs: *USS Astoria, USS Chicago, USS Navajo*, and *USS Sands.*
Medical Officer to CO USS *Chicago*. "Report of Killed and Wounded." August 10, 1942.
Senior Surviving Officer USS *Quincy* to CinCPac. "Report of the Engagement the Morning of August 9, 1942, off Guadalcanal Island in which the U.S.S. Quincy Participated." August 16, 1942.
"Translations from Daily War Reports of the 25th Air Flotilla, August and September, 1942." Records of Japanese Navy & Related Documents, Translations, 1941–1946. Naval Historical Center. Washington, DC.
"War Diary *Kako* from 7–10 August 1942, Solomons Sea Battle." Records of Japanese Navy & Related Documents, Translations, 1941–1946. Naval Historical Center. Washington, DC.
War Diaries: *USS Buchanan, USS Chicago*, Task Force 62.

Documents and Official Reports

Bates, Richard W., and Walter D. Innis. *The Battle of Savo Island, August 9, 1942: Strategical and Technical Analysis.* Newport, RI: U.S. Naval War College, 1950.
Biographical Sketch of Captain Frank Elliot Shoup, Jr. Operational Archives Branch, Naval Historical Center, Washington, DC.
Biographical Sketch of Captain Howard Douglas Bode. Operational Archives Branch, Naval Historical Center, Washington, DC.

Biographical Sketch of Vice Admiral Ralph O. Davis. Operational Archives Branch, Naval Historical Center, Washington, DC.

Bureau of Ships, United States Navy. "War Damage Report #29: Loss of the USS Astoria (CA-34)." 1942.

———. "War Damage Report #37: USS Chicago (CA-29) Loss in Action." 1944.

Combat Narrative Number VIII: The Japanese Evacuation of Guadalcanal. Washington, DC: Office of Naval Intelligence, United States Navy, 1944.

Dyer, George. *The Amphibians Came To Conquer: The Story of Admiral Richmond Kelly Turner.* Vol. 1. Washington, DC: United States Navy, 1972.

Hepburn, Admiral Arthur J. *Report of Informal Inquiry into the Circumstances Attending the loss of U.S.S. Vincennes, U.S.S. Quincy, U.S.S. Astoria, and H.M.A.S. Australia, on August 9, 1942, in the Vicinity of Savo Island (Solomon Islands).* Washington, DC: Navy Department, Headquarters of the Commander in Chief, 1943.

Hough, Frank O., Verle E. Ludwig, and Henry I. Shaw. *History of U.S. Marine Corps Operations in World War II.* Vol. 1. *Pearl Harbor to Guadalcanal.* Washington, DC: Historical Branch, G-3 Division, Headquarters, U.S. Marine Corps, 1958.

Lewis, Winston. *The Battle of Savo Island.* Washington, DC: Office of Naval Intelligence, United States Navy, 1943.

Miller, John Jr. *Guadalcanal: The First Offensive.* Washington, DC: Historical Division, United States Army, 1949.

Secretary of the Navy. *Register of the Commissioned and Warrant Officers of the Navy of the United States, Including Officers of the Marine Corps.* Washington, DC: Government Printing Office, 1942, 1943.

"Service Record of Roy Taylor Spurlock." St. Louis, MO: National Personnel Records Center.

United States Congress Joint Committee on the Investigation of the Pearl Harbor Attack. *Pearl Harbor Attack. Hearings before the Joint Committee on the Investigation of the Pearl Harbor Attack.* Vol. 26. Washington, DC: U.S. Government Printing Office, 1946.

United States Strategic Bombing Survey (Pacific), Naval Analysis Division. *The Interrogations of Japanese Officials.* Vols. 1 and 2. Washington, DC: Government Printing Office, 1946.

Ware, Leonard. *The Landing in the Solomons.* Washington, DC: Office of Naval Intelligence, United States Navy, 1943.

"U.S. Navy Record of Officers: William Greenman." St. Louis, MO: National Personnel Records Center.

Articles

"Astoria Survivor Tells of Jap Attack in Savo Island Battle." Undated newspaper article. Box 5, in Record Group 24. Records on the Bureau of Naval Personnel: Ships Stations, Units and Incidents, Causality Information, 1941–45. National Archives II, College Park, MD.

Bartsch, William. "Operation Dovetail: Bungled Guadalcanal Rehearsal, July 1942." *The Journal of American Military History*, April 2002.

"Cruiser Chicago Sinks with Guns Blazing at Japs." *Chicago Tribune*, February 21, 1943.

Daley, Lt. Joseph R. "Shot Down in Flames." *Cosmopolitan*, April 1943.

"40,000 Join Navy in Month, Four Times Usual Rate." *New York Times*, January 8, 1942.

Hirama, Rear Admiral (JMSDF) Yoichi. "Japanese Naval Preparations for World War II." *Naval War College Review*, Spring 1991.

Johnson, Tim. "Veteran's Ship Comes In." *The Daily Nonpareil*. Council Bluffs, IA, December 3, 2000.

———. "Dinovo Survived Torpedo Attack." *The Daily Nonpareil*. Council Bluffs, IA, August 11, 2003.

LaVo, Karl. "The Destroyer Aviator." *Naval History*, December 2006.

"Lt. Ferneding, Injured in Action, Home on Leave." Undated newspaper article courtesy of Tom Ferneding.

"Navy Officer Credits Twin's Transfusion with Saving His Life." Undated newspaper article courtesy of Tom Ferneding.

"New Training Program for Candidates, Ensigns, U.S. Naval Reserve." *Information for Naval Personnel, Bulletin Number 292,* May 31, 1941.

O'Connor, Raymond G. "The American Navy, 1939–1941: The Enlisted Perspective." *Military Affairs*, October, 1986.

Ohmae, Captain Toshikazu. "The Battle of Savo Island." *United States Naval Institute Proceedings,* December, 1957.

Roberts, Carol. "When Boys Became Men of War." *San Louis Obispo Tribune*, September 26, 1999.

Schenck, Earl. "Action in the Pacific." *Liberty*, July 31, 1943.

Wharton, Don. "Eddie Armes: Naval Veteran at 19." *Look*, December 29, 1942.

Interviews, Correspondence and Oral Histories on *Astoria* (CA-34)

Alair, Gene. Telephone interview and letters to the author.

Armes, Edward. Telephone interviews with author.

Bouterse, John M. "Confessions of a Navy Chaplain." Manuscript. Courtesy of Lee Davis (daughter).

Douglas, George. Telephone interview with author and correspondence.

Eugene Hardy Collection (AFC/2001/001/20428), Veterans History Project, American Folklife Center, Library of Congress.

Ferneding, Thomas. Telephone interview with author and correspondence.

Fritz, John. Narrative sent to author.

Hobson, Belcher. Telephone interviews with author.

Juarez, Henry. Telephone interviews with author.

Kuphaldt, William. Narrative from 1993 sent to author by daughter.

Powell, John. Telephone interviews with author.

Santos, Abe. Telephone interview with author.

Schiller, Bob. Telephone interviews with author.
Spurlock, Roy. *First Savo: The Lost Battle.* Unpublished narrative. Courtesy of the Columbia River Maritime Museum.
Torsch, Theodore. Telephone interviews with author.
Tunnell, Richard M. Telephone interview with author.
Yeamans, Don. Telephone interviews and correspondence with author.

Interviews, Correspondence and Oral Histories on *Chicago* (CA-29)

Blumhorst, Harry. Telephone interview with author.
Dinovo, Frank. Telephone interview with author.
Fortney, Howard. Telephone interviews and correspondence with author.
Germann, Charles. Interview with author.
Goldsmith, Charles. Telephone interviews with author.
Grady, Bill. Telephone interview with author.
King, Art. Telephone interviews with author.
Maysenhalder, Ken. Telephone interviews with author and unpublished narratives sent to author.
Pursley, George. Unpublished narrative sent to author and telephone interviews with author.
Sheble, Thomas. Telephone interviews with author.
Tuccitto, Fred. Telephone interviews and correspondence with author.
Wallace, Don. Unpublished narrative sent to author, correspondence and telephone interview.

Internet Sources

"Astoria (CA-34)." http://www.history.navy (accessed November 22, 2006).
"Chicago (CA-29)." http://www.history.navy (accessed November 22, 2006).
"Conference on the Limitation of Armament, Washington, November 12, 1921– February 6, 1922." http://ibiblio.org/pha/pre-war/1922/nav_lim.html (accessed April 30, 2007).
Dictionary of American Fighting Ships. http://www.history.navy.mil/danfs/index.html. (accessed on various dates 2006–2007).
"Gene Lyle Alair." http://www.lonesailor.org (accessed June 12, 2007).
"Japanese Naval Ordnance." http://combinedfleet.com (accessed January 25, 2008).
Kittredge, George W. "Savo Island: The Worst Defeat." http://www.navalinstitute.org/NavalHistory/Articles02 (accessed October 22, 2006).
"Military Training Program Records, 1941–1949." www.library.northwestern.edu/archives/findingaids/military_training_programs.pdf (accessed June 22, 2007).
"U.S. Navy Shipboard Radars — CXAM." http://www.history.navy (accessed July 3, 2008).
U.S.S. Estes, A History. http://www.ussestes.org (accessed June 28, 2008).
"Vice Admiral Robert C. Giffen, USN (1886–1962)." http://www.history.navy (accessed November 2, 2006).
"World War II Shipbuilding in the San Francisco Bay Area." www.cr.nps.gov (accessed November 14, 2006).
Wukovits, John. "Battle of Rennell Island: Setback in the Solomons." http://www.historynet.com (accessed May 4, 2005).

Index

Adell, Cecil 83, 91, 171, 173, 197
Alair, Gene 20–21, 36, 45, 54, 83, 96, 118–119, 122, 132–133, 145–146, 157, 163, 199
Alchiba 154, 157, 163
American Legion 163
American Samoa 6, 33
Annapolis, Maryland 17–18, 204
Aoba 75–77, 84–85, 88, 91, 97–99, 107, 112, 118, 158
Argonne 169
Arizona 29
Armes, Edward 22, 71, 82, 137, 150–151, 199
Astor, John Jacob 7
Astoria: abandonment of 139–140, 155–157; armament 8, 39, 41–42, 55–56, 83, 96, 105, 114, 118; commissioning 7–8; crew 9; description 8–9, 40–42, 83, 96; dimensions 7; early operations 16–17, 28–29, 38; effort to save 131–133, 142–149, 151–155; sunk 156–157; under fire during Savo Island battle 98–100, 103–105, 110–112, 115, 118, 120, 135–136, 140
Astoria, Oregon 7, 17, 44
Australia 34, 37, 51, 60, 79–80, 85, 87, 161

Bagley 52, 79–80, 85, 88, 99, 106, 132–134, 144, 149, 151–154, 162–163, 203
Baker, George 119
Balint, Steve 89, 91
Bartholomew, Albert 186
Betelgeuse 46
Betty bomber (plane) 59–60, 68, 181–182
Blough, Ike (Ira) 21, 139
Blue 84–86, 160
Blumhorst, Harry 22–24, 51, 184, 194, 197, 199
Bode, Howard 27, 37, 46, 51, 59, 65–66, 80, 83, 89, 94, 158–161, 169, 171–173, 200
Bougainville Island 33, 60, 62, 64, 76, 78, 158, 201, 203
Bouterse, Matthew 25–26, 28–30, 36, 43, 49, 55, 70, 83, 134, 139, 141, 153, 163–165, 200
Bremerton, Washington 7
Britten, Elizabeth 6
Brom, Leo 105, 110
Brown, James 139–140
Bruning, Robert Jr. 44, 60, 64
Buchanan 154–157, 163, 201
Burkey, Noel 95, 99–100

California 27, 186
Campbell, William 44, 56–58
Canberra 34, 37, 48, 79–80, 85, 87–90, 93–94, 97, 100, 159–161; *see also* Savo Island, Battle of
Chaumont 10, 19
Chenango 177, 179–180, 188–189
Chevalier 187
Chicago: abandonment of 191–197; armament 8, 39–40, 66, 92, 172; commissioning 6; crew 9; description 6, 8–9, 12, 38–40; dimensions 6; early operations 10, 27–28, 38; effort to save 185–186, 189–190; emergency repairs after Savo Island battle 159, 169; repairs at Mare Island 170–173; return to war zone 176–177; sunk 191; torpedoed during Savo Island battle 89–92; torpedoed near Rennell Island 180–183, 185, 191
Chokai 75–77, 84–85, 87–88, 90, 97–99, 104, 106, 112, 116–117
Cleveland 177, 182
Coe, Benjamin 149–150
Columbia 177, 182
Conway 198
Cookatoo Island *see* Sydney, Australia
Coral Sea, Battle of 28, 35, 59, 66
Cruisers: early development 5; life aboard 8, 41; treaty cruisers 6
Crutchley, Victor 34, 37, 46, 51, 79–80, 84–85, 87, 160–162
CXAM radar 10, 60, 65, 172, 181, 184, 191

Daley, Joseph 61–62, 91
Datko, John 96
Davis, Ralph 172–173, 176–177, 181–183, 185, 190–191, 200
Davison, Walter 116
Dewey 46, 55, 71
Dinovo, Frank 171–172, 176, 184, 193–194, 197–198, 200
Douglas, George 138, 163

Eaton, William Guy 105, 110
Edmands, Allen 56, 82, 125
Edwards 188, 191, 198
Ellet 160
Enterprise 34, 54, 71, 178, 188–190
Espiritu Santo, New Hebrides 162, 188, 197–198, 201

Ferneding, Thomas 110, 118, 164
Fletcher, Jack 34, 36, 71, 117
Florida Island 37, 54, 62, 65, 67–68, 86, 161
Flower, Charles 127–128, 152–153
Fortney, Howard 13–14, 40, 81, 89–90, 171, 184–185, 193, 197, 200
Fritz, John 157
Furutaka 75, 84–85, 88–90, 97, 158

George Elliott 70–71, 79, 87
Germann, Charles 14, 38, 81, 90–91, 160–161, 171, 175, 186–187, 189, 192–193, 201
Getting, Frank 80, 88
Gibson, Jack 21, 113, 135–136, 142, 155
Giffen, Robert 177–179, 187, 189–90
Golden Gate Bridge, San Francisco 175–176
Goldsmith, Charles 184, 187, 190, 196–197, 201
Grady, Bill 22–24, 27, 34, 40, 45, 59, 81, 90, 171, 185, 190, 197, 201
Great Depression 10, 17
Great Lakes Naval Base 14–16, 26, 171
Greenman, William 35–36, 37, 49, 53, 54, 56–57, 64, 69, 73, 78, 80–81, 83, 95–97, 100, 103–105, 110–111, 116, 118, 124, 128, 130–134, 144–145, 147–150, 152, 154–155, 157, 163–164, 201
Guadalcanal: American landing on 37, 55–56, 62; American rehearsal exercise for invasion *see* Koro Island; American voyage to 37, 46–52; description 33, 36–37; Japanese air attacks 59–62; Japanese invasion 33; Japanese reaction to American landing 59–62; strategic importance 33
Guantanamo Bay, Cuba 10

Halliburton, Richard 17
Halsey, William 188
Hardy, Eugene 121
Harris 23, 24
Hawaiian Islands 6, 14, 17, 23; *see also* Pearl Harbor, Hawaii
Hayes, John 95, 107–108, 111, 115, 142, 146–148, 154
Healey, Vincent 82, 114, 125–126, 133, 136, 150
Helm 60, 79–80, 85, 98, 100, 106, 150, 154
Henderson 28
Henley 51, 60
Hepburn, Arthur 162, 200
Higai, Joji 182
Hobart 34, 37, 48, 51
Hobson, Belcher 132–133, 138, 148, 157
Hong Kong 17
Hopkins 149–150, 154
Hughes, Charles Evans 5
Hull 46, 79–80
Hunter Liggett 80, 162

I-169 47
Indiana 178

Japanese Cruiser Force 76–77, 84–87, 158
Jarvis 70, 79–80
Johns, Walter 101–102, 136
Juarez, Henry 24–25, 36, 41, 43, 67, 82, 113, 140–141, 148–149, 155–156, 201

Kako 75, 77, 84–85, 90, 92, 97–98, 106–107, 110, 112, 158
Kanawha 46
King, Art 10–12, 27, 39, 44, 65–66, 81, 91–92, 160, 173, 177, 186, 189, 195–196, 201
King, Ernest 162
Kinugasa 75, 84–85, 92, 97, 104, 107, 112, 116, 158
Koro Island, Fiji 37, 43–47, 79, 198
Kuphaldt, William 119–122, 130, 153, 164–165, 202

La Vallette 188–193
Lexington 22, 28
Little Rock, Arkansas 22, 23
Look magazine 199
Los Angeles, California 20, 24
Louisville 177, 179, 182, 185, 187, 189
Louisville, Kentucky 10, 82, 173
Lozano, Lawrence 148–149
Lunga Point, Guadalcanal 37, 55, 61, 70–71, 87, 97, 162, 178

Mare Island Navy Yard 6, 10, 11, 16, 170–171, 173–174, 197, 203
Marzetta, Dante 96, 101, 111–112, 124
Maysenhalder, Ken 14–15, 27, 39, 54–55, 66, 93–94, 171, 184, 194–195, 202
McAnney, Victor 29, 49, 165
McCampbell, Gaylord 123, 154, 163
McCawley 34, 37, 48, 62, 86, 161–163
McGrath, Raymond 101, 105, 124–125, 131–132
McKay, Leila 7
McLaughlin, Art 21, 25, 99, 113
McNulty, J.T. 107–108
Memorial Continental Hall 5
Midway, Battle of 29–30, 33, 35, 52, 75
Mikawa, Gunichi 75–77, 84–88, 94, 97, 117, 158
Minneapolis 20, 35
Mobile, Alabama 23
Moore, John 158
Mugford 18, 46, 49, 62, 162
Munson, Henry 76

Navajo 188–193, 197
Naval Academy (United States) 18, 27, 35, 172
Neosho 13
Nevada 22, 24, 28, 35
New York 20
Nimitz, Chester 162, 201
Norfolk, Virginia 10, 11, 13
North Carolina 178, 200
Northern Force 79, 85–87, 94, 97–99, 106–107; *see also* Savo Island, Battle of
Noumea, New Caledonia 28, 33, 162, 170, 178, 198, 199

Ohmae, Toshikazu 75
Oklahoma 22, 27, 35
Omaha, Nebraska 16, 2004
O'Reilly, Edward 127

Panama Canal 11, 17, 200
Patterson 79–80, 85, 87–89, 92, 99, 103, 106, 158–160, 162

Index

Pearl Harbor, Hawaii 15, 19, 28, 30, 34–36, 46, 162, 199–201, 205; attack on 22, 24–25, 38, 56, 60, 75, 120
Perkins 27
Philippines 17, 20
Platte 46
Port Moresby, New Guinea 28
Portland, Oregon 17, 19, 205
Powell, John 18–19, 36, 42, 56, 61, 63, 67–69, 83, 96, 121–124, 128, 132–133, 153–154, 163, 202
President Jackson 162–164
Price, Walter 150
Puget Sound Navy Yard 7, 200
Pursley, George 15–16, 184, 197–198, 203
Putman, Walter 95, 100, 105, 110

Quincy 37, 44, 46, 48, 51, 54–55, 64, 79–80, 85, 98–100, 103–107, 111, 117, 124–125, 137–140, 152, 162; *see also* Savo Island, Battle of

Rabaul, New Britain 33, 47, 59–60, 64, 67, 75, 78, 117, 158, 178, 181
Radke, Roy 95, 100, 105, 111
Rainier 46
Ralph Talbot 84–86
Rennell Island 50, 181, 187, 198; Battle of 180–185, 190–192, 198
Riddell, Robert 121, 130
Riefkohl, Fredrick 79–80, 85, 94, 103–104, 106
Root, Edmund 8
Russell Islands 51, 60

S-38 76
S-44 158
Salt Lake City 18, 34, 43
San Cristobal Island 33, 162, 180–181
San Diego, California 12–14, 17, 23, 29, 34, 201–203
San Francisco 20
San Francisco, California 8, 12, 14, 17, 36, 170–171, 173, 175–176, 202
San Juan 51–53, 59, 64, 95, 97, 154, 160–161
San Pedro, California 10, 13–14, 16
Sands 188, 191, 197–198
Santa Cruz, California 12
Santos, Abe 73, 109, 141–142, 149, 163–164
Saratoga 34, 36, 43, 50, 54, 60–61, 71, 178, 203
Savo Island 37, 51, 53, 77, 79–80, 84–87, 95, 97, 117, 132, 150, 154, 158–159, 161, 177, 198, 200; Battle of: aftermath 158–162, 165, 176–177, Allied night dispositions 79–80, 84–86, Allied reconnaissance of Japanese cruiser force 76, battle north of Savo Island 97–99, 106–107, battle south of Savo Island 87–88, 91, 103–105, *Canberra* sunk 160, composition of forces 75, 85, Japanese night fighting tactics 76–77, 84, 98–99, Japanese planning 75–77, *Quincy* Sunk 117, *Vincennes* Sunk 117; *see also* Northern Force; Southern Force
Scanland, Francis 28, 35, 42
Schiller, Bob 19, 40, 70, 82, 125, 133
Selfridge 50, 55, 160
701st Air Group (Japanese) 182
705th Air Group (Japanese) 181

Sheble, Thomas 174–176, 183–184, 193, 197, 203
Shoup, Frank, Jr. 35, 45, 135–136, 138–143, 148, 155, 164, 203–204
Simmons, M. H. 6
Sinclair, George 132, 153
Smith, Donald 144
SOC seaplane 40–41
Southern Force 79, 85–88, 91, 94, 132, 161; *see also* Savo Island, Battle of
Spurlock, Roy 44–45, 47, 61, 68, 81, 83, 127–130, 133, 154, 163, 204
Suva, Fiji 27, 46
Suwannee 177, 188
Sydney, Australia 28, 47, 169–170, 189

Task Force 18 177–178, 181–182, 188, 190
Task Force 61 34, 50, 54
Task Force 62 34, 37, 43, 46–50, 51, 61, 64–65, 70–71, 80, 162–163
Taylor 188
Tenryu 75, 84–85, 88, 92, 97, 106, 158–159
Topper, James (John) 95, 97, 99–100, 103, 105, 115, 124, 130–131, 144–147, 154–155
Torsch, Theodore 82, 136–137, 163
Treaty for the Limitation of Armament of 1922 *see* Washington Naval Treaty
Truesdell, William 52–53, 96, 101, 103, 107, 111–112, 117–119
Truk, Caroline Islands 47
Tuccitto, Fred 16, 39, 45, 54, 66, 93–94, 161, 170, 194, 198, 204
Tulagi Island 33, 37, 47, 50–51, 53–55, 57–60, 62–63, 64–66, 71, 75–77, 86, 97, 99, 162
Tunnell, Richard 18, 40, 44, 54, 56–58, 67, 69–70, 82, 125, 133, 204
Turner, Richmond Kelly 17, 34, 37, 46–47, 51, 56, 62, 64, 66–71, 78–80, 85–87, 144, 150, 159, 161–162

Val dive bomber (plane) 60, 62
La Vallette 188–193
Vandergrift, Alexander 34, 80, 86, 161
Vincennes 37, 44, 48, 54–55, 64, 70, 79–80, 85, 87, 91, 94–95, 97–100, 103–107, 117, 124, 137, 140, 152, 161–162; *see also* Savo Island, Battle of

Wake Island 28, 204
Wakefield, Ellis 118, 131
Walker, Frank 87–88
Wallace, Don 12–13, 34, 39, 92–93, 170–171, 196–197
Waller 181–182, 191, 194, 198
Washington, District of Columbia 5, 25, 27, 201, 203
Washington Naval Treaty 5
Wasp 34, 65, 71, 78
Wellington, New Zealand 34
Wharton 165, 201–202
Wichita 177, 179, 182, 185, 189–190
Wildcat fighter plane 50, 54, 60–61
Willman, Donald 122–123, 125–126
Wilson 80, 85, 98–99, 106, 133, 140, 150, 154, 162
World War I 5, 10, 27, 35, 77, 149

Yamada, Sadayoshi 59, 64
Yeamans, Don 17–18, 22, 40, 69, 100, 110, 118, 132, 144, 148, 156–157, 205
Yokohama, Japan 17
Yorktown 28–30
Young, Julian 110–111

Yubari 75, 84–85, 88, 92, 97, 158
Yunagi 75, 84–85, 87, 117

Zeilin 46
Zero fighter plane 60–61, 64, 68, 70